# About ISTE

The International Society for Technology in Education (ISTE) is the trusted source for professional development, knowledge generation, advocacy, and leadership for innovation. A nonprofit membership association, ISTE provides leadership and service to improve teaching, learning, and school leadership by advancing the effective use of technology in PK–12 and teacher education.

Home of the National Educational Technology Standards (NETS), the Center for Applied Research in Educational Technology (CARET), and the National Educational Computing Conference (NECC), ISTE represents more than 85,000 professionals worldwide. We support our members with information, networking opportunities, and guidance as they face the challenge of transforming education. To find out more about these and other ISTE initiatives, visit our Web site at **www.iste.org**.

As part of our mission, ISTE Book Publishing works with experienced educators to develop and produce practical resources for classroom teachers, teacher educators, and technology leaders. Every manuscript we select for publication is carefully peer-reviewed and professionally edited. We look for content that emphasizes the effective use of technology where it can make a difference—increasing the productivity of teachers and administrators; helping students with unique learning styles, abilities, or backgrounds; collecting and using data for decision making at the school and district levels; and creating dynamic, project-based learning environments that engage 21st-century learners. We value your feedback on this book and other ISTE products. E-mail us at **books@iste.org**.

# About the Editors and Contributors

## Editors

**Arlene Borthwick** (aborthwick@nl.edu) is Department Chair and Associate Professor, Integrated Studies in Teaching, Technology, and Inquiry, at the National College of Education at National-Louis University (Chicago). Following public-school teaching (Grades 5–6), she began her career in higher education by coordinating technology-related continuing-education activities for K–12 teachers at Kent State University and the University of Tulsa. She is the past president of ISTE's Special Interest Group for Teacher Educators and a member of the Editorial Board of the Journal of Computing in Teacher Education. She has served as the Program Chair for AERA's Action Research SIG and as a member of the Program Committee for the National Educational Computing Conference. Her research activities include participation as an AT&T Fellow at the Research Center for Educational Technology at Kent State University (2005–2006) where she worked with elementary teachers and students on multimedia authoring. Additional areas of research include use of handheld computers for assessment, design of online instruction, and the process of school-university collaboration for school improvement.

**Melissa Pierson** is Director of Teacher Education and Associate Professor of Instructional Technology at the University of Houston. She teaches both undergraduate and graduate students, and both technology and teacher-education courses, a natural way to ensure technology integration. Her current research interests include the integration of technology, pedagogy, and content (Technological-Pedagogical-Content-Knowledge, or TPACK) in teacher education, and the use of inquiry and action research to inform novice teachers technology integration practices. She has directed grant projects aimed at restructuring preservice technology instruction, and has both led and participated in national and local educational technology organizations and initiatives. Her scholarship includes books, chapters, articles, and conference presentations in the field of educational technology.

# Dedication

This volume is dedicated to the past presidents of ISTE's Special Interest Group for Teacher Educators (SIGTE) whose leadership, guidance, and enthusiasm supported the professional development of their colleagues, including both of us.

—*Arlene & Melissa*

> Tony Jongejan
> Henry Kepner, Jr.
> Charlotte Scherer
> Neal Strudler
> Marianne Handler
> Keith Wetzel
> Marjorie DeWert
> Dale Niederhauser
> Ann Cunningham

# Contributors

**Ann Barron** is a Professor in the Instructional Technology program at the University of South Florida. She teaches graduate-level courses related to Web design, instructional design, distance learning, and multimedia development. Ann has published several books in the field of educational technology and numerous research articles in national and international journals. Her research interests focus on the use of audio in online learning and trends in the integration of technology in K–12 schools.

**Robert Bowe** works and teaches at National-Louis University, where he has been the Academic Technology Facilitator for the National College of Education since 2000. While working on his doctoral degree in curricular design, he has also been involved in a professional development grant in which 80 faculty members participated. Bowe has assisted faculty in their development of technology-infused classroom activities, electronic portfolios, assessment practices, and online teaching. Prior to his work at NLU, he taught K–8 students for eleven years in public schools in the Chicago area. As a teacher and technology coordinator, he has experience in a variety of educational settings.

**Sally Brewer** is an Associate Professor at the University of Montana, where she teaches library media and technology courses and is the NCATE coordinator. Sally has been involved in planning, developing, and delivering workshops for inservice teachers and teacher educators for more than 15 years. Her workshops have focused on multimedia tools, digital storytelling, school library Web sites, and distance education. She helped design UM's Masters in Education program with an option in Instructional Design for Technology and has developed several of the required technology courses. Her current research focuses on assessment and the role of the librarian in virtual K–12 schools.

**Scott W. Brown** is a Professor of Educational Psychology at the Neag School of Education at the University of Connecticut. He has published three books/monographs on issues related to educational psychology, and published more than 90 refereed journal articles and book chapters in the fields of educational psychology, educational technology, learning, and cognition. He has presented more than 200 papers at professional conferences. In over 20 years of service at the University of Connecticut, he has held positions both as the Director of the Bureau of Educational Research and Service and as the department head for Educational Psychology.

**Joanne Carney** is an Associate Professor of Instructional Technology and Elementary Education at Western Washington University. For three years, she was an evaluator for the NO LIMIT! project, which she writes about in this volume. In a previous faculty position, Carney directed a large-scale PT3 project. She presents frequently on instructional technology and teacher learning and assessment. Publications include "Integrating Technology into Constructivist Classrooms: An Examination of One Model for Teacher Development," which received a research award from ISTE's SIG for Teacher Educators. Carney herself has 16 years of experience in PK–12 education and ten years as a teacher educator.

**Craig A. Cunningham** is an Associate Professor in the Technology in Education Program at National-Louis University, where he also teaches courses in the history and philosophy of education. Cunningham holds a PhD in the Philosophy of Curriculum from the University of Chicago, where he worked as director of curriculum at the Chicago Public Schools/University of Chicago Internet Project (CUIP) prior to joining National-Louis University in 2004. Cunningham's research interests include emergent technologies for online education, the applications of shared inquiry in teaching and learning, and the history of moral education.

**Ronnie Davey**, a former English teacher in secondary school, has for the last decade been a teacher educator, first at the Christchurch College of Education and now at the University of Canterbury in New Zealand. She is the immediate past president of the New Zealand Association for the Teaching of English (NZATE), and has published both school texts on New Zealand fiction writers and academic papers on ICTs and teacher education. Her research interests include new literacies and English education, preservice and inservice teacher education, and professional identity. Davey is currently engaged in a major national research project investigating effective practice in inservice teacher education (INSTEP).

**Kara Dawson** is an Associate Professor of Educational Technology in the School of Teaching and Learning at the University of Florida. She serves as the program coordinator for the face-to-face and online programs there. Her research relates to investigating innovative ways in which technology supports teaching and learning processes. She has special interest in how teacher inquiry can be used to document the impact of technology on student achievement and in partnerships between K–12 and university programs. She serves on the Editorial Board for the Journal of Computing in Teacher Education (JCTE) and the Journal of Research on Technology in Education (JRTE).

**Judy T. DiLeo** has worked in public education since 1988. As a teacher of students with specific learning disabilities, she has taught children ages 5 through 18. She currently teaches English as a Second Language in grades K–12. Since the early days of the Apple II and Macintosh, she has included technology in daily instruction. In her role as technology coordinator, DiLeo helped teachers and students integrate technology across the curriculum. Her article in this book underscores the importance of appropriate support in technology implementation and details one district's process for enhancing techno-skills among teachers for the purpose of improving achievement among learners.

**David R. Erickson** is an Associate Professor in the Department of Curriculum and Instruction at the University of Montana. David served as the Director of Professional Development for the Montana TALES Grant from 2000 to 2003. His research focuses on professional development in teaching mathematics and using educational technology, including teacher change as required by advances in technology tools for teaching. He believes that the use of graphing calculators and handheld computer–algebra systems provide symbolic-manipulation opportunities for everyone. Appropriate use of such technologies is critical for sustaining forward progress in education.

**Maryanne Fazio-Fox** has worked for more than a decade with K–University instructors to conceptualize, produce, and pilot technology-integrated curricula. She served for several years as the lead instructional designer at the Office for Teaching and Learning Effectiveness (OTLE) at Northern Arizona University, where she actively participated in the design and production of more than 100 Web courses. At NAU, she also developed a faculty-training model to aid instructors in making the transition from face-to-face to technology-aided instruction. Recently she has served as a professional-development specialist and curriculum designer for grant-funded technology-integration projects in K–12 schools.

**Vince Ham**, a former Rhodes Scholar, was educated at the University of Canterbury, New Zealand, and Oxford University in the UK. After a long career as a history teacher and teacher educator in educational computing, Vince left the academy to be a founding Director of CORE Education in Christchurch, New Zealand. CORE Education is an independent, not-for-profit research, development, and consultancy centre specialising in e-learning. Vince's research areas are practitioner research methods, teachers' professional learning, large-scale programme evaluation, and the effective integration of new technologies into formal teaching and learning. He has published widely in the e-learning and teacher education fields, and serves on the international editorial boards of several journals on education and e-learning.

**Mary Lane-Kelso** advises and teaches courses in educational technology and curriculum development as well as the integration of technology in schools at Northern Arizona University's Educational Technology Master's Program. She also works with several educational technology grants throughout the state. Lane-Kelso's research interests include the application of pedagogical principles and learning theories to the design and development of online learning environments that include professional development and global education. She is also interested in the integration of technology into nontraditional learning environments as well as issues related to digital equity and education for sustainability.

**Kimberly A. Lawless** is an associate professor of Educational Psychology and Language, Literacy, and Culture at the University of Illinois at Chicago. Lawless studies how individuals acquire and comprehend information from nonlinear digital environments, focusing on how aspects of the learner, the media, and the task influence navigational strategy and learning outcomes. She has published more than 90 articles in these areas and procured over four million dollars in grant funding.

**Sarah McPherson** is an assistant professor and chair of the graduate program in Instructional Technology at New York Institute of Technology. Prior to coming to NYIT, she was the Associate Director of the Johns Hopkins University Center for Technology in Education and led the Maryland Technology Academy in partnership with Towson University and the Maryland State Department of Education. She teaches courses in technology for diverse learners and integrating technology into language arts. McPherson is a former board member of MICCA, the Maryland ISTE affiliate, and currently serves on the board of directors of NYSCATE, New York's ISTE affiliate.

**Dianna L. Newman** is a Professor in the Department of Educational and Counseling Psychology and the Director of the Evaluation Consortium at the University at Albany/SUNY. In that capacity, she has served as an external evaluator on multiple K–12 technology-integration projects. Her major areas of research include systems change analysis, technology usability, and the longitudinal impact of technology integration.

**Rae Niles** has been in public education for more than 20 years. She currently serves as the Director of Curriculum and Technology for Sedgwick Public Schools, USD 439 in Sedgwick, Kansas. Rae has been a keynote speaker and presenter for several state, national, and international conferences, sharing how students are seamlessly using technology in Grades K–12 and how access to wireless, mobile technology changes teaching and learning for both the student and the teacher. She has also collaborated with Apple Computer, Follett Education, McNeil Lehrer, and the Learning First Alliance.

**Thomas L. Otto** is the principal of Withcott State Primary School in Queensland, Australia, and has 30 years' experience as a principal in primary and secondary schools. His EdD at the University of Southern Queensland investigated the beliefs of principals about teaching with ICTs. He is currently undertaking a PhD project to develop a framework for designing and sustaining constructivist learning environments. The field work for this project has provided significant professional development opportunities for teachers and school administrators across the state, including the classroom implementation of student-centred ePortfolios. Otto has contributed several papers at AACE and ACCE conferences.

**Josh Radinsky** is an Assistant Professor of the Learning Sciences at the University of Illinois at Chicago. He teaches courses in research on learning environments and social studies education, and conducts research in collaboration with teachers in Chicago Public Schools. His research uses sociocultural and cognitive theoretical frameworks to study how students learn to reason with visual data, with an emphasis on history and the social sciences in elementary, secondary, and undergraduate settings. His research and development projects include Teaching and Learning with Geographic Information Systems (http://litd.psch.uic.edu/gis) and GIS for History (www.gisforhistory.org).

**Cathy Risberg** is an educational consultant with 15 years of teaching experience in public and private schools. As the owner of Minds That Soar, LLC, she specializes in providing academic advocacy services for gifted and twice-exceptional children and their families. Along with Dinaz Tambe and Arlene Borthwick, she implemented a 2001 Palm Education Pioneer grant in two third-grade classrooms, and she participated in collaborative research with Arlene Borthwick in 2002–2003. This research focused on conditions necessary for successful implementation of new technologies and examined obstacles to and benefits of using handheld computers as identified in a case study.

**Louanne Smolin** is currently an adjunct faculty member at National-Louis University. Prior to that, she was Clinical Associate Professor of Curriculum and Instruction in the Department of Education at the University of Illinois at Chicago. She specializes in the use of technology in K–8 classroom contexts, with a particular emphasis on community partnerships designed to facilitate teacher development in technology integration. She has published articles and book chapters related to professional development and technology integration. She has also presented her work at numerous national and international conferences.

**Linda S. Tafel** is a Professor at National-Louis University. Her research focuses on leadership and school change within and across cultural settings. Tafel's areas of professional expertise include educational leadership and administration, curriculum planning and evaluation, teacher education, teacher education accreditation, licensure and certification, and the professional development of teachers and school leaders. She has explored the work of educational leaders in Germany, Poland, Thailand, and China and is currently engaged in supporting the work of a network of principals in Poland. She continues to explore and use new technologies through the creation of learning communities, both face-to-face and online.

**George D. Warriner II** has been in public education for 17 years as a classroom teacher, coach, and administrator. Currently he is the Coordinator of Instructional Technology and Interventions for the Sheboygan Area School District in Wisconsin, where he established the Instructional Technology Mentor Program, enhancing the classroom instructional strategies of more than 200 teachers over the last ten years. He also is the founder and administrator of a charter high school that utilizes personalized curriculum and online courses. George earned his MS in Instructional Communication and Computing from the University of Wisconsin–Madison and his doctorate in Educational Technology from Pepperdine University. His interests include sustaining innovations in school districts and personalizing education for students according to their interests and abilities.

**Derek Wenmoth** is the Vice President of the Distance Education Association of New Zealand as well as the Director of e-Learning at CORE Education. He is a past recipient of the Peter Brice Award (from The Pacific Circle Consortium) in recognition of his achievements in fostering inter-cultural understanding through distance education in the Asia-Pacific region. Derek's research interests are in the application of new technologies to distance education, (online) communities of practice, and national policy development in e-learning. Derek writes and manages a widely read blog on e-learning (http://blog.core-ed.net/derek/).

**Diane Yendol-Hoppey** is an Associate Professor in the School of Teaching and Learning at the University of Florida. Her research focuses on job-embedded professional development and supervision that integrate the tools of mentoring, peer coaching, teacher research, professional learning communities, lesson study, and research in action. Her work involves cultivating rich contexts for teacher learning through school–university partnerships and the development of teacher leadership that is powerful enough to contribute to school improvement. Her research has appeared in such journals as Teachers College Record and Journal of Teacher Education. She is the co-author of three books published by Corwin Press.

**Nicole Zumpano** has taught for 15 years in Chicago Public Schools. She is a National Board Certified teacher, and holds a masters degree in Administration and Supervision. She plays an active role within her school as a Local School Council representative, grade-level chairperson, and liaison for the school's relationship with Chicago Communities In Schools. She individually designed and maintains the school Web site as well. Nicole was a participant in the Web Institute for Teachers and went on to be a mentor in the program for the next five years. She has won several grants that benefit her students, including one with NASA, and currently holds a fellowship with the Teachers Network Leadership Institute.

# Contents

# Introduction to Professional Development Strategies in Educational Technology

*Arlene Borthwick*
National-Louis University

*Melissa Pierson*
University of Houston

## Purpose, rationale, value

In an effort to assist those who are (or will be) responsible for planning, implementing, and/or assessing professional development in educational technology, this text provides an overview of professional development (PD) programs that have demonstrated long-term success through assessment of outcomes to provide recommendations for future effective professional development efforts. In the past, PD programs in educational technology have often focused on developing teacher competency in using specific hardware and software applications. By contrast, the models described in this text focus on approaches that expand teachers' knowledge, skill, and confidence in using technology tools in teaching and learning environments, with the focus on improving teaching and learning rather than on the technology use. Some teachers may be hesitant or even resistant to trying new instructional methods, yet the introduction of new technology tools in the classroom, accompanied by the appropriate professional development, may enable these teachers to implement student-centered constructivist approaches (Matzen & Edmunds, 2007). Although there is no one "right" approach to working with teachers, professional developers will increase their chances for success in developing a PD program for their local context when they base their work on a solid theoretical background of adult learning theory and organization development, along with an understanding of lessons learned from the practice of others through the years. This text aims to assist professional developers in just this way—through the guidance of fellow practicing professionals involved in innovative programs being implemented both nationally and internationally.

## Content of the book

The book is divided into three sections: (1) a set of introductory chapters that provide a history of professional development in educational technology as well as a grounding in the literature on adult learning and organizational climate for effective professional development; (2) chapters on successful and cutting-edge professional development models that describe program planning, implementation, and assessment; and (3) a closing chapter that highlights lessons to be learned by professional developers through reading this book. The professional development models included in the text represent long-term projects from which the authors could discuss observed outcomes (e.g., changes in learning environments) and recommendations for successful future implementation. The models involve a variety of information and communication technologies and the work of colleagues across the United States, Australia, and New Zealand.

## Background chapters: History, adult learning, organization development

Chapters 1 through 3 frame the concept of educational technology professional development with an introduction (for novice professional developers) or an update (for experienced professional developers) to the history and research on professional development in educational technology, adult learning theory, and organizational context (school, district, and beyond) for successful professional development of teachers.

## Models of professional development

Chapters 4 through 12 discuss selected professional development programs, grouped by general descriptive category: Working with In-House Leadership (chapters 4 through 6), Peer Coaching (chapter 7), Learning Circles (chapter 8), Action Research (chapter 9), Outside Leaders and Partners (chapter 10), Networked Learning Communities (chapter 11), and Systemic Change (chapter 12). Chapter authors chronicle the development of these programs along with significant outcomes. Although chapters are labeled as particular models, many of their approaches are hybrids involving more than one form of professional development (e.g., the approach described in chapter 11 includes online communities as well as on-site mentors).

## Lessons learned: Charting your path to success

In the final chapter Pierson and Borthwick conclude the book by highlighting lessons learned from each chapter, reviewing common and disparate elements of the models discussed, and identifying themes that emerge throughout the chapters.

## Special chapter features: Literature Essentials and Getting Started Resources

Each chapter in the "Models of Professional Development" section is presented against the backdrop of selected relevant literature in boxed features labeled *Literature Essentials*. Rather than a comprehensive literature review, *Literature Essentials* situate each model in the collective experience and recommendations of researchers to enlighten your interpretation of the specific model and to inform the design and implementation of future professional development activities.

The intent of this text is that you will be interested, inspired, and intrigued to consider how elements of the models presented here might be applied to your own context. When you are ready to learn more about specific topics discussed in chapters 1 through 3, or one of the professional development models discussed in chapters 4 through 12, get started on your journey right away with the *Getting Started Resources* section at the end of each chapter. Chapter authors have identified and annotated resources helpful to successfully implementing professional development strategies akin to the methods discussed in their chapters.

## Where should I start? PD models at a glance

You are encouraged to explore the background material and the PD models in any order as needed to support your growth as a professional developer. The Professional Development Models At a Glance table is intended to guide your exploration by outlining key characteristics of each model, including professional development activities, technologies, underlying framework, and assessment tools.

As you read, you will find that chapter authors share both knowledge and insights as they discuss key strategies, critical moments, challenges, and benefits of implementing professional development models in a specific context. Further informed by up-to-date literature on adult learning, organization development, and the historical underpinnings of professional development in educational technology, we hope that you will move forward with confidence as you plan PD activities to improve teaching and learning through the integration of information and communication technologies.

## Audience for the book

The intended audience for this book is district and building-level professional developers, administrators, teacher-leaders, and technology committees responsible for planning professional development activities; and private, government, university, and agency consultants and researchers who design, implement, and assess the process and outcomes of professional development. The book will also be appropriate as a text in educational technology graduate programs or educational administration professional development courses and workshops.

*The Editors wish to acknowledge the guiding hand of Marianne Handler, Professor Emerita at National-Louis University, in developing the proposal and selecting chapters for this book.*

# Professional Development (PD) Models At a Glance

| Chapter | Title | Model | PD Activities |
|---|---|---|---|
| 4 | Designing and Sustaining Constructivist Learning Environments | In-house leadership | Sharing cases; workshops; information booklet; Web site; e-mail discussion list |
| 5 | Technology Apprentices, SWAT Teams, and Using Students for Professional Development | In-house leadership | Students as technology mentors for teachers and peers |
| 6 | Sustaining an Innovative Professional Development Initiative: Key characteristics to consider | In-house leadership | Peer-mentors; curriculum integration through understanding by design (UbD); year-round PD including graduate credit; mentor presentations at conferences |
| 7 | Peer Coaching and Technology Integration: Insights from three projects | Peer coaching | Peer coaching; inter-school peer mentoring; personal trainers |
| 8 | Digital Storytelling Promotes Technology Integration | Learning circles | Developing digital stories; ongoing mentoring |
| 9 | Teachers Doing IT For Themselves: Action research as professional development | Action research | Teaching mentoring; action research |
| 10 | Higher Education Institutions as Partners for Technology Professional Development | Working with outside leaders and partners | Intensive summer programs; collaborative curriculum design; mentoring |
| 11 | How Do We Support Teacher Learning Online and On-site?: Lessons learned from Washington's Networked Learning Community | Networked learning communities | Helping teachers establish a vision, situating learning in teachers' work, providing authentic audience for sharing |
| 12 | Ensuring Integration of Teacher Changes: What practices will make sure that professional development takes a hold? | Systemic change | Varied (as implemented in 50 grant-supported projects) |

| Technologies | Framework | Assessment Tools | Selected Lessons Learned |
|---|---|---|---|
| e-Portfolios | Constructivist learning environments; case based reasoning | Case stories, workshop feedback, e-Portfolio implementation | Long-term program with large impact possible through limited number of well-planned PD sessions |
| Laptop initiative for curriculum integration | Appreciative inquiry | Student and teacher focus groups | Stages of implementation led to paradigm shift of teacher-student roles |
| Variety of classroom tools; mentor e-mails and chats | Activity system | Journal entries, e-mail, online survey and structured interviews | Expect stages of PD program to include implementation "dip" |
| Internet resources | Job-embedded support | Peer coaching checklist matrix; survey and interviews; NCREL Learning with Technology tool; teacher feedback; review of teacher-designed materials | Peer coaching is successful when context includes well-designed materials, exemplary pedagogical strategies and receptive school culture |
| Multimedia; audio and video-tape; online databases and other Internet resources; software applications such as PowerPoint, Photoshop or iMovie, and digital tools, such as digital camcorders or scanners | Situated cognition | Doug Johnson's Code 77 rubrics; TAGLIT teacher survey; individualized multimedia technology learning plan (IMTLP); summative sharing and reflection; direct observation, journals, and interviews | Teachers are successful when they learn technology through an authentic teaching application, supported through a learning community |
| Variety of information communication technologies (ICTs), especially eLearning | Reflective inquiry | Teacher self-study and research reports | Action research, supported by external mentoring, allows teachers to focus on own teaching practice beyond technology use |
| Web-based materials | School–university collaboration | Surveys, reports from mentors, observations, document analysis, formal external evaluation, | Partnerships with higher education afford resources that allow for success of K–12 PD |
| Online communication tool | Web-based learning communities | Teacher logs, case studies, interviews, lesson design, conference presentations | Success of online learning communities requires appropriate communication tools and structured learning activity, as well as connection with existing learning communities, peer experts, and initiatives |
| Varied (as implemented in 50 grant-supported projects) | Three I Model of Systems Change: Initiation, Implementation, Impact | Meta-analysis of 50 cases | Sustainability: PD without systems change is not effective |

# section I
# Background Chapters

## History, Adult Learning, and Organization Development

### chapter 1
Professional Development
in Educational Technology
What have we learned so far?

### chapter 2
Using Adult Learning Theory to Frame
and Support Professional Development
What should we know?

### chapter 3
Establishing an Organizational Climate
for Successful Professional Development
What should we do?

**chapter 1**

# Professional Development in Educational Technology
## What have we learned so far?

*Robert Bowe*
*National-Louis University*

*Melissa Pierson*
*University of Houston*

## abstract

THE INTRODUCTORY CHAPTER sets the stage with a brief overview of major initiatives and trends in professional development in educational technology during the first two decades of computers in schools. After a discussion of the importance of educational-technology professional development, this chapter will outline related theoretical models that have guided our understanding of, and provided a roadmap for, countless initiatives encouraging effective technology use. The chapter concludes with a review of the literature on strategies for increasing teacher adoption of technology in the learning environment.

When Irving Independent School District in Texas started its 1-to-1 laptop initiative in 2001, they needed to design technology training for 9,600 users over the next four years. The district's long-term goals included changing the very ways that teachers approached teaching and learning, so initial training targeted toward how to use the laptops in the classroom was crucial. Venturing into this new realm of learning opportunities dictated that teachers be prepared in new and different ways, including how to model best practice activities in the form of face-to-face interactions and online video clips. Much of the training focused on progressive concepts, such as learning to guide the students, as opposed to directing them; maintaining student interest in learning; and creating activities that seamlessly integrate technologies into the existing curriculum. The final results were transformative. Not only did the students learn more (Owen, Farsaii, Knezak, & Christensen, 2005), but students were reported to be more motivated and engaged. Teachers affirmed that the availability of technology became a benefit of their job and for many was a motivator for continued employment at this particular school district. Some teachers even observed that having such a technology-rich environment gave the Irving schools a hiring advantage with which other districts could not compete.

In districts with goals as progressive as those of Irving Independent School District, teachers attend workshops throughout the year designed to help improve their teaching. These workshops, interchangeably called *inservice education, teacher training, staff development, professional development,* or *human resource development* (National Staff Development Council [NSDC], 2006), may consist of single days of training that are often unrelated to each other. A common format is a guest speaker who dominates the entire day with a steady delivery of information. This single-day, one-size-fits-all model assumes that the audience of teachers use similar teaching methods with identical groups of students. As a result, there is very little change to overall teacher attitudes or skill levels with regard to the use of technology. Recently, though, this approach is morphing into models characterized more by personalized just-in-time instruction and ongoing support. Increasingly, teachers are encouraged to self-reflect and exchange ideas with one another concerning new teaching strategies. As we will see in this book, such an interactive approach is becoming one of the most effective tools for encouraging teacher change.

This chapter provides an introduction to educational-technology professional development, highlighting effective approaches that have been tested throughout computer technology's opening decades in schools. Though professional development of technology skills can be provided in a range of formats, such as demonstrations or hands-on workshops, it is important to avoid assuming that rows of computers are the most important ingredient. In fact, a room that is designed for participants to talk, share techniques, and collaboratively pose and answer questions about their technology-enriched lessons can be of far greater value. Major contributing theoretical frameworks, such as teacher learning, dissemination of innovation, and change theory, will be discussed as key ingredients to creating sound and effective strategies for increasing teacher adoption of technology in the learning environment.

# Why is professional development vital to effective technology use?

Investing in long-term professional development goals such as those of the Irving Independent School District means relying on the professionalism and expertise of each teacher, not only in the areas of content and pedagogy, but also in the appropriate use of technology (Mishra & Koehler, 2006; Pierson, 2001). To positively affect teacher action in the classroom, teachers must be convinced that these new instructional technologies (IT) will actually lead to increased student learning. Once a teacher has created a personal goal of using technology, learning new technical skills is one thing, but learning how to effectively teach with IT is something entirely different.

The National Staff Development Council (NSDC) recommends that 25% of professional development time be devoted to learning and collaborating with colleagues (NSDC, 2006). This recommendation is evident in some countries where teachers are required to spend only 15 hours per week in the classroom and the rest of the time planning, meeting with colleagues, continuing their education, contacting parents, and working with students (Darling-Hammond, 1998). Asian countries such as Japan and Korea are reported to allocate a much larger amount of a teacher's schedule to professional development than their American counterparts. In these countries, approximately 60 days a year are set aside for new teachers to spend working with other teachers, parents, and students in a nonteaching setting (Bond, 1998). New teachers in American public schools, on the other hand, are often turned loose in their classrooms, only to be heard from again on the day they quit (Brown, 2003).

What many people outside the educational community fail to realize is that the single greatest impact on improved student achievement is increased teacher education. The qualifications of the teacher constitute 44% of the impact on student learning (NSDC, 2006). Joellen Killion, Director of Special Projects for the NSDC, states that the ultimate goal of any educational professional development is to improve student achievement, which can be accomplished in three ways: (1) increasing teacher content knowledge, (2) changing teachers' attitudes about their content areas, and (3) expanding the teacher's repertoire of instructional practices (Killion & NSDC, 2002). Clearly, then, IT professional development would overlay the goal—increasing the meaningful use of technology—with both content and pedagogy.

Not only does technology offer a variety of instructional options to teachers, it additionally motivates students who are accustomed to electronic devices in their everyday lives. And yet, one study (Sparks, 2006) reported that only 7% of schools have teachers who are technologically advanced enough to effectively integrate technology into their lessons. Lawless and Pellegrino (2007) believe it is unclear that students will "have access to teachers who know how to use that technology well to support 21st-century learning and teaching" (p. 578). This works against a long-held Vygotskian belief that teachers need to be aware of sociocultural influences on their students to maximize each student's understanding of the curriculum and the world around them (Vygotsky & Cole, 1978). This same study found that 36% of schools provide no professional development for technology and another 29% provide only 1–14 hours a year. It labeled teacher development as the "biggest technology challenge" facing schools. Even William Bennett, the former Secretary of Education, who stated that there was no significant evidence that most uses of computers significantly improve learning, conceded that "[when] teachers aren't trained to teach differently with the help of [computer] equipment, all too often they end up forfeiting its latent benefit and allowing students to play games or roam the Web" (Bennett, 1999).

If the primary purpose of professional development is to improve the learning outcomes of students, then the first goal of any professional development model should be to change the way each teacher actually teaches (Guskey, 2002). Initial tangible differences in the ways teachers conduct their classes as a result of a workshop might entail using a computer with a projector to demonstrate a science simulation, or it might include guiding students to do research independently at the Library of Congress's Web site. A logical next goal is that teachers take time to analyze the overall effect of any new approach on student learning, such as by gathering frequent feedback directly from students. Teachers too often abandon a new approach because they have not taken the time to examine the end results on students. Even if student learning has increased, teachers still may find it difficult to make changes in their teaching permanent.

Studies have suggested that the effects of good professional development alone are reason enough to provide training whenever possible. One study showed that schools in which teachers had technology training and used computers to teach higher-order skills also enjoyed lower student absenteeism and higher teacher morale (Schacter, 1999). The study also found that students of teachers who had received any kind of staff development in computer technology during the past five years outperformed students whose teachers had no educational technology training. In fact, eighth graders whose teachers had technology training were found to be one-third of a grade level higher than those whose teachers lacked this training.

## Theoretical support for educational technology professional development

During the first two decades of rapid growth of IT use by classroom teachers, a number of theoretical models emerged to describe developmental levels of teachers' progress in learning to teach with technology over a period of time, including changes in instructional practices, attitudes, concerns, and adoption of innovations. These models have guided our understanding of, and provided a roadmap for, countless initiatives encouraging effective technology use. Primary in all of these models is the acknowledgement that change is a process that takes time and requires constant support in order for the individuals attempting to change to be successful.

## Stages of concern

Starting in 1981, Apple Inc. created opportunities for educators to observe and develop their own methods of teaching to take advantage of the many benefits that technology offers. During its 10-year research project, the Apple Classrooms of Tomorrow (ACOT) studied the changes in instructional beliefs and practices of elementary and secondary teachers and their students due to the infusion of an exceptional amount of technology. A primary outcome that emerged over the multiple-year study was a set of five *Stages of Concern* of individual teachers as they grew comfortable with using technology (Sandholtz, Ringstaff, & Dwyer, 1997).

The first stage, *Entry*, addresses the uncertainty teachers may feel about their own ability to use the new technology in their classrooms. Professional developers should be aware of teacher confidence levels as well as getting teachers to focus on careful planning. The next stage, *Adoption*, describes skills and strategies for effectively coping with challenges that arise during a lesson. During the *Adaptation* stage, teachers began making the technology work for them, getting past issues of teaching the technology and back to teaching content. Teachers also reported that administrative duties, such as record keeping and test creation, were made easier and less time-consuming by use of the technology. *Appropriation* is the stage at which technology is used effortlessly as a tool for teaching. If these developmental stages are achieved, the teacher can progress into the *Invention* stage, in which a new learning environment is developed as a context for using technological resources. Outcomes from the research showed that technology can positively impact the classroom climate and the capabilities of students (Sandholtz et al., 1997). In addition to outlining the various phases through which teachers progress, Sandholtz, Ringstaff, and Dwyer outline the types of support teachers require during these phases, including emotional support (Entry), with the later addition of technical assistance (during Adoption), opportunities for instructional sharing (during Adaptation), and the option of team teaching (during Appropriation and Invention). Apple's success also inspired other technology companies to create their own educator development projects, such as Intel's *Teach to the Future* and IBM's *Reinventing Education*, although not until years later.

## Concerns-based adoption model (CBAM)

The Concerns-Based Adoption Model (CBAM) (Hall & Hord, 1987) has guided professional developers by describing *Stages of Concerns* and *Levels of Use* of teachers engaged in a process of change related to technology. Professional developers who understand where each teacher is in the change process are more likely to be successful than those who plunge headlong into the content of a session with little or no attempt to get to know each participant. Listening to the types of questions being asked and the ways each teacher is using technology allows the professional developer to accurately understand which stage each teacher is in. In general, teachers at the beginning of a change process ask more self-oriented questions, about how a new technology will help them personally

(*Awareness, Informational, Personal*). Once they have developed a base of initial confidence, teachers' questions become more task-oriented, related to how they use the tool and why they are having particular challenges (*Management, Consequence*). And, toward the end of the process, teachers tend to alter their perspective to look toward their work with others and the larger impact of the use of the technology on students (*Collaboration, Refocusing*).

Together with teacher questions, the CBAM Levels of Use taxonomy describes how teachers use technology tools in different ways as they move through a change process, which has specific implications for the individualization of professional development. Over time, teachers work to implement what they have learned in authentic classroom settings and must continue to have access to and guidance from a professional trained in effective technology use. Beginning users (*Non-Use, Orientation, Preparation*) require information and specific plans to use the technology. As they develop more skill and confidence, tool usage becomes the norm (*Mechanical, Routine*), meaning professional developers may need to combat teachers' beliefs that they have already learned all there is to learn. At latter stages of the process (*Refinement, Integration, Renewal*), teachers again open up to considering further changes in their own practice. Professional developers must monitor the Stages of Concern and Levels of Use of their participants over the course of several months or years.

## Diffusion of innovations

From Everett Rogers (2003), professional developers have learned that the adoption of innovations is dependent on several interrelated models of change. Individual teachers themselves, as adopters of new technology innovations, fall into predictable categories that describe their comfort with and level of adventurousness toward the uncertainty of newness. *Innovators* are at the cutting edge, latching onto new instructional technologies first. The majority of teachers will fall into one of three middle categories: *Early Adopters, Early Majority*, and *Late Majority*. Bringing up the rear are the *Laggards*, who tend to resist new innovations and frequently pose the largest challenge to professional developers. The decision process that an individual teacher goes through to adopt an innovation also follows a developmental pattern through the stages of *Knowledge, Persuasion, Decision, Implementation*, and *Confirmation*. And each innovation itself possesses attributes that make it more or less desirable to an adopter: *Relative Advantage, Compatibility, Complexity, Trialability*, and *Observability*. Those who are conducting professional development sessions are often placed in the role of "Change Agent," a role described by Rogers as one that changes or shifts during the diffusion process, a role that eventually leads to working oneself out of a job as others become more proficient.

## Four-stage professional renewal cycle

Kansas State University faculty members Gerald Bailey and Dan Lumley (Bailey & Lumley, 1997) revisited this model, initially developed by Joyce and Showers (1988), which is designed to describe how educators interact with new educational materials and strategies. At the beginning of the cycle, participants interact and share ideas about the new material (*Information*). The next stage gives an opportunity for the group to see the new teaching approach in action via an actual lesson or possibly a video recording (*Demonstration*). Time is then devoted to practicing this new approach so that each participant gets a chance to experience it firsthand (*Practice*). After the practice, it is important for the participants to come back together to share their experiences. The final stage is to pair each participant with a coach who is well trained in the new teaching approach. It is at this stage that the participant works out specific details that apply to his or her teaching environment (*Feedback*).

## Knowledge, attitude, skill, aspiration, and behavior (KASAB)

A common model of planning for professional development is *Knowledge, Attitude, Skill, Aspiration*, and *Behavior*, or KASAB (Killion & NSDC, 2002). The KASAB model helps professional developers understand how teachers move beyond merely creating a path to achieving a specified goal. In this model, professional developers focus on having teachers learn more about a topic (*Knowledge*). Once the teachers experience the possibilities, they are motivated (*Attitude*) to learn more about the topic. After taking time to build their skills (*Skills*), the teachers are further motivated to develop lessons themselves using their newly acquired skills (*Aspiration*). The resulting behavior is that teachers will change how they teach (*Behavior*).

## New consensus model: Individual and collaborative inquiry

In 2002, one Minnesota school established a project that required long-term participation from its teachers. Small groups of teachers collaboratively investigated pedagogical and content issues to bring about a change in teaching practice (Hughes, Kerr, & Ooms, 2005). This project was based on the new consensus model of Hawley and Valli (1999) in which teachers were asked to choose their own topic of study and collaborate in small groups. Teachers then took part in a careful self-reflection, taking stock of their own beliefs and specific approaches to teaching. Detailed discussions as a group included considering alternatives to current practices and possible effects of each change. Finally, the new practice was integrated into a lesson plan and taught in a classroom. Final discussions with the group about the effect of this new lesson helped to fine-tune the lesson for use in subsequent classes.

# Professional development frameworks

Through the late 1990s, educational technology workshops could be categorized by a framework of four types of professional development activities (Bailey & Lumley, 1997). The first of these four, *Administrative Productivity*, has gotten a lot of attention recently, especially due to the demands of the United States of America No Child Left Behind (NCLB) legislation, which requires large amounts of student data to be collected and analyzed to guide the curriculum. Workshops in this category include training in software designed to increase the everyday functioning of the school, including automated attendance, record keeping, and maintaining a Web site. The second of these four types of workshops is referred to as *Teaching and Learning*. This is professional development designed specifically to help the teacher with the effective application and integration of technology resources into existing curriculum. The third type of workshop can be labeled *Curricular Production–Tools*. Training in this category mainly includes the prepackaged software programs that are sold to schools as a conveniently organized method of teaching, tracking, and reporting student progress. Some of these are better known as Integrated Learning Systems (ILS), which consist of a wide variety of bundled activities and corresponding testing and remediation alternatives. Workshops on production tools have seen a resurgence recently, once again due to the recent NCLB legislation. Finally, the fourth type of workshop deals with the concept of *School Restructuring*. With the advent of the digital age, schools are finding they need to reform their practices to address the overall effects technology is having on our society. As a method of reform, it is important to start a dialogue with teachers, students, and community members about how schools can best meet these new challenges. NCLB has had an effect here, also, by discouraging this conversation. NCLB's focus on frequent and high-stakes assessment is challenged by opponents who believe over-reliance on high-stakes testing may lead to inaccurate conclusions and be potentially harmful to teaching–learning environments. However, as we have seen, there are school district plans, such as Irving Independent School District's constructivist model, that embrace progressive approaches to professional development and school reform.

As the field of educational technology professional development has evolved, Judy Harris, a former teacher and now a professor at the College of William and Mary, has suggested a more sophisticated framework focusing on teacher action and context (2007). She contends that there are five general types of professional development models:

- Group training, which involves demonstrations or instructor-led hands-on activities;

- Individualized learning, or independent exploration;

- Collaborative observation and analysis, a more involved model that may involve school visits, mentoring, peer coaching, and critical friends;

- Inquiry/Action research, requiring systematic data collection and analysis; and

- Collaborative development/improvement, which takes the form of group projects or problem-solving.

Lawless and Pellegrino (2007) largely concur that high-quality professional development must "[be] longer in duration (contact hours plus follow-up), provide access to new technologies for teaching and learning, actively engage teachers in meaningful and relevant activities for their individual contexts, promote peer collaboration and community building, and have a clearly articulated and a common vision for student achievement" (p. 579). Harris (2007) suggests that although professional development can vary by purpose, objectives, content, grade levels, pedagogies, models, and assessment, effective sessions are all: (1) conducted in school settings; (2) linked to school-wide change efforts; (3) teacher-planned and teacher-assisted; (4) differentiated learning opportunities; (5) focused around teacher-chosen goals and activities; (6) exhibit a pattern of demonstration/trial/feedback; (7) concrete; (8) ongoing over time; and (9) characterized by ongoing assistance and support on-call. However, because factors such as availability of technology, school climate, or participants' experience can vary, professional developers must match the type of professional development to teachers' learning preferences, the goals of any professional development, and the specific context. This matching requires professional developers to select, combine, and sequence goals and models to fit the specific professional development situation.

## Strategies for increasing teacher adoption of technology

On a basic level, the field of education has reached a consensus about what is considered best practice regarding educational technology professional development. In short, professional development will result in the adoption of the desired skill or practice when active participants are the focus of standards-based, integrated content that is continually assessed for effectiveness on many measures.

### Focus on participants

Professional developer Angela Peery (2004) compiled a list of the qualities used by teacher-participants to describe an effective professional development experience. The descriptors predominantly focused on treating teachers as professionals who are fully able to make effective decisions about their classroom lessons. Words such as *congenial, no pressure, validation, trust, informative, flexible,* and *clear purpose* all describe workshops that respect teachers in their roles of decision-maker and caretaker.

Workshops held by RAND/CTI (Glennon & Melmed, 2000) contributed three additional insights that increased effectiveness of professional development. These include providing: (1) adequate time for teachers to acquire skills and plan the school's programs and activities, (2) assistance that is keyed to the needs of the teachers and administrators at times they need it, and (3) a clear vision concerning the purposes and the educational goals that guide the program of the school and classroom.

As studies have shown, a high level of anxiety about computers detracts from the ability to learn skills, and even creates a resistance to learning. In addition, those who are confident of their own ability with computers have been shown to persist at computer-related tasks longer than those who are not (Sam, Othman, & Nordin, 2005). Making participants comfortable—such as by offering food and drink, interacting with the participants, and acknowledging the different needs and skills of each attendee—is an effective initial strategy.

Teachers rarely have the opportunity to come together and converse about their teaching (Vanatta, Banister, Fischer, Messenheimer, & Ross, 2005). When teachers are allowed to come together and share ideas, participants often find so much in common with one another that they readily find answers to problems with which they have struggled. Collaboration can happen on a large scale, such as by having an entire group of teachers travel to a conference together (Rhine & Bailey, 2005), which can introduce an immediate level of bonding that strengthens a group's ability to exchange ideas and critique new approaches, as well as serves as the foundation for future change. However, smaller-scale collaborative techniques can be just as powerful. Reading and discussing a common book (Joyce & Showers, 2002), participating in a teacher support network or community of practice (Killion, 2007; Niesz, 2007), or frequenting social networking sites for educators (e.g., eduwikius.wikispaces.com or www.infinitethinking.org) can allow teachers the time for shared experiences and development. The ability of a group to bond and length of the program were also found to be critical to the long-term success of any training program (McPherson, Wizer, & Pierrel, 2006). In order to help preserve bonding between participants over time, online discussion boards and e-mail discussion lists can be established.

## Broad participation

To be fully effective, the exchange of ideas should take place not only among teachers, but also with administrators and other specialists (Fullan, 1982). Technology coordinators and computer-lab teachers play an important role in sharing ideas with general-education teachers about enhancing the curriculum with technology. When professional development is being planned and carried out, or even when a subject-area curriculum is being mapped out, having a technology specialist on hand to answer questions is invaluable. Without this integration of school personnel, curriculum designers often do not take the crucial step of adding specific technology-enhanced activities. The use of technology may be intended, but there are no specific software or activity needs identified to help achieve the desired learning outcomes.

Administrators can also participate by evaluating teachers specifically on how well they integrate technology into lessons. Too often, when a principal or other teacher evaluator sees a computer on and students busy using it, they assume legitimate curricular goals are being met. Of course this is not always the case. With the proper training and awareness of teacher technology use standards (e.g., NETS•T, International Society for Technology in Education [ISTE], 2008), teacher evaluators can more easily spot appropriate and effective uses of technology. By devoting a section of the evaluation process to technology as a teaching tool, evaluators can motivate teachers to integrate new skills they have learned in workshops. As a follow-up activity with the teacher, the well-trained evaluator can then make suggestions about how to improve the lesson.

## Isolated versus integrated teaching of technical skills

One of the ongoing debates of technology-related professional development planning is whether helping to develop a wide array of computer skills among teachers will actually lead to increased usage of technology in the classroom. One approach focuses on teaching all of the capabilities of a software program, regardless of whether those features will ever get used. Another approach argues that, after receiving an overview of the software, participants can explore the features of the software as needed. A third approach is to wait for the group to convene and decide according to their needs. That would require the planners of the sessions to tailor staff development to individual teachers or small groups of teachers rather than provide a one-size-fits-all generic model (Sparks, 1998). Darling-Hammond (1998) explains that choosing the appropriate foundation-building skills is integral to a good start. Without a basic foundation, participants may find themselves overwhelmed. Educator Mike Schmoker promotes a slightly different approach. He believes that participants are just as able to learn, if not more so, if basic skills are unveiled during times of challenging activities (Schmoker, 1999). He also points out that low-performing participants stand to gain the most from approaches that incorporate basic skills into complex, higher-order-thinking skills.

There are two common scenarios in which training takes place: demonstration by a presenter or hands-on training. One assumption is that workshops in which participants are led through a step-by-step process in a hands-on environment will result in a very successful start. However, when people are simply asked to follow directions, they are doing very little to internalize the learning experience. Relatively little cognitive processing goes on when a person is just following directions. Professional development support must include giving teachers time to experiment, permission to change the way they do things, and the opportunity to make mistakes along the way (Sparks, 1998). In the act of listening to directions, the learner may never feel truly involved, ask questions, or even become curious about the process. On the other hand, if the training requires the participants to watch a demonstration first, followed immediately with hands-on time, then the responsibility and desire to complete the task is turned back to the participant (Darling-Hammond, 1998). Perhaps even the anguish of being frustrated lends itself to the learning process because it draws the learner into the learning process in a much more active way. In addition, it can be argued that the participants learn more because they know they have to rely on themselves to complete the task and not just follow the rote, verbal directions from the trainer.

# Assessment of effectiveness

As we enter the 21st century, research describes the most effective professional development, leading to the most lasting results, as possessing a common set of qualities: (1) long term participation; (2) focus on specific content and/or strategies rather than being general (Fishman, Marx, Best, & Tal, 2003); (3) collaborative participation, as in communities of practice (Borko, 2004; Grossman, Wineburg, & Woolworth, 2001; Little, 2002); (4) coherence; and (5) involving active learning (Desimone, Porter, Garet, Yoon, & Birman, 2002; Garet, Porter, Desimone, Birman, & Yoon, 2001).

Guskey (2000) recommends further that evaluation of professional development examine five areas: (1) participants' reactions, (2) participants' learning, (3) organization support and change, (4) participants' use of new knowledge and skills, and (5) student learning outcomes. The major challenge that remains is measuring the effectiveness of educational technology professional development on teaching and student learning. Despite countless professional development efforts that have been standards-based and aimed at teachers' developmental levels, the inconsistent mix of evaluation methods makes it nearly impossible to attribute any positive (or negative) effects to any specific professional development experience, due either to a lack of a comparison group or because professional development is often instituted as part of a wider reform strategy (Snow-Renner & Lauer, 2005; Spillane, 1999). Additionally, challenges in determining effectiveness lie with how greatly varied the actual quality and makeup of professional development opportunities are, as well as with the use of measurement tools that are not aligned with the specific goals of the professional development (Snow-Renner & Lauer, 2005). Lawless and Pellegrino (2007) provide recommendations for future research on educational technology professional development, highlighting the need to focus interrelated systems to assure that outcomes were the direct result of professional development as opposed to other variables, and further noting the lack of experimental studies and the lack of data collected from students.

Ultimately, although research generally shows that students learn more and are more actively engaged when teachers learn more and are more actively engaged, and despite the addition, and even integration, of instructional technologies, basic instructional practices persist (Mitchum, Wells, & Wells, 2003). A key to this inability to convince teachers to significantly change the way they teach by incorporating modern technologies is the fact that the field of educational technology research lacks proof that using technology leads to increased achievement (Kerr, 1991). In the climate of accountability present in the early 21st century, this absence of causal effects of technology on achievement after considerable technology expenditures—despite myriad isolated positive descriptive studies—makes a continued focus on professional development for educational technology a challenge for districts. Many administrators assume that once their teachers can send an e-mail or make an electronic presentation, they have arrived as a technology-using district and no longer require professional development. There is thus a continued need for accurate assessment of teacher needs and teacher growth as it relates to technology use.

# Focus on standards

During the early part of the 21st century, professional development efforts, along with most education initiatives, were significantly influenced by the development of, and almost universal adherence to, standards in all content and professional areas. The International Society for Technology in Education (ISTE) has become the leading professional organization for technology-using educators. Starting in 1998, ISTE developed the now widely accepted National Educational Technology Standards not only for students, but also for teachers and administrators. Known, respectively, as NETS•S, NETS•T, and NETS•A, these standards are written with the goal of improving teaching and learning by advancing the effective use of technology in education.

The *Framework for 21st Century Learning* outlines the competencies that need to be developed to enable today's students to be digitally literate, inventive thinkers, effective communicators, and highly productive (Partnership for 21st Century Skills, 2008). If teachers are not introduced to these competencies and related standards during professional development workshops, fundamental changes, such as the ones happening in Irving Independent School District, will not become as commonplace as they need to be. The Partnership for 21st Century Skills remind us that we live in a knowledge-based, global society that requires shifts in school policy and practices.

# Conclusion

Many veteran teachers can recall a time in their careers when a specific type of technology was introduced at their schools, only to be given up within a few years for the next innovation. Whether the technology was too complex, was never fully adopted by faculty, or was replaced by newer technology, the whole process may have created negative feelings toward technology as a whole. Stories like this are a challenge for professional developers to overcome. Teachers may recall giving up a great deal of their personal time to learn and integrate a promising new technology only to find that it did not deliver what was promised.

As educators consider new models of professional development such as those presented in this book, and as they identify goals and strategies to achieve an ideal balance of individualization and group participation, they will need to actively study the effects of professional development on teaching and learning. Certainly, the field of education has come a great distance in understanding the range of best practices regarding educational technology professional development. However, consensus on a research agenda in this field will allow us to seek to understand the role of the individual and context in the race to develop 21st-century teachers who guide and shape student learning.

## GETTING STARTED RESOURCES

ACOT. (2007). *Apple classroom of tomorrow.* Retrieved October, 2007, from www.apple.com/education/k12/leadership/acot/

This is the home for the groundbreaking 10-year research and development project sponsored by Apple Inc. A library archive provides easy access to related project reports and articles.

ALTEC. (2003). *Exhibit: ALTEC learning interchange.* Retrieved October, 2007, from http://ali.apple.com/ali_sites/hpli/exhibits/1000097/Introduction.html

By all accounts, the PT3 program was the single largest impetus for the growth of technology-related professional development. This site is the best remaining archive of the funding model, notable and enduring projects, and related resources and assessment tools.

Lamb, A., & Johnson, L. (2007). *Teacher tap: Professional development resources for educators & librarians.* Retrieved October, 2007, from http://eduscapes.com/tap/

Providing easy access to practical, online resources and activities, the Teacher Tap is a free professional-development resource that helps educators and librarians address common questions about the use of technology in teaching and learning.

NSDC. (2007). *Welcome to NSDC.* Retrieved October, 2007, from www.nsdc.org

The National Staff Development Council (NSDC) has the stated purpose of "ensuring that every educator engages in effective professional learning every day so every student achieves." The site highlights projects, publications, conference information, online communities, and the "Professional Development IQ Test" that assists district leaders in exploring the relationship between professional development and student learning.

Partnership for 21st Century Skills. (2008). Retrieved April 6, 2008 from www.21stcenturyskills.org

Informed school and district leaders can use the *Framework for 21st Century Learning* to redefine what it means to be educated. The framework integrates key student outcomes of learning, including core subjects; life and career skills; learning and innovation skills; and information, media and technology skills with necessary support systems of learning environments; professional development; curriculum and instruction; and standards and assessment. The framework encourages educators at all levels to consider the use of 21st century skills to help facilitate change in education.

**chapter 2**

# Using Adult Learning Theory to Frame and Support Professional Development

## What should we know?

*Linda S. Tafel*
*National-Louis University*

## abstract

 THIS CHAPTER PRESENTS a review of the foundational theories underlying adult learning theory, considers the current application of these theories to our work in professional development, and reconsiders these theories in light of the context for our work with adults in schools, school districts, and other educational institutions. Based on implications drawn from this literature for working with both individuals and organizations and from recent change theory literature, the author offers a framework for "working together" that provides readers a helpful background for crafting professional development aligned with adult learning theory.

# Where do we begin? A scenario

It is a Friday in late fall, the first of two regularly-scheduled inservice days in the Happy Valley School District. Following a two-hour morning meeting with all teachers and aides in the auditorium, twenty teachers from Grades K–12, most of whom chose this breakout session as their #2 or #3 choice on the needs assessment, assemble in the cramped computer lab on the first floor of the building for a session called, "Making the Most of Technology: New Tools for Teachers," to be conducted by Mary Maude, a professor from the local university. A week later as she reviews the session evaluation forms, the district superintendent concludes that Dr. Maude will not be invited back and that it will take a miracle to move the resistant faculty toward the district's long-stalled goal to integrate technology across the curriculum. She sighs and shakes her head, wondering, "Where do we go from here?"

Is this a typical scenario? Are the flaws in this model atypical or overstated? Every day, teachers and leaders I work with report that our designs for professional development continue to *work on* adult learners—still training them, herding them into small rooms to learn on demand, viewing them as having deficits, and providing them with generic skills that are disconnected from their real needs and the needs of their students. Fifteen years ago, a colleague and I proposed, as an alternative, a framework for *working with* teachers (Tafel & Bertani, 1992) that was based on principles of adult learning theory. My experiences with teachers and leaders in school settings and my own experiences as an adult learner and learner with and about technology affirm these principles.

Preparing this chapter has allowed me to once again reflect on the foundational theories of adult learning (Knowles, 1973; Kegan, 1982) and the latest reconsiderations of these theories (Knowles, Swanson, & Holton, 2005; Merriam, Caffarella, & Baumgartner, 2006) to identify the implications for the context of our work with adults in schools, school districts, and other educational institutions. In this chapter, I outline considerations that might guide our thinking about adult learning as we plan for, implement, and evaluate professional development (Lindstrom & Speck, 2004). I also link key ideas about adult learning to the rich, but still emerging, literature on change theory, especially as applied to our work in schools and as professional developers (Fullan, 2004; Senge, Scharmer, Jaworski, & Flowers, 2004; Wagner et al., 2006). Near the end of the chapter I will offer a framework for *working together*—for designing professional development around key principles of adult learning and change theory in an attempt to provide a lens for looking at both the design and the outcomes of our professional development efforts. Along the way, I will return to the scenario above to illustrate how the use of this framework might significantly enhance our work.

# Adult learning: Individual or social/group/organization focused?

Nearly every resource about adult learning theory begins by citing and summarizing the work of pioneer Malcolm Knowles (1973) or by contrasting adult learning with children's learning. Knowles, to his credit, focused on adults and how they best learned. Based on his studies with adults—primarily older adults in nonschool settings, he found that adult learners were autonomous and self-directed; had accumulated a foundation of life experiences and knowledge; and were goal-oriented, relevancy-oriented, and practical. He also found that adults wanted to be shown respect for their knowledge, their abilities, and their experience. In proposing his theory of "andragogy," Knowles (1973) contrasted the teaching of adults with other forms of pedagogy (Merriam, Caffarella, & Baumgartner, 2006).

## Individual focus

Knowles' principles have been repeatedly referenced in the last 25 years and often applied to adult learning in school settings. Additionally, Kegan's (1982) work on adult stages provided a useful analysis to frame and support guidelines and later undergird the initial standards for professional development (NSDC, 1994). During the decades of the 1980s and 1990s, these principles often became translated into practices centering on individual needs assessments, maximum degrees of choice, and a focus on individual educator growth. In the last ten years, this individual focus has gradually been eroded as the new version of these standards emerged (Sparks & Hirsh, 1997; NSDC, 2004). Professional development is now "driven by *student* learning" [emphasis mine] and adult learning in schools focuses on "what *must teachers know and do* to ensure student success" [emphasis mine] (Hirsh, 2001, p. 10).

My experience tells me it is essential to return to what we have learned from the pioneers in adult learning and think *first* about the individual adult learners we are working with, *then* about the school context. Creighton (2003) provides vivid descriptions of adult learner attitudes and behaviors run amok during technology planning and implementation. In discussing "resisters" and "saboteurs," he details what we can expect to happen when we focus on training, not education, and in the process ignore or rush past the individual in an effort to get started with changing schools and classrooms. In the scenario posed at the start of the chapter, the faulty assumption of the planners was that giving teachers a choice was analogous to really listening to teachers *before* providing teachers with what someone thought each of them needed to move their technology knowledge and skills forward. In thinking about the adult learner—the individual—reflect on the following questions:

- To what degree have I, as a professional developer, taken into account the individual needs of these adult learners?

- To what degree and toward what purpose is the adult learner/teacher motivated to learn?

- What is the relationship between what we are doing in our professional development efforts and the individual teacher's *definition of self as teacher, self-esteem* or *status*?

- To what degree does the teacher seek out self-directed opportunities to increase the understanding and application of new technologies? How can we recognize, capitalize on, or redirect this evidence of self-direction?

- Have I taken into consideration the individual's experience, interests, and unique background as teacher and learner?

- To what degree will the teacher likely acquire the new knowledge or skills and apply it immediately?

- How do I provide "scaffolding" for the new learning that this adult has just experienced?

- How do I provide time for these adults to construct meaning of what they are learning? To integrate it with their previous knowledge? To use the new learning for themselves and with their students?

- How do I provide support for this adult's learning—through mentoring, coaching, community-building?

With our reflections in mind, let's consider Daloz' question: "Where are [adult learners] going and who are we for them in their journey?" (1999, p. 5). Perhaps this sounds like too big a question for the planner of professional development or the technology coordinator, or Dr. Mary Maude from the posed scenario. If we do not consider the individuals, their "story," their "path," their "journey," and our role in this adult development process, then we are doomed to continue or, worse yet, revert back to the *working on* model characterized by "depersonalized activities that reflect a generic 'one size fits all' perspective" where "the leader knows best and denigrates previous experiences and knowledge" (Tafel & Bertani, 1992, p. 44) of the adult learners.

As we support individual learning and change, we must keep in mind the tension that learning new technology or skills often causes for adults. On the one hand, some teachers will respond well and be naturally motivated when they see that what they are learning will help them be better teachers and meet the needs of learners. On the other hand, teachers may demonstrate outright signs of anxiety or mask their concern through disinterest, distraction, or inattention. Those planners who both understand and use the natural anxiety from adults who are faced with learning something new will provide an early and appropriate safety net—providing ways for individual learners to express both their learning goals and their concerns. Knowing early on who is feeling what about the new challenges can help us guide the adult learning process more appropriately and respectfully.

Although a number of studies focused on the technology anxiety of preservice and inservice teachers during the late 1990s (Ayersman, 1996; Laffey & Musser, 1998; Ropp, 1999), little recent research provides evidence about anxiety among practicing teachers as technology becomes more widely used at both school and home. Of particular interest to me are the possible differences between teachers who are new to the profession and digital natives, and veteran teachers who are digital immigrants. This said, I strongly urge technology leaders to look for emerging leadership among all age and experience segments of a teaching force. I agree with Creighton (2003), "Resisters display immediate opposition [but] they possess untapped energy and creativity often ignored by leaders" (p. 60). I have found that anxiety and resistance are both fleeting and recurring phenomena during the course of change efforts and innovation. I have seen early trailblazers hit the wall at the implementation phase of a technology integration effort. Conversely, I have seen the slow starter blossom into a leader just in time to ignite a new round of enthusiasm for a stalled effort.

In order to minimize anxiety, it is particularly important to scaffold learning experiences for adults who are entering into new territory with technology. The best models I have experienced begin with conversation; hook learners by letting them feel initial success, and move slowly enough to instill confidence but whet the learner's appetite for what's next. Reinforcement is the key. Bravos for engagement, trying it out, and small successes will go a long way in keeping the anxious adult learner feeling safe and respected.

For now, we close with two ideas that we will return to later in the chapter. First, I suggest that by "engendering trust, issuing a challenge, providing encouragement, and offering a vision" (Daloz, 1999, p. 31) to adult learners, we might be able to honor and engage individuals in their own growth as adults and professionals. Second, I believe that foundational to our professional development work with *groups* of teachers—whether in learning communities, teams or whole school faculties—is our work with *individual* adults—each unique, learners on their own journeys and developing along their own paths. Adult learning theory would challenge us to truly accept adults in a *becoming* mode: able to change, learn, improve, and to plan experiences that are carefully and collaboratively tailored to meet individual needs.

## Social/group/organization focus

Fullan has noted the powerful effect on individual motivation, creativity, and innovation from the dominant school culture (Sparks, 2003; Fullan, 2004). Therefore, we must also consider the degree to which our work with adult learners takes place within a social setting—in most cases a school or district—where core values, cultural norms, and a history of honoring (or not) adult learning principles exist. Our program design must continue to consider adult learning theory as we engage adults in learning together: collaborating, setting goals, planning in teams, moving toward implementation, and charting their progress. When thinking about the relationship between the individual and the school culture and context, consider a second set of questions:

- How would I characterize the relationships between adult learners in this school culture? What is the foundation for our work moving forward?

- Who sets the course for learning in this school?

- Are adults used to learning together? If so, what have they learned? What processes are in place?

- Do adults set individual or collective professional learning or development goals?

- What experiences have the adult learners had in working together toward shared goals?

- To what degree and toward what purpose are groups of adults *motivated* to learn together?

- To what degree do groups of teachers seek out common opportunities for their work?

- How has the school used each individuals' experiences, interests, and unique background to support or foster collaboration or common purpose?

- How much time is provided for adults to learn together?

- How would adults define the word "change" in the context of this school?

- On a scale of 1–5 (with 5 exemplifying solid relationships, common purpose and moving toward action or change together), how would you rate this school culture as a learning culture?

As I think about adult learners at work within the larger school culture, I have found Kegan's (1982) framework very helpful. In analyzing the relationship between adult development within the surrounding environment—schools included—we must consider three processes: *confirmation*, *contradiction*, and *continuity*.

The reader must determine whether schools today confirm an individual teacher as a human being, as a professional, as a decision-maker, and as a leader. By transcending and de-emphasizing the role boundaries between leaders and teachers, and by involving teachers in the designing and planning of their own professional development, we can foster and support a culture of *confirmation*. As we recognize and celebrate the experience and knowledge of adult learners and as we use these as the basis for moving the organization forward, we further confirm adults.

Kegan's second process, *contradiction*, provides a wonderful terrain on which to explore the concepts of both individual and organizational growth. It is in the "gap between person and world, things as they might be and things as they are" (Daloz, 1999, p. 187) that real opportunity for personal and system change emerges. In two more recent books, Kegan and his Change Leadership Group colleagues have provided a guide for exploring this gap by focusing on individual and organizational assumptions and immunities to change that get in the way of moving change forward. It is in exploring the contradictions between the "as is" and the "to be" that we find both personal and collective possibility and momentum for our work (Kegan & Lahey, 2001; Wagner et al., 2006).

The third process, *continuity*, a concept first introduced by Dewey (1938) as he explored the differences between experience, education, and mis-education, is further developed by Kegan when he talks about the bridging of individual and organizational worlds (Kegan, 1982; Wagner et al., 2006). Fullan (2004) and others have claimed that barriers to such bridging or continuity must be addressed by systematically improving trust and relationships between and among all adults connected with schools: teachers, leaders, and parents. Donaldson (2006) warns that we cannot move to action in common (addressing organizational goals) unless we ground our work on relationships (between and among individuals) and purpose in common. But existing structural barriers often make it difficult for people to have time to get together or work together regularly, to learn about each other through learning together, and to "be" in relationship with one another. Further, cultural barriers—the way we define teachers' roles, responsibilities and status—within schools cause teachers to resist new ways of learning together. In order to provide continuity for adult learners, we must adopt models for simultaneous learning, supporting the individual, the individual in relationship with others, and in relationship to the larger organization. Such models will be about relationship building, collective work, and sustainable change (Fullan, 2004; Donaldson, 2006).

In short, leadership grounded by adult learning theory would engage individuals and groups within schools differently—ways that return us to a fuller, more comprehensive definition of adult learning that has emerged since Knowles' foundational work, focusing on both individual learning and the social or school context.

## Innovation from the perspective of adult learning theory

Bringing about innovation, whether at the individual or organization–school level, presents a daunting challenge for the professional developer who remains committed to modeling adult learning theory. Because our work with and around technology and professional development is, at its core, centered around leading change, I believe it would be helpful to frame a discussion around Rogers' five perceived attributes of innovation and draw implications for our new work:

1. *Relative advantage* [of an innovation] is the degree to which an innovation is perceived as better than the idea it supersedes.

2. *Compatibility* is the degree to which an innovation is perceived as consistent with the existing values, past experiences, and needs of potential adopters.

3. *Complexity* is the degree to which an innovation is perceived as difficult to understand and use.

4. *Trialability* is the degree to which an innovation may be experimented with on a limited basis.

5. *Observability* is the degree to which the results of an innovation are visible to others. (2003, pp. 15–16)

Each of these attributes informs our work with individuals and among groups of teachers we work with. In considering the *relative advantage* of learning and using new technologies in the classroom, a teacher will weigh the relative merits of the new versus the status quo. Though many teachers will express a desire to break the isolation of their classroom routine, just as many may complain about the amount of time and energy it takes to plan, implement, and assess the impact of new technologies on student work. Many teachers want to know and use the latest technology, but want to learn it painlessly and quickly. Professional developers need to be able to demonstrate, in concrete ways, the relative advantages of the latest software and online learning strategies. It's not enough to talk about the advantages; these must become real—and quickly—for individuals and groups of teachers.

The *compatibility* of an innovation calls upon us to be key observers and data collectors within increasingly complex organizations. Few individuals and organizations are really ready for the change we will lead. Do we ignore the readiness levels and move forward? Not without eyes wide open. The professional developer needs to be keenly aware of the existing values, the past experiences, and needs of both individuals and the organization. When someone like Dr. Mary Maude in the introductory scenario is brought in from the outside, she likely will not spend much time in unearthing the history of technology innovation within the district. She also may not have any data about the needs of each of the individuals or the nature of the school improvement plan. And so, she plunges ahead, delivering a "one size fits none" workshop, aiming down the middle, hitting few targets. Professional developers must become data specialists, collecting, analyzing, and using data about adult learners, the organization, and student learners to make sure innovation has a good chance of success.

More often than not, the *complexity* of an innovation is difficult to understand. I am often struck by my own feelings of being overwhelmed by the "too much, too fast" that comes with complex new technology. I often have expressed the thought, "What if we do half of what you have planned for us today?" I find that those who know and are able to do the latest software, grading program, or courseware are often more excited to show off their facility with the technology than help others, who know little and are begining the journey. If we keep Kagen's principle of confirmation in mind, we will emphasize the relationship between what is known and the new, then simplify, scaffold, and "chunk" the new learning so that individuals and groups continue to feel challenged but not flooded with angst and insecurity. We must also continue to assess the knowledge and skills of each learner so that pioneers stay challenged and can move ahead while those who are taking a bit longer to grasp the innovation are feeling supported, mentored, and on track.

Rogers' notion of *trialability* calls upon us to know about what motivates each individual we work with and challenges us to find creative ways to foster experimentation. For me, this translates into emphasizing the fun, the newness, the excitement, the possibility of the innovation. Undaunted technology trainer beware! This means we cannot run over individuals or organizations with our own agenda, knowledge, and skills. It also means we must create space for adult learners, either alone or acting together, to make the innovation their own—to construct their own meaning and apply the innovation in new ways. When we foster a culture of experimentation and creativity, ownership results.

Persistence, patience, and consistent focus on progress are the keys to supporting *observability*. Through modeling, applauding, and benchmarking innovation, leaders stay relentlessly attuned to both the "here and now" and the "to be." I have found it helpful to coach technology leaders to phase in their plans or programs: identify several goals for "now," more goals for "soon," and a larger set of goals for "later." The tendency is to want too much, too soon, and become frustrated when we expect monumental change faster than can reasonably be expected. In working with individuals and groups, we must consistently ask, "What are you seeing that indicates that change is happening?" We must collect artifacts: exit slips, journal reflections, work products, focus group notes, and other data that support formative assessment. By encouraging reflection and making progress tangible, we can chart a course of accomplishments and progressive growth that everyone can celebrate. Momentum builds and innovation grows strong roots deep within the culture.

## Working together: Foundational assumptions for professional development leaders

Rather than present a list of dos and don'ts, a checklist or a rubric to apply as we analyze the "adult learning fit" for our programs, I propose a set of assumptions that I hope will guide our thinking, our designing, and our planning. This framework builds on and extends the contrasting models of *working on* and *working with* people and organizations (Tafel & Bertani, 1992). In the left hand column of Table 2.1, I present a set of *Processes and Practices That Seem to Ignore What We Know About Adult Learning*. In the right column, I present a set of *Emerging Processes and Practices for Reflective Consideration* by those who would do better. In the discussion that follows, I describe what professional development might look like if the *Emerging Processes and Practices* were honored.

**Table 2.1** | Contrasting processes and practices

| Processes and Practices That Seem to Ignore What We Know About Adult Learning | Emerging Processes and Practices for Reflective Consideration |
|---|---|
| The adult learner is objectified; planners make assumptions about what learners know and are able to do; planners make assumptions about learners' degree of motivation, level of interest, previous experience, personal and professional goals. | Learning, by all adults and children within and across the school community, is the focus of our collective work. |
| Knowledge rests with leaders, trainers, those who have status or those who have been "trained" to train others. | Knowledge and expertise rests within each member of the school community and our goal as a learning community is to use this knowledge and expertise as our shared resource. Each adult envisions themself as a leader for learning in some area. |
| There is not enough time for learners to prepare for, engage, learn, practice and reflect on new knowledge or skills. | Processes around learning, continuous development and collaboration are honored and adequate time for this work characterizes the school culture. |
| There is little bridging or continuity between adult learning for individuals and larger organizational learning processes. | Each member of the organization understands how their own learning is connected to the learning of students, teachers, leaders and others within the school community. |
| The school or district is a learning organization in name only; learning efforts are scattered and unfocused. | The school or district is future-focused and has established processes that allow for learning to occur across the community; all learners model an enthusiasm for individual and organizational growth. |

# A different scenario

It is a Friday in late fall, the third late-start day purposely scheduled for teachers in the Happy Valley School District to support their work toward their professional development goals. Today, the focus is on each teacher's technology goal, linked closely to the school's literacy improvement goal. Activity abounds! As we walk through the elementary school, we see small groups of teachers meeting in grade-level teams to discuss sample lessons they posted last week to a new district Web site aimed at sharing best practices. Volunteer teacher leaders and literacy coaches facilitate the groups. In the computer lab, the six members of the intermediate science team meet with Dr. Mary Maude, who, at the team's request, has agreed to spend this year facilitating hands-on sessions and making follow-up classroom visits to support the use of new technology tools for assessing learning. Across town at the high school, cross-disciplinary teams consider a draft of new technology standards for high-school graduates. A task force of students, teachers, administrators, and community members has responded with enthusiasm to the charge by the superintendent to define technology literacy. By ten o'clock, notes from each of the team meetings around the district and electronic feedback surveys are available electronically to the district's Professional Development Committee. The notes indicate the progress made in today's sessions and identify what is needed to move closer to achieving personal and school goals during the next late-start day.

If this chapter has succeeded in helping the reader understand and reflect on principles of adult development, then it is possible to envision and actualize such a radically different scenario within each school setting. Here, teachers' learning is the essential focus if student learning is to be enhanced. By engaging each adult in his or her own learning and by supporting an every-learner-a-leader culture, meaningful, job-embedded focus becomes the cornerstone of professional development.

Gone is the sit-and-get paradigm where knowledge and expertise lie beyond the passive participant. In our radically different scenario, the important developmental work of the individual and school is transparent, public, and shared among collaborative team members who have embraced similar important goals. Time is both valued and reorganized to allow for good work to take place at the beginning of a school day. In this case, late-start days are bunched at the beginning of the school year to jump-start school improvement efforts in August, September, and October focused around the literacy theme. Teachers have found authentic, personally relevant ways to weave their individual professional development goals together with the goals of others at their grade level or across the school, resulting in a deeper understanding of the relationship between the part (individual growth) and whole (school change efforts) (Wagner et al., 2006).

This scenario presents a hopeful outlook as these teachers and schools move from the "as is" to the "to be." No longer are teachers *worked on*. They are working together and growing as individuals. No longer is the school organization's culture pushing back against change efforts. The collective energy, collaborative work, and common purpose are altering the way adults are in relationship with one another as professionals and the way work gets done. This new scenario is possible if we use adult learning theory as a foundation for our work.

## GETTING STARTED RESOURCES

Brookfield, S. D. (2006). *Skillful teacher: On technique, trust and responsiveness in the classroom* (2nd ed.). San Francisco: John Wiley and Sons.

Pioneer adult educator Brookfield brings his most passionate self to this newer edition of his inspired book. Of particular interest are chapter 5 where he discusses "adjusting teaching to the rhythms" of adult learning and chapter 11 where he focuses on "overcoming resistance." A teacher's teacher, Brookfield captures both the joy and challenge of working with adults and calls us to take the "higher road" in our work.

Caffarella, R. S. (2001). *Planning programs for adult learners: A practical guide for educators, trainers and staff developers* (2nd ed.). New York: John Wiley and Sons.

A step-by-step guide is often helpful for those new to program planning or for veterans who need a road map for keeping year-long or multi-year projects "on course." Grounded in adult learning theory, clearly written and filled with activities, this book deserves a place on the bookshelf for use as a handy reference.

Knowles, M. S., Swanson, R. A., & Holton, E. F. (2005). *The adult learner: The definitive classic in adult education and human resource development* (6th ed.). Amsterdam: Elsevier Science and Technology Books.

Significantly updated by Swanson and Holton, this latest edition of the late Malcolm Knowles' foundational work on adult learning and development provides updated additions from Knowles himself, explanation and elaboration on adult learning theory since 1979, and an excellent section on the tensions in and continuing questions for the field.

Lindstrom, P. H., & Speck, M. (2004). *The principal as professional development leader.* Thousand Oaks, CA: Corwin Press.

In every rich chapter of this book, the words "technology leader" could substitute for "principal." Especially helpful is chapter 1 where the authors present and discuss the "components" of high-quality professional development and introduce their model-leader as designer, implementer, and reflective practitioner. In subsequent chapters, each of these components are detailed, providing leaders with a template for action grounded in the principles of adult learning theory and sound professional development practices.

Merriam, S. B., Caffarella, R. S., & Baumgartner, L. M. (2006). *Learning in adulthood: A comprehensive guide* (3rd ed.). San Francisco: Jossey-Bass.

This recently updated classic provides a good overview of the "big ideas" in the field of adult learning. More importantly, a frequent reading of the foundations detailed here will keep those who would "do" professional development for adults centered on what we know and are coming to know about adult learning. Certainly there is much to support the Emerging Processes and Practices for Reflective Consideration described in this chapter.

**chapter 3**

# Establishing an Organizational Climate for Successful Professional Development

What should we do?

*Arlene Borthwick*
*National-Louis University*

*Cathy Risberg*
*Minds That Soar, LLC*

## abstract

IN THE CONTEXT of schools as organizations, this chapter discusses key factors that can promote or impede the success of professional development efforts. Drawing on a synthesis of existing research complemented by interviews of leaders in educational technology (interviewed by one of the authors), the chapter reveals the type of organizational culture and the leadership practices required to support technology adoption and curricular integration by teachers. Key elements include: balancing organizational change with individual change, establishing learning communities as social networks for influencing change, and assessing both classroom outcomes and organization conditions.

Why does the use of new technology seem so effortless and sustainable in some environments when, in other environments, there seems to be a level of combined resistance, hostility, and fear by teachers, administrators, or both? Based on our own experiences (Borthwick & Risberg, 2003), we knew that successful adoption and diffusion of new technologies had something to do with the organizational climate but we wanted to delve deeper, to identify key elements for success.

> Establish a climate where technology is just used and infrastructure is just there and… supported.
>
> — Dr. Craig Cunningham, National-Louis University

So we set out on a journey to uncover the factors that would help educators establish the optimal organizational climate for successful professional development. With tape recorder in hand, one of the authors interviewed seven Chicago-area educators and received answers from two others via e-mail. These nine respondents included, at that time, one technology teacher, three technology directors (one retired), one building principal and one former building principal, two district administrators, and one university faculty member. (Several have since retired or changed positions, as reflected with their quotes later in the chapter). Following animated conversations in coffee shops and offices and through e-mail responses, we soon realized that we were finding common themes (Risberg, 2006). We subsequently sought to ground our conclusions in the existing literature. Themes we identified and quotes from those interviewed are included at the beginning of appropriate sections of this chapter, followed by a summary of recent literature on organizational change.

## Look beneath the surface

What we discovered is that the optimal organizational climate for educational technology professional development is multifaceted and influenced by a complex set of factors. Faced with the responsibility for getting a group of teachers to integrate technology in their instructional settings, we may feel that we are stirring up the waters, swimming upstream, or facing unknown deeper currents. Deep inside we might be plagued with doubts, similar to what we might experience snorkeling while vacationing in Hawaii. We might decide to stay strictly within our own comfort zone and inadvertently be faced with a limited view of what lies beneath the surface.

Just as the scuba or deep-sea diver charts the waters, checks the weather, and assesses the boat crew and diving equipment, so the professional developer works with district and school personnel to examine the context, culture, and conditions (Wagner et al., 2006) that affect technology integration for improvement of teaching and learning. Although as professional developers, we might like to simply focus on the dive itself (our PD training activities), we must examine the waters (context), weather (culture), boat and equipment (conditions), and crew (competencies) to survive and enjoy the dive.

# Examine context, culture, conditions, competencies

With initial funding from the Bill and Melinda Gates Foundation, the Change Leadership Group at Harvard's Graduate School of Education has worked with schools and districts to identify and implement strategies for systemic improvement. Their book on Change Leadership (Wagner et al., 2006) and Web site (http://www.gse.harvard.edu/clg/news1a.html) provide templates for a variety of diagnostic exercises for both teams and individuals, including procedures for taking a closer look at an organization's context (social, historical, and economic context), culture (shared values, beliefs, expectations, behaviors), conditions (time, space, resources), and competencies (skills, knowledge). This picture of the existing organization can then be contrasted with a projected picture of what the culture, conditions, and competencies would need to be in order to overcome a specific problem or achieve a specific goal. In terms of educational technology, a major problem might be the lack of use of technology by teachers and students and a major goal might include professional development to enable effective use of technology by teachers and students to improve student learning.

# Consider the larger context

School organizations exist as dynamic and open systems. As described by Wagner et al. (2006), a district's context involves social, historical, and economic milieux at the community, state, and global levels. In his best-selling book, *The World Is Flat*, Thomas Friedman (2006) looks at the world we live in today, providing a unique perspective and lens to view school organizations. He calls this the era of Globalization 3.0 and describes a new world order that had its beginnings in 2000. According to Friedman:

> It is now possible for more people than ever to collaborate and compete in real time with more other people on more different kinds of work from more different corners of the planet on more equal footing than at any time ever in history of the world—using computers, e-mail, fiber-optic networks, teleconferencing and dynamic new software. (p. 8)

Clearly these changes have enabled and empowered individuals to become global collaborators in a global marketplace, shrinking our new "flat world" so that the exchange of goods and services, information, and money flow across borders more freely than ever before in our history.

It is within this global context that we find ourselves. As Friedman states, "We are now connecting all the knowledge centers on the planet together into a single global network which … could usher in an era of prosperity, innovation and collaboration by companies, communities and individuals" (p. 8). The implication of all this is that our graduates will be competing for jobs that did not exist when they entered high school, jobs that will be increasingly dependent upon the use of technology tools and related skills. Yet the dilemma our schools face is the inescapable realization that the current industrial model in place in most of our high schools neither reflects nor prepares students for the knowledge economy.

## Balance organizational change with individual change

Leadership for change involves working with both the organization and the individual. As long ago as 1955, Bakke described the work setting as one where the organization operates on the individual and the individual operates on the organization, as each seeks maximum self-actualization. Like Bakke's seminal work, Adamy and Heinecke (2005) discuss the dichotomy of organizational and faculty needs and influence on innovation. "While individual adopters make use of innovations in their own way, that use is shaped in part by the extent to which organizational attitudes and resources support individual efforts" (p. 251). Adamy and Heinecke identified three main organization-level factors in play:

1. availability and use of technology resources, including technological support;

2. faculty relationships with key technology players; and

3. the organizational attitude or culture in terms of technology use.

> Making it OK to take risks and have encouragement of administration … Nurture those who have propensity [for new technology] and try to move them along.
>
> —*Larry Cline, retired Technology Director, Wheeling (Ill.) District 21.*

Although technology planners frequently assess teacher–student access to, and skill levels in using, hardware and software, they may overlook the second and third items listed above—faculty relationships and organizational attitude, both of which can be expected to influence individual commitment. The work of Harvard's Change Leadership Group suggests that training sessions or even curricular planning sessions may not elicit commitment to change, because of underlying assumptions or competing commitments of the participants. Wagner et al. (2006) refer to these as immunities to change and outline such additional barriers to change as the tendency to react to immediate demands, focus on external compliance issues, and the isolation in which many teachers work (closed-door classrooms). In contrast, the Change Leadership Group advocates the establishment of role-alike communities of practice to encourage collaboration and engagement, and a singular focus on teaching and learning throughout all meetings.

## Develop shared values

Without a doubt, the values held by school administration and staff are a key component in establishing an optimal organizational climate for successful professional development. Just as personal values and beliefs determine how we act as individuals, the values of any institution guide its actions and influence its climate. Interviews with educators confirmed that is important to:

- Foster a climate of trust, collaboration, and professionalism.

- Promote technology-related risk-taking among teachers on behalf of students.

But in many schools, the process of building trust, promoting collaboration, and encouraging professionalism is not at the top of the list. The inescapable reality of high-stakes testing has altered the climate of our schools and our classrooms and placed a national focus on assessment results. Yet as a result of this focus on improving test scores and learning for all students, establishing relationships and building trust have never been more important. Effective school leaders have learned this fact well. They strive to listen to their students, staff, and parent community to validate perspectives as well as empower and encourage member participation. The power of the community to transform teaching and learning has been a focus of researchers who have looked at ways to improve our schools. According to Barth (2006):

> A pre-condition for doing anything to strengthen our practice and improve a school is the existence of a collegial culture in which professionals talk about practice, share their craft knowledge and observe and root for the success of each other. Without these in place, no meaningful improvement—no staff or curriculum development … no sustained change is possible. (p. 13)

> Having a climate where it's OK to disagree … There is value in the conversation and discussion where people have different perspectives.
>
> —Phil Collins, Assistant Superintendent, Glenview (Ill.) District 34

This collegial culture does not represent the way all schools are run. For some schools, the organizational climate is one that encourages a sense of isolationism. It is as Richardson (2003) describes, "as the way in which many Americans—teachers and other professionals included—approach their work. In schools, it is abetted by the egg-crate environment and the practice of 'closing the door' " (p. 402). Fortunately, an increasing number of researchers have concluded along with DuFour (2004) that "educators must stop working in isolation and hoarding their ideas, materials, and strategies and begin to work together to meet the needs of all students" (p. 11).

Meeting the needs of a student population that differs in interests, learning styles, and readiness is not an easy task. When there is support of technology risk-taking by teachers on behalf of student learning, these needs can often be met. However, as Schmoker (2006) points out, "Few teachers see themselves as inventive, adaptive professionals upon whom improvement primarily depends" (p. 117). Instead, many of today's teachers are urged to turn to carefully scripted curriculum guides and time-intensive achievement-test preparation as the answer for improving student learning.

Nevertheless, numerous educators, like Glenview (Ill.) Assistant Superintendent Phil Collins, have learned a crucial lesson regarding the role of a school's values and the exploration and use of new technology. Collins confirmed how important it is to trust and support technology trailblazers and encourage them to help move others down the technology road. Without such support, not many educators can afford to take the risks related to being a "technology renegade" and go it alone.

# Establish learning communities as social networks for influencing change

Where individual teachers are organized into teaching teams, they are empowered by their administration to see themselves as both capable and responsible for improving both teaching and learning. This theme was a thread in many of our conversations with practitioners. They agreed it is vital to:

- Involve all constituents by seeking out and using their input.

- Provide on-going, on-demand differentiated training, support, and coaching for teachers.

As far as professional development for strengthening instruction, Wagner et al. (2006) recommend PD that is "primarily on-site, intensive, collaborative, and job-embedded ... designed and led by educators who model the best teaching and learning practices." (p. 31). Author Mike Schmoker, in *Results Now* (2006), emphasizes professional learning communities as the "best, most agreed-upon means by which to continuously improve instruction and student performance" (p. 106). Schmoker suggests that critical teams are teacher teams that meet regularly to discuss standards, decide upon curriculum, and participate in short-term cycles of "implementation, assessment, and adjustment" of instruction (p. 107).

Penuel, Sussex, and Korbak (2005) suggest that reform is a social process and that decisions about "what materials to use, how to prepare teachers to enact reforms, and teacher preparation activities are themselves social activities" (p. 5). Even further, based on their review of "prior research on large-scale school reforms," these SRI researchers note that "teachers' collaboration with colleagues around what and how they teach precedes observable changes in classroom practice and is a primary mechanism that drives the implementation of reforms" (*Social Capital for Technology Integration*, 2003–2007, p. 1).

> At [a teachers'] in-service, have a [technology] gallery walk ... Teachers bring in samples of ... student/teacher work and put it on display and share ideas.
>
> — *Dr. Debra Hill,*
> *National-Louis University,*
> *and former Superintendent,*
> *Northfield (Ill.) District 31*

Douglas Reeves (2006) confirms that teachers will most often rely on trusted colleagues for assistance with new instructional programs and technologies, rather than the help desk or technology department. Too often, Reeves concludes, leaders rely on hierarchical communication to influence change in schools, ignoring the fact that "organizations function not as hierarchies, but as networks" (p. 34). As far as dealing with "toxic hubs" (negative participants who may derail change efforts), Reeves suggests making staff development activities optional. However, implementation of small, instructionally focused teacher teams (Schmoker, 2006) may reduce "toxic" participation. Other opportunities for teacher-based sharing may also encourage teacher interest. Akin to Debra Hill's suggestion (see sidebar) for a gallery walk, Reeves encourages publishing a "Best Practices Book" featuring teacher contributions at the end of the school year and providing copies to new and seasoned teachers.

# Develop a learning organization and systems thinking

The use of authentic listening and collaboration are certainly key elements in transforming schools into true learning organizations. When this transformation occurs, it becomes easier to facilitate the establishment of the optimal organization climate for professional development. Leaders in the field indicated it is important to:

- Value conversations and discussions where people have different perspectives.

- Listen to what is being said on the surface and search for underlying meanings.

> A culture of concern...It's all about relationships. We couldn't get teachers to do things unless we care about each other.
>
> —Dr. Joanne Rooney,
> Co-Director, Midwest
> Principals' Center

Peter Senge's (2006) concept of a learning organization encompasses several of the elements described by the practitioners we interviewed in preparing this chapter. Senge suggests that as today's organizations become more networked, hierarchical models of management are decreasing, "potentially opening up new capacity for continual learning, innovation, and adaptation" (p. xvi). He also connects organizational learning to individual learning, noting "reciprocal commitments" between the individual and the organization (p. 8). In a learning organization, planning is equated to learning, with corporate planning viewed as institutional learning.

Senge outlines three "core learning capabilities" for teams within a learning organization: aspiration, reflective conversation, and understanding of complexity. Five disciplines (akin to subject areas in a school curriculum) provide the underlying theories and methods that enable development of these core learning capabilities:

1. personal mastery based on commitment to lifelong learning (aspiration),

2. shared vision (aspiration),

3. uncovering and discussing mental models including assumptions and generalizations (reflective conversation),

4. team learning (reflective conversation); and

5. systems thinking (understanding complexity).

Senge (2006) points out that each of the disciplines "has to do with how we think and how we interact and learn with one another" (p. 11). Of course, participants in an organization must not only understand the discipline but practice (follow) it. Senge highlights the "Fifth Discipline"—systems thinking—as the essential component, reminding us that organizations operate as systems and that practice of the disciplines will operate as part of that interrelated system. In *Schools That Learn, A Fifth Discipline Fieldbook* (Senge, Cambron-McCabe, Lucas, Smith, Dutton, & Kleiner, 2000), Senge and his co-authors provide methods and techniques for implementing (practicing) the five disciplines in schools and universities and tools (diagrams) for making sense of systems in operation, as well as stories and reflections by field-based educators.

## Integrate the work of technology departments

Larger school districts often employ one individual to oversee information technology services and another to oversee instructional technology. Although information services departments have existed since the 1970s, instructional technology departments did not emerge until the 1990s. "Many districts hire curriculum specialists and technology specialists and hope they work together. Sometimes they do; sometimes they don't" (Byrom & Bingham, 2001, p. 15). In a study of seven Colorado schools, Robbins (2000) examined the integration of subcultures of these departments, one charged with supporting technology infrastructure and administrative uses of technology and the other responsible for planning and staff development for classroom and library applications of technology. When integration of the two departments was higher, indicators for technology performance (as outlined by the North Central Regional Educational Laboratory) were also higher. Among important factors to departmental integration were frequent meetings of the technology department heads as well as cooperative planning and project implementation. "For planning to affect cultural integration, it must be broad based and inclusive, allowing all participants to feel as if they are contributing, which leads to support of future implementation projects" (p. 120). Robbins also recommended analysis of organizational structure and related technology mission statements, along with distribution of resources necessary to support technology-related services.

## Examine how leadership is distributed

According to the educational leaders interviewed, the willingness to redefine leadership models of yesterday to reflect current research on leadership is a basic feature of the optimum organizational climate. The lesson shared by these individuals is a simple one:

> Involve leadership at all levels in modeling technology use and promoting technology adoption.

In *Breakthrough*, Fullan, Hill, and Crévola (2006) suggest that "leadership is the turnkey to system transformation" (p. 88). Further, they advocate "distributive leadership" through which leaders "help develop other leaders" (p. 92). According to the SouthEast Initiatives Regional Technology in Education Consortium's (SEIR*TEC) *Lessons Learned* (Byrom & Bingham, 2001), effective decision-making and subsequent integration of technology into schools is handled best when leadership roles are shared, "School technology committees can play an important role in making decisions that reflect the needs of a total school community" (p.5).

> It is important for administrators to follow the teachers' lead and then support it.
>
> — *Principal, Stevenson High School, Lincolnshire, Ill.*

Spillane (2006) defines leadership activities as those "designed by organizational members to influence the motivation, knowledge, affect, or practices of other organizational members" (p. 11). In his classic work on diffusion of innovations, Rogers (2003) refers to champions—those

> The way to get buy-in is to involve teachers in the process. You need to listen carefully to them. Find out what they are looking for help with in terms of overall program and activities. Help make the matches between what they are looking to do and how the technology can help.
>
> —*Phil Collins, Assistant Superintendent, Glenview (Ill.) District 34*

who are able to "overcome indifference or resistance that the new idea may provoke in an organization" (p. 417)—and confirms that champions do not necessarily have to be in positions of power. Reeves (2006) recommends that administrators become talent scouts and listeners, searching out and learning more about the teaching strategies and opinions of in-house experts. Administrators need to listen to teacher concerns and extend the necessary support to their faculties to address the natural barriers to technology integration: lack of time, training, resources, and technical support (Fisher & Dove, 1999).

Where Fullan, Hill, and Crévola (2006) refer to "distributive leadership," others use terms such as shared leadership, collaborative leadership, and transformational leadership. Spillane (2006) explains the differing implications of each of these terms, concluding that the important thing is to examine *how leadership is distributed*. Rather than resting within a single individual, such as the principal, Spillane describes leadership as taking "shape in the interaction of leaders, followers, and their situation" (p. 14). He recommends that leaders review evolving routines and tools that are designed to support leadership interactions, focusing on leadership practices rather than roles, processes, or structures.

In his discussion of the role that organizational leaders play in shaping an organization's culture, Daft (1989) summarizes research by Harrison Trice and Janice Beyer in which they identified four types of cultural leadership:

1.  Leaders who create culture (founders, entrepreneurs in a young organization)

2.  Leaders who embody culture (those who preserve prevailing values)

3.  Leaders who integrate culture (those who develop consensus and harmony)

4.  Leaders who change culture

Spillane (2006) notes that "school leaders are often rebuilding, if not building, the proverbial plane as they fly it. Design and redesign are central in the work of leadership" (p. 93). Dynamic leadership practices must shift to assure the right players (including teachers and students), motivation (group dynamics that assure engagement and effort), and policies (for example, professional development opportunities and scaffolding for emerging leaders, and district compensation policies). Along with Rogers (2003), Daft (1989) notes that leaders may include those who are not officially designated as leaders. The use of new technology tools results in the transfer of "expert power" to teachers—and often even to students. This is seen by some staff and administrators as a disruption of power and a change in "control over and access to the form and flow of information" (Hodas, 1993, p. 11). These changes in power and information flow may be perceived as a direct challenge to authority and status.

# Develop a shared vision

Casting a wide vision that leads to stakeholder buy-in can be a daunting task for any leader of any organization. According to our interviews, effective leaders take into consideration many factors, including the following:

- Developing a shared vision.

- Focusing on what's best for students.

- Valuing curriculum mapping to ensure that technology use is curriculum-driven.

From the research and experience of administrators, we can learn a valuable lesson about casting a vision. It is not really about technology but about quality teaching and quality curriculum. According to Schmoker (2006):

> A common, high-quality curriculum is just as important to the team itself. Without it, team members lack a shared focus; they can't even work together effectively. Leaders must arrange for teacher teams to map out a common schedule for teaching standards they themselves select to teach in each course. (p. 129)

This curriculum map becomes a powerful tool and a visual representation of the school's vision and desire to do what is best for students.

Yet for some schools, the vision is not on curriculum or related collaboration and technology innovation. Rob Luby, a retired technology director we interviewed, offered a dose of reality faced by many teachers today in public schools concerning No Child Left Behind. With a sharp focus on testing, technology tools are often not utilized fully to provide for curriculum access or acceleration to meet diverse learning needs. Nevertheless, many educators would agree with Joanne Rooney that integrating technology is based on "what you believe in and what you are as a school." Her staff's central belief was that the kids deserved the best, and so technology use was grounded in the belief that these tools would provide the best learning opportunities for their students.

*Don't push for technology integration but push for improved student learning.*

*— Dr. Craig Cunningham, National-Louis University*

In some ways, building vision is a two-way street. Vision establishes direction and direction establishes vision. According to Fullan, Hill, and Crévola (2006), "Shared vision and ownership are less a precondition for success than they are an outcome of a quality process. Successful systems build vision and ownership through the quality of their learning processes and corresponding results" (p. 88).

# Assess both classroom outcomes and organizational conditions

The impact of standards-based curriculum in public schools and the emphasis on assessment and test data analysis has resulted in similar goal-setting and assessment when planning for educational technology and professional development. Leaders in the field indicate the importance of:

- Establishing expectations and specific goals for technology use.

- Collecting assessment data to inform decisions regarding use of technology as instructional tools and need for further teacher training.

- Articulating clear-cost benefits to stakeholders including teachers, students, administrative leaders, and the local community.

In our role as professional developers, we have responsibility for assessment at two levels: the classroom level and the organizational level. As described earlier, assessment of student outcomes is critical to decision-making for the next steps in classroom instruction (Fullan, Hill, & Crévola, 2006; Schmoker, 2006). By involving teachers in the evaluation of student learning in relation to existing technology use, teachers will be more open to understanding the implications of educational technology use and its potential for improving learning and developing creativity of all students. The belief that students are "benefiting more from the innovation than from past practices" (Owston, 2003, p. 159) is a key component of sustainability. Review of assessment data should also help to balance the influence of teachers' personal perspectives, needs, and biases. One problem, though, is that educators may lack knowledge or models and tools to track the impact of technology use on teaching and learning (Byrom & Bingham, 2001).

> Bottom line …
> are they using it …
> do you see it being
> used in the classroom?
>
> — Larry Cline,
> retired Technology Director,
> Wheeling (Ill.) District 21, on
> assessing the use
> of technology

Although not labeled as assessment, examination of organizational climate has been the focus of this chapter and can be aided through the use of Senge's (2006) *Fifth Discipline* diagrams and techniques, the Change Leadership Group's approach to documenting the 4 Cs (context, culture, conditions, competencies), a study of how leadership is distributed (Spillane, 2006), and awareness of social networks for dissemination of innovative instructional strategies (Reeves, 2006; Penuel, Sussex, & Korbak, 2005). The impact of professional development on classroom outcomes represents yet another facet of assessment, a facet addressed in this book's subsequent chapters on models of professional development.

Bruce Joyce (2004) reminds us that "replicating successful efforts in new settings is difficult and tricky work" (p. 82). He cautions that those responsible for implementing school improvement efforts should assume that they "have imperfect strategies to work with" (p. 78) and study the implementation and outcomes to increase effectiveness. In addition to examining workplace norms, conceptual framework or rationale underlying an innovation, and leadership support, Joyce recommends that professional developers shift their roles from providers or presenters "to working colleagues who will inquire with the teams of which they are a part" (p. 81). Such teams should include both teachers and administrators. "Whatever change strategy is used, what happens needs to be studied intensively and the information used to improve the process and get better results" (p. 82). In terms of funding such inquiry, SIER*TEC (Byrom & Bingham, 2001) recommends that 10% of project budgets be devoted to project evaluation.

We have learned that change is a slow process, often taking three to five years (Byrom & Bingham, 2001). What makes it so hard? Hodas (1993) observes that schools view change as both a disruption and a criticism and possess a "natural resistance to organizational change" (p. 2). Such a school culture stands as a barrier to those introducing new technology. Because technology is never value-free, professional developers may experience "technology refusal" when the users realize that implementing new technologies requires "the acquisition of an entirely new set of skills and world outlook" (p. 9). Likewise, Spitzer and Stansberry (2004) point out that instructional technology represents a change in the way teachers and school officials operate. They stress the importance of the school culture in bringing about or blocking change and indicate that for teachers, change is promoted by experiential reflection (akin to Senge's (2006) "reflective conversation"), continuing education, and the school culture. Spitzer and Stansberry confirm that "teachers use instructional technology because they believe they should and they believe there are benefits to doing so" (p. 777). This brings us back full circle to the importance of assessment of classroom outcomes. Problems with sustainability arise, according to Rogers (2003), when the innovation does not seem to match an organization's stated or unspoken goals for technology use and when potential consequences of continued use of the innovation are seen as more detrimental than beneficial. He cautions that we often underestimate the level of effort required for successful use of technology.

> Teachers must realize how changing what they are doing is beneficial to the kids.
>
> — *Rob Luby, retired Technology Director, Barrington (Ill.) District 220*

Fullan's et al. (2006) "breakthrough" system for improving classroom instruction highlights the intersection of classroom outcomes and professional learning, focusing on three core components:

1. personalization (individualization or differentiation of instruction for students),

2. precision (use of formative assessment for informing everyday instruction), and

3. professional learning (daily teacher learning in context).

They emphasize that "professional learning 'in context' is the only learning that changes classroom instruction" (p. 25) and that teacher learning is "a never-ending proposition" (p. 87). Other key elements of a "breakthrough" system include: changes in behavior that lead to changes in beliefs, school-based learning communities, and lateral capacity building where schools (or districts, states, nations) learn from each other. "Schools have a moral and intellectual responsibility to learn from other schools and agencies and to contribute what they know to others" (p. 95). At the heart of the "breakthrough" system, then, is the moral purpose of education focusing on student, teacher, and organizational learning.

# Conclusion: Anchoring professional development activities for success

The distinction between staying on the ocean's surface and diving deeper can be a useful metaphor as we examine what to do when establishing an organizational climate for successful professional development. As proposed in this chapter, we need to explore organizational context, culture, conditions, and competencies (Wagner et al., 2006); social networks; organizational vision, values, learning, and structure; distribution of leadership; and systems for assessing and sustaining effective use of technology by teachers and students to improve student learning. When we venture far beyond and beneath our initial observations, we begin to perceive the facets, interactions, and complexity of organizational climate. In these previously uncharted waters and at these new depths of awareness and understanding, we can gradually establish an optimal organizational climate. And, though we intermittently anchor our work, we can anticipate setting sail for new territory as we stay alert to changing circumstances.

As you dip your foot to test the waters, here are a few recommendations for a successful launch:

- Working with a small group of stakeholders, discuss the school's context and existing learning culture and envision elements needed to support the professional learning culture you would like to establish.

- Identify existing and desired conditions (infrastructure, resources) and competency levels of faculty, staff, and students.

- Conceptualize professional development activities as part of an interconnected system.

- Balance organizational (school or district) vision and needs with the vision and needs of individual teachers.

- Take advantage of social networks as a way to achieve professional development goals. Work with instructional teacher teams to circumvent the impact of negative participants.

- Avoid being the sole leader. Encourage other in-house experts—including teachers and even students—to take on leadership roles.

- Plan to assess the impact of professional development activities by documenting changes in classrooms (changes in the teaching-learning environment and student learning outcomes) and in organizational conditions and culture.

- Encourage a spirit of inquiry as technology instructors, teachers, and administrators work together to achieve a shared vision for use of technology in support of curricular goals.

*The authors wish to acknowledge the kind contribution of Michael Simkins, Project Director for the Technology Information Center for Administrative Leadership (TICAL), in the conceptualization of this chapter.*

## GETTING STARTED RESOURCES

Byrom, E., & Bingham, M. (2001). *Factors influencing the effective use of technology for teaching and learning: Lessons learned from the SEIR\*TEC Intensive Site Schools.* Durham, NC: SouthEast Initiatives Regional Technology in Education Consortium.

Byrom and Bingham share eight lessons learned from their intensive work with 12 school sites over a period of five years. This booklet (only 24 pages) is a must-read for administrators and technology coordinators and is also available at www.serve.org/seir-tec/publications/lessons.pdf

Change Leadership Group. (2007). *Reinventing leadership in K–12 education: News and resources.* Retrieved August 11, 2007, from www.gse.harvard.edu/clg/news1a.html

Harvard's Change Leadership Group Web site includes templates for a variety of diagnostic exercises for both teams and individuals, including procedures for taking a closer look at an organization's context, culture, conditions, and competencies. Consult the Wagner et al. text, *Change Leadership*, for additional guidance.

Owston, R. (2003). School context, sustainability and transferability of innovation. In R. Kozma (Ed.), *Technology, innovation and educational change: A global perspective. A report of the second information technology in education study, Module 2* (pp. 125–161). Eugene, OR: International Society for Technology in Education.

Based on 174 cases from 28 countries, Owston defines key factors for sustainability of ICT innovation, including teacher, administrative, and student support of the innovation; professional development; external sources of support; policies that promote technology use; and adequate funding. Factors enabling transferability (similar application in other settings within the same country) included the amount of available resources and condition of the infrastructure, the perception of the innovation by administrators and teachers as appropriate and useful in another context, and the existence of a technology plan supporting innovation in ICT.

Schmoker, Mike (2006). *Results now: How we can achieve unprecedented improvements in teaching and learning.* Alexandria, VA: Association for Supervision and Curriculum Development.

Schmoker believes change is dependent upon a willingness to look honestly at the realities of our schools and consistently utilize basic and effective teaching strategies. Equally important is a collaborative environment that focuses on building a sound curriculum; enables teacher dialogue to develop and assess standards-based lessons; and routinely honors, recognizes, and celebrates teacher and student success in the classroom.

Senge, P. M. (2006). *The fifth discipline: The art & practice of the learning organization* (2nd ed.). New York: Doubleday.

This very readable text provides an introduction to the five disciplines of Senge's systemic view of a learning organization. The companion resource text, *Schools That Learn*, provides examples and activities for understanding and enabling schools to become learning organizations.

# section II
# Models of Professional Development

## WORKING WITH IN-HOUSE LEADERSHIP

## TEACHER DEVELOPMENT THROUGH PEER COACHING

## TEACHER DEVELOPMENT THROUGH LEARNING CIRCLES

**chapter 4**

# Designing and Sustaining Constructivist Learning Environments

*Thomas L. Otto*
*Withcott State Primary School,*
*Queensland, Australia*

## abstract

A PROFESSIONAL DEVELOPMENT Framework emerged in a project to support teachers in their classroom implementation of ePortfolios. The framework is a checklist of questions to design, evaluate, and sustain a Constructivist Learning Environment (CLE). Activities include an investigation of the issue and context, access to a library of cases and information resources, skill development in the use of tools, and social and contextual support (Jonassen, 1999). Case Based Reasoning (CBR) is a key feature, with teachers accessing cases to complement their own experience. The author applies his inside knowledge as a school principal and utilizes local expertise and resources.

As a school principal, I have observed that the delivery of professional development is often fragmented, learning is not sustained, and there is no record of successful new practices. From my studies I became interested in the potential of a Constructivist Learning Environment (CLE) (Jonassen, 1999) as an instructional design for professional development activities. A CLE supports teachers in their learning, and teachers can apply the same design principles in their classrooms. That is, teachers would learn as we would have them teach. The Information and Communication Technologies (ICTs) skills that teachers develop while participating in a CLE could also be applied in the classroom.

## LITERATURE ESSENTIALS

## *Constructivist Learning Environments (CLE)*

Wilson (1995) defines a CLE as "a place where learners may work together and support each other as they use a variety of tools and information resources in their guided pursuit of learning goals and problem solving activities" (p. 5). For example, the key learning goal in the project described in this chapter is the classroom implementation of ePortfolios. Teachers have an active role in identifying issues with ePortfolios that are important to them and in controlling how those issues will be explored (Ravitz, Becker, & Wong, 2000). Content knowledge and cases provide background information and potential solutions (Jonassen, 1999). Learning experiences are related to the context of a teacher's everyday work through reflection and interaction with peers (Ravitz et al., 2000).

Project planners design activities in a CLE around five elements (Jonassen, 1999) by:

1. investigating the **issue**, the context, and the learners,

2. assembling a **library of cases**,

3. collating **information resources**,

4. developing skills in the **tools** needed to participate in learning and to perform new practices, and

5. providing **social and contextual support** to sustain change.

I searched for a suitable project to field-test a CLE, and like many educators became intrigued by the potential of student-created ePortfolios. It is a deceptively simple concept in that students digitally record their achievements. But on reading the work of Barrett (2003) and others, it soon became apparent that the classroom implementation of ePortfolios changes the way teachers teach. Later I conducted many workshop sessions and found that teachers grasped the concept of ePortfolios quickly. Furthermore, they were motivated to develop their understanding of a range of educational concepts supported by ePortfolios such as multiple intelligences, higher order thinking, and student engagement.

The sustaining of professional learning had to be an important feature of the ePortfolio Project, because it takes teachers a long time to implement the practices in their classroom. Bain (1999) addressed this issue in his investigation of learning innovations in higher education, and recommended that professional development projects be designed around four phases. The Professional Development Framework (see Table 4.1) that emerged during the ePortfolio Project was my adaptation of Bain's phases. I developed the framework as a checklist of questions to guide the design, evaluation, and sustaining of a CLE. In the model, learners are encouraged to take responsibility for their own learning and to apply their learning to solve issues in their classrooms and schools.

**Table 4.1** | The professional development framework

| |
|---|
| **PHASE 1: Investigate and Plan Activities—Design the Constructivist Learning Environment** |

**1.1  The Issue and Context**

*1.1.1  The Issue*
a. What is the issue?
b. Why is the issue important?
c. What data supports the importance of the issue?

*1.1.2  The Changes*
a. What are the new practices?
b. How are the new practices different?
c. How do the new practices fit the context?

*1.1.3  The Learners*
a. Who are the learners?
b. What beliefs do the learners hold that will affect the implementation of the new practices?
c. What skills and experiences do the learners have and need to implement the new practices?

*1.1.4  Engaging the Learners*
a. What is so compelling about the issue that will engage the learner—i.e., what does the learner gain?
b. How will the learner be encouraged to engage with the issue?
c. How will learner engagement be sustained?

*1.1.5  The Context of the Professional Learning*
a. Where will the professional learning take place and how will this affect the learning?
b. What aspects of the learners' workplaces will impact on the learners' capacity to learn?

**1.2  Related Cases**

a. How will learners access similar cases?
b. How will learners be encouraged to use the principles of Case-Based Reasoning?
c. How will the new cases be recorded, stored, and accessed?

**1.3  Information Resources**

a. What information will learners need?
b. How will learners access information at a time of their choosing?
c. What support will learners need to understand the information and how it should be used?

*(Continued)*

**Table 4.1** | *(Continued)*

| |
|---|
| **1.4  Tools** |
|     a. What physical, thinking, and communication tools will learners use? |
|     b. How will learners develop skills in these tools? |

| |
|---|
| **1.5  Social and Contextual Support** |
|     a. What factors will affect implementation? |
|     b. What support will learners need and who will provide that support? |

| |
|---|
| **PHASE 2: Trial, Reflect, and Modify—Evaluate activities with a group of learners** |
|     a. Is the assessment of activities workable and what changes need to be made? |
|     b. Are the activities workable and what changes need to be made? |
|     c. Will the activities achieve the desired learning outcomes? |
|     d. Is the assessment of learning outcomes workable and what changes need to be made? |
|     e. Will the learning outcomes have the desired effect on practices? |

| |
|---|
| **PHASE 3: Implement and Reflect—Evaluate the effectiveness and efficiency of the project** |
|     a. How effective and efficient was the project in changing practices? |
|     b. What are the recommendations for planners of similar projects? |

| |
|---|
| **PHASE 4: Sustain, Monitor, and Share—Sustain learning and share new practices** |
|     a. What needs to happen to sustain learning and changes in practices? |
|     b. What were the benefits to the organization? |

# The ePortfolio Project

As both researcher and principal, I took a leading role in the ePortfolio Project by: coordinating activities; preparing funding submissions; presenting sessions at workshops; arranging planning committee meetings; responding to participant queries; and assembling, reproducing and distributing an information booklet and CD. Jonassen and Rohrer-Murphy (1999) agree that a CLE may only be studied "in real life practice" (p. 68) with the researcher taking the role of active participant. *Active* means more than being a teacher or administrator implementing ePortfolios, although I did so at my school. It means taking advantage of every opportunity to promote the project and to improve its outcome (Jonassen & Rohrer-Murphy, 1999). As a consequence, the project grew from the involvement of only a few local schools to include teachers and administrators across the state.

My full-time responsibilities as a primary school principal caused some activities to be delayed and the project might have otherwise progressed at a faster rate or with more intensity. However, the project was authentic and reflected limits to the time that principals have available to support large-scale initiatives. My inside knowledge as a principal enabled the project to be effectively promoted to schools and allowed me to participate in conversations with district and state education officers.

# Planning

As with any professional development, the purpose of the ePortfolio Project was to change teaching practices. Changing teaching practices is complicated because teaching involves complex tasks (Nespor, 1987). For example, teachers had many teaching objectives throughout their working day besides implementing ePortfolios and they could not be certain when the objective of ePortfolio implementation had been entirely achieved. Further, a successful ePortfolio in one context may need to be refined to be successful in another context. Therefore, professional development had to be systematically planned so that these and other variables were taken into account, and had to be sustained so that learning was reinforced over time allowing for experimentation and reflection.

The design of activities also had to address the four sources of information that influence teacher self-efficacy (Bandura, 1986). First, teachers had to observe ePortfolios in action. Second, teachers had to enact teaching with ePortfolios. Third, teachers had to be convinced about the merits of ePortfolios. The fourth source of information concerns affective states. For example, the stress of learning new ICT skills and changing familiar practices may cause teachers to avoid implementing ePortfolios. These sources of information can be referred to simply as *seeing*, *doing*, *hearing*, and *caring*. *Seeing* and then *doing* the new practice provides the crucial link between teachers knowing about the new practice and actually changing their own practices. Teachers are motivated to take on new practices if they understand the potential of the new practices to improve outcomes for children (Cuttance, 2001), and therefore they needed to *hear* about the merits of the new practice. That is, teachers need to know why ePortfolios are important, and be perturbed by the gap between what they *are* doing in the classroom and what they *could be* doing in the classroom (Jonassen, 1999). The project planners had to *care* about teachers as learners because changing from a familiar to an unfamiliar practice can be a disconcerting experience. A teacher's repertoire of practice is built over time around beliefs about what "constitutes content and content coverage, [and] what comprises learning and engaged time" (Ertmer, 1999, p. 48). Challenging those beliefs had to be accompanied by reassurances that the value and outcomes of ePortfolios were viewed favorably by colleagues.

With these principles in mind, I called a meeting of teachers and administrators from the local area who were interested in the implementation of ePortfolios. This meeting was attended by 30 people, which provided an early indication that the project was going to be well supported. I spoke about the concept of ePortfolios and a teacher gave a presentation as a case. Participants provided suggestions about the type of professional development activities they would like to have arranged, and a small planning committee was established.

The committee was made up of administrators from a secondary school, a special school, and one small and one large primary school, and representatives from the District Education Office and the Toowoomba Technology Mathematics and Science Centre of Excellence (TTMSCE). At the beginning of each year an e-mail would be sent to schools to advertise the dates of the four workshops and other activities for the whole year. The committee would meet before each workshop to fine-tune the sessions and to review the evaluations of previous workshops. The commitment of committee members contributed to the sustaining of learning over an extended period of time.

Teachers who participated in the project took on the role of researchers (Mattingly, 1991) as their vision of what could be achieved through ePortfolios was refined during the course of the project. They analyzed their context, designed ePortfolio frameworks, and devised solutions to issues that were specific to their context. During this period of learning and experimentation, they had to manage teaching responsibilities that included a mix of new and old practices. As Schmidt (2000) explains, professionals "handle situations for which there are no techniques. They must develop their own kind of artistry, involving reflecting in practice in the midst of intense activity without interrupting the flow" (p. 269).

## Activities

There were five major activities in the ePortfolio Project, with each addressing a number of elements of the CLE (Table 4.2). For the most part, teacher participation in these activities was voluntary, though I was invited to conduct all-in-one sessions with the whole staff in some schools.

**Table 4.2** | Activities in the ePortfolio Project

| Activity | Elements of the CLE *(identified in italics below)* |
|---|---|
| **1.** Workshops | Before each workshop commenced, participants informally shared stories about their progress and concerns over coffee (*social support*). The whole group would meet for 45 minutes to have the concept of student-created ePortfolios explained (*the issue*), for *information* to be distributed, and for teachers to present their work as cases. Participants would choose one of three sessions conducted by local experts for 75 minutes of skill development in ICTs at basic and advanced levels (*tools*). |
| **2.** All-in-One Sessions | I conducted 60–90 minute presentations that addressed all elements of the CLE. I would explain the concept (*the issue*); present cases; distribute *information*; demonstrate ICTs (*tools*); reassure teachers about their capacity to implement ePortfolios and provide sources of *social and contextual support*. |
| **3.** Information Booklet | A comprehensive source of *information* about ePortfolios including guides in the use of ICTs (*tools*). |
| **4.** Web Site | The Web site included a definition of an ePortfolio and its advantages (*the issue*), the *information* booklet; an annotated list of Web sites (*information and cases*); a library of *cases* from the project; tutorials in ICTs (*tools*); and sources of *social and contextual support*. The Web site could be accessed online and was also distributed to schools on CD. |
| **5.** E-mail Discussion List | A source of *social and contextual support* through communication with others and facilitators. |

### Workshops

Workshops were held after school and on whole days set aside for staff development. These events became very popular, and 90 or more participants would respond to a single advertising e-mail. A local high school provided the venue, and the format for the first workshop became the pattern for future sessions. We always started with an informal discussion during a cup of coffee and snacks, and then the whole group would meet for 45 minutes. I would briefly review the concept of ePortfolios and distribute the information booklet for participants who had not attended previous workshops. I would explain the design of the CLE and the concept of case-based reasoning (CBR) to enhance metacognition. That is, by understanding the processes involved in their own learning, it was assumed that teachers would be able to apply the same principles in their teaching. A teacher or group of teachers would be contacted several weeks before the workshop and asked to present their classroom work on ePortfolios as a case. For the next 75 minutes participants would choose one of three hands-on sessions in computer labs conducted by local expert teachers. The hands-on sessions ranged from basic to advanced levels and focused on a particular aspect of ICT such as movie and image editing, Photo Story, file management, and PowerPoint. Participants evaluated each workshop and provided suggestions for future workshops. Careful attention to organization ensured that sessions flowed well and started and finished on time, and that equipment was working.

---

**LITERATURE ESSENTIALS**

## *Case-Based Reasoning (CBR)*

Teachers access the library of cases to view examples of how other teachers have solved similar issues in their classrooms. According to Aamodt and Plaza (1994), the case library supports the four steps in case-based reasoning (CBR).

1. **Retrieve.** Learners access a case that solves a similar problem to the one they are encountering.

2. **Reuse.** Learners apply the solution in the case and their own experience to try to solve the problem.

3. **Revise.** Solutions are revised until the problem is solved.

4. **Retain:** The new case is stored for others to access.

CBR scaffolds learner memory because processes in a case are recalled when solving a problem. Cognitive flexibility is enhanced because cases provide different perspectives and interpretations of a problem and its solution (Jonassen, 1999).

The informal sharing session at the beginning of workshops had an important role in the CLE. Implementing new practices involves taking risks and support may be needed if processes are unfamiliar and results uncertain. Teachers reported their appreciation of this time and the effort taken to provide a well-presented workshop.

At the first two workshops, teachers were invited from outside the district to present their work as cases until there were sufficient local cases to present and discuss. A funding grant allowed teachers in six schools to be reassigned from their normal teaching duties for several days to plan the implementation of ePortfolios in their classrooms. Those teachers spoke about their work as cases at the workshops. Teachers reported that they liked to see and hear what other teachers were doing and gained a better understanding of the concept and its potential. There are many issues to solve in the implementation of ePortfolios and teachers felt reassured that everyone was in a similar situation and that an ePortfolio framework for a classroom or school could take years to develop. The cases were motivating and generated ideas and goals, and teachers responded to subtle and difficult to describe aspects, such as the changed relationships between children and teachers and student-centered learning. Teachers appreciated the practical aspects of the hands-on components, which supplemented the theory in the information booklet. They also understood the need to share their work, which is an important aspect of a CLE. This was particularly noticeable in that teachers who were normally reluctant to talk in front of their peers readily accepted the opportunity to share their work as a case and spoke excitedly about their achievements and the concept of ePortfolios.

The elective hands-on ICT skills sessions were presented by volunteer teacher experts, who talked as teachers to teachers. They were enthusiastic about the topic, and there was a strong sense of presenters and participants learning together. Participants recognized that presenters were giving up their time to support others and were forgiving of any lapses, though the pace of a presentation was frequently raised as an issue. Many teachers preferred presenters who ensured that everyone in the computer lab had performed and understood a task before moving on to the next task. Presenters who moved at a faster pace were successful if they could carry their audience along with enthusiasm. It was difficult to meet the needs of every individual, even by breaking into three groups of 30 with a choice of basic to advanced skill development. The best we could hope for was that there was something for everybody.

### Tools for learning: Skill-building workshop sessions

Jonassen (1999) describes the three groups of tools that learners apply in a CLE: cognitive (knowledge-construction) tools, static and dynamic knowledge modeling tools, and conversation and collaboration tools. So that the groups of tools could be easily remembered by teachers, I adopted the terms *physical tools*, *thinking tools*, and *communication tools*. Each of these three groups of tools was addressed in skill building sessions at the workshops.

*Physical tools* are the objects used to perform a task. For example, ePortfolios may require the use of a Web cam, digital and movie camera, audio recorder, scanner, printer, headphone, microphone, data projector, memory stick, external hard drive, and software such as PowerPoint and Microsoft Producer (to create multimedia presentations), Windows

Movie Maker (movie editor), IrfanView (image editor), Audacity (audio editor), and Photo Story 3 (to create slideshows).

*Thinking tools* (e.g., word processors, databases, spreadsheets, and the Internet) enhance learners' performance and their ability to access and gather information. Thinking tools also help learners to visualize and organize new practices (Jonassen, 1999). For example, Inspiration software is a useful concept mapping tool for teachers and students to plan the structure of ePortfolios and for students to plan the projects included in ePortfolios. Another example of a thinking tool is the following list of questions that I assembled to stimulate reflection and to aid teachers in their planning. The list below was distributed at workshops and included in the booklet and CD.

1. What purposes would ePortfolios serve in your classroom or school?

2. Who is the audience and how will they view ePortfolios?

3. What elements need to be included in the design of your ePortfolios?

4. What software would be used to create artifacts and view student work?

5. What ICTs are available or need to be purchased?

6. What skills need to be developed?

7. How will data be stored?

8. Will your ePortfolios be teacher centered or student centered?

9. How will you monitor the curriculum to ensure outcomes are being addressed?

10. What changes will occur in teaching practices when ePortfolios are implemented?

The *communication tools* used by teachers to communicate and collaborate with each other and with facilitators were e-mail and e-mail discussion lists, and did not require skill building.

## Other workshop opportunities

The Toowoomba Technology Mathematics and Science Centre of Excellence (TTMSCE) is a federally funded support body for teachers, and as a principal, I had worked on other projects with the coordinator. As a result of our discussions, he recognized the potential of the ePortfolio project to support one of his own objectives in developing the ICT skills of teachers. Consequently, the TTMSCE provided several thousand dollars in funding each year and invited the planning committee to organize workshops at the annual TTMSCE conference. On those whole days of professional development we offered streams of sessions with each devoted to an aspect of ePortfolios (e.g., teachers talking about their work as cases, and hands-on ICT skill development).

An idea that came from a member of the planning committee was to offer workshops called an *ePortfolio Playground*. These after-school workshops were informal and teachers could *play* with various ICT hardware and software and bring along their work on ePortfolios to receive help from experts and peers.

## All-in-one sessions

As the activities of the ePortfolio Project became known around the district, I was called upon to give presentations at school staff meetings and to student teachers at the local university. These sessions were also organized around the five elements of a CLE. In fact, whenever I am in a teaching situation or discussing pedagogy with teachers, I mentally check to ensure that each element is addressed.

I began the all-in-one sessions by giving a simple explanation of the concept of ePortfolios. This was followed by a demonstration of two cases of ePortfolios to provide an immediate sense of what ePortfolios looked like. The first ePortfolio I presented was teacher-centered and depicted a series of videos taken by a teacher over the course of a year to demonstrate a child's reading development. The second ePortfolio was student-centered and was developed by a child with little input from the teacher. These cases provided discussion points and illustrated how ePortfolios lie on a continuum from teacher-centered to student-centered, with each having inherent advantages and disadvantages. The information booklet was distributed and the basic concept of ePortfolios expanded and discussed.

The rest of the session was taken up with a demonstration of software and hardware. There was insufficient time at these sessions for hands-on experiences, but I was able to undertake a comprehensive overview of the required resources. Many teachers were not aware of the ICTs now available that provide off the shelf solutions to problems: for instance, external hard drives for data storage. I assembled a portable kit of ICT equipment and demonstrated each application using a laptop and data projector.

Special attention was given to the affective state of participants because technology can be overwhelming. I used an analogy to suggest there was only a swimming pool of things to learn about ICTs. Although there is a lot of water in a pool, it is not as overwhelming as an ocean. After demonstrating that the skills in one application applied to other applications, the analogy could be reduced to a bathtub of things to learn. I always tested the equipment beforehand to ensure that it worked first time every time, though with plug and play this was rarely a problem. Participants were assured that for every problem there was a solution, and that their problems were likely to be experienced by many others. For example, information about ICTs and responses to error messages were readily available via Google. It was explained that ICTs are sold worldwide to people of all ages and experience levels, and are becoming easier to use, cheaper, and more durable. It was also pointed out that computer stores were filled on weekends with their students and parents, who were using these tools in their everyday lives.

The versatility and adaptability of ePortfolios became obvious as I was kept busy giving presentations to teachers from early childhood, primary, secondary, and special schools. I submitted reports to senior education officers and would raise the topic at every opportunity. Principals became aware of my work and would arrange for me to talk to their staffs. The education authority funded 50 principals from all parts of the state to visit my school in groups for an all-in-one session, and I have taken the presentation on a state-funded road show to schools in rural and remote areas.

The Regional Technology Manager invited me to train as a presenter for the ICT Pedagogical Licence. This new approach to ICT professional development introduced by the education authority was compatible with the work we had achieved in the ePortfolio Project. Teachers would attend a three-day workshop, and as a presenter I was able to introduce the concept of an ePortfolio and a CLE. The teachers would prepare an ePortfolio reflecting their beliefs about teaching with ICTs and include samples of their students' work in ICTs. The teachers' ePortfolios would be assessed and successful applicants would receive an ICT Pedagogical Licence.

## Information booklet

I compiled a booklet that summarized the literature on ePortfolios and contained all of the information teachers would need in the early stages of implementing ePortfolios. Teachers could use the booklet later in the implementation process to reflect on what had been achieved and what was still possible to achieve. The title of the booklet, *ePortfolios: A Learning Tool*, was intended to highlight the role of ePortfolios in enhancing student learning rather than just serving as an administrative tool to track student progress. Information in the booklet was presented as a series of dot points (bulleted items) and in tables so that teachers could peruse and retrieve the information quickly, including:

1. a definition of an ePortfolio,
2. types of ePortfolios and their purposes,
3. the role of ePortfolios in assessment,
4. links to other initiatives or concepts in education,
5. software and hardware and how these are used,
6. the content of ePortfolios,
7. stages of development of ePortfolios,
8. strategies to evaluate ePortfolios,
9. issues that may need to be resolved, and
10. a plan of action.

The booklet section on software and hardware was continually updated as new ICTs were developed and prices generally became cheaper for better-quality and faster equipment. I browsed computer shops to keep abreast of the latest trends and this information was valued by teachers, particularly those in isolated areas. Teachers can introduce ePortfolios to their classrooms in stages and at their own pace, and the information booklet was useful in providing ideas about how they could move to the next step in their learning and development. I would point out to teachers that the booklet was a background resource for their learning and not a textbook for instruction, which is an important distinction in a CLE.

## Web site

I collated the information resources and cases presented during the project for a Web site. The Web site was accessible only to participants and was constructed so that it aligned with the five elements of a CLE listed below:

1. The issue: a definition of ePortfolios and the benefits of ePortfolios.

2. Information resources: the information booklet and annotated list of Web sites.

3. Cases: presentations by teachers as written and video cases.

4. Tools: list of questions to guide planning (*thinking tool*) and tutorials on using ICTs (*physical tools*).

5. Social and contextual support: options for support and how to support others (e.g., people to contact and how to subscribe to the e-mail discussion list).

The recording and storing of cases of new practices on the Web site represented the final step in the case-based reasoning (CBR) process, retaining new cases for others to access. By accessing these cases, teachers could observe ePortfolio practices they had not previously considered, they could compare their own progress with the achievements of others, and they could be reassured that the concept of ePortfolios as an innovative teaching practice was viewed favorably by their colleagues. The cases also provided a bank of solutions for teachers if they had problems implementing ePortfolios (Jonassen, 1999), and contributed to organizational memory so that what was achieved in the project is accessible for others in Queensland learning projects. (Because the site is only available to employees of Education Queensland, there were fewer demands on screening content; the intent was for professionals to view the work of other professionals on this restricted site.)

Each case had a brief explanation including the issue, the context, the new practice, and the effect of the new practice. Enough detail was provided so that teachers could identify with the issue and solution and interpret similarities and contrasts with their own context. The quality of cases was considered more important than quantity, and new cases were continually added and old cases removed. Visual aids such as photos or video clips were powerful and provided a lot of information quickly. The enthusiasm of teachers talking about their work on video was stimulating, and teachers viewing the videos identified with the language and stories.

In order to build a case library it was necessary to identify skilled practitioners (Jonassen & Hernandez-Serrano, 2002). The concept of a *knowledge scout* (Jonassen, Wang, Strobel, & Cernusca, 2003) was applied successfully in the ePortfolio project and members of the planning committee or participants at workshops would nominate practitioners as potential presenters of exemplars. *Knowledge scouts* also sourced interesting articles on the topic for sharing at workshops, on the Web site, or by e-mail.

Using my office computer, I copied the Web site onto hundreds of CDs and printed labels and covers, and I distributed these free to schools and individual teachers. This process was used as an example at workshops that professional-looking material can be produced using the software and hardware commonly found in schools.

### E-mail discussion list

An e-mail discussion list was used as a means of communication between participants and facilitators. Even though it proved effective in advertising events and sharing information and resources, this tool was not used to its potential. The discussion list was one aspect of the project that suffered from time constraints in my dual role as principal and researcher, and I should have delegated responsibility for its management to a person with an interest in this form of communication. A record of e-mail discussions, though, proved to be useful data to indicate participant areas of need.

## Data collection

Though the CLE was made up of a variety of activities to address each of the five elements, it was also viewed as a whole system (Salomon, 1991). Therefore an evaluation of new knowledge, understanding, and skills attained in each activity told only part of a participant's story of development. Of importance was the participant's identity as a learner and the changes in practices implemented as a result of his or her learning (Greeno & the Middle School Mathematics Through Applications Projects Group, 1998). The Professional Development Framework (see Table 4.1) was a valuable guide in the design of data collection tools to investigate the effectiveness of both discrete activities and the project as a whole. These tools included surveys, observations, teacher and school cases, videotapes of teacher presentations, interviews, and documents.

Data were collected over time to fully understand the consequences of changed teaching practices, including the impact on schools (Bober, 2001). For example, a teacher reported that her practices had changed so much that it created problems for teachers who took over her class during absences. Her integration of ICTs had changed the way knowledge was managed in her classroom (Bober, 2001). When a critical mass of teachers reached this point, there was pressure for change to be adopted across the whole school.

Workshop participants rated sessions on a five-point Likert scale, provided comments, and nominated topics for future workshops. The cases presented by teachers at the workshops gave a detailed account of their changed practices and personal journey of change. The teachers' levels of confidence in presenting their work indicated their self-efficacy in performing the new practices. The two strong messages that emanated from peer presentations were that obstacles could be overcome, and that *if I can do it, anyone can.* Informal discussions with individual and small groups of participants at the gathering before workshops commenced and other, more formal, interviews provided valuable feedback. For example, a teacher became enthused about the concept of ePortfolios at the first workshop and over the following weeks applied his considerable experience in ICTs to build an impressive approach to the classroom implementation of ePortfolios. An interview provided insights into his motivation and how he planned to realize his vision for ePortfolios throughout his whole school.

Data collection was enhanced by my close involvement in the project. I was already aware of likely data sources, and could take advantage of any opportunity to supplement the data. For example, administrators provided valuable information about their vision for ePortfolios in their application for a funding grant to pay for teachers to be reassigned from their normal classroom duties. Information in the funding application was compared with the ePortfolio frameworks that were implemented in those schools after participation in the learning activities. In addition, comprehensive follow-up surveys of principals and project managers provided data on observed changes in teaching practices, management issues, and needs for additional progress. This comparison highlighted the nature of learning as a journey. All of the schools made progress towards the goal of implementing ePortfolio frameworks, but to reach that goal takes time and the commitment of motivated individuals.

As this was my doctoral research project, data were collected, recorded, and analyzed in detail. Nevertheless, the principles involved apply to any project. That is, professional development activities should be evaluated and the results used to inform future activities. As well, there is a need to look beyond the evaluation of discrete activities to include an evaluation of the effect of the activities on classroom practices.

## Results

The network has operated continually since July 2004, with four after-school and two whole-day workshops organized each year. I was also invited to give presentations about ePortfolios at individual schools and for clusters of schools. Although this does not appear to be a lot of activity, teachers and administrators needed time to absorb the concept, gather resources, develop requisite skills, and experiment with ePortfolios in their schools. From the outset I was determined that the project was going to be sustained, and therefore the quality of activities in meeting the needs of teachers was more important than frequency. Teachers took more than two years to be confident in learning requisite skills in using ICTs and changing their practices, and therefore a lot of activity would have been overwhelming.

Participants readily identified with belonging to a learning network, although the name of the network changed to reflect the makeup of the group and the requirements of funding submissions. For example, the current name for the network is the *ePortfolio Alliance*, simply because a major source of funding established alliances among schools to facilitate professional development.

Workshops were free because teachers volunteered to present cases and provide expertise, and meals and expenses were paid from grants. Teachers did not have to approach their school administration for funding to attend, and registrations for workshops were easier to manage without money being involved. The project was promoted in district newsletters and mentioned at every opportunity such as meetings of teachers and administrators. The project developed a reputation that activities were well organized and worthwhile and that it was sustained. Participants who were later involved in other ICT learning projects realized the benefits of their work in the ePortfolio project, and how their new knowledge and skills could be applied in other situations. Many participants also had no trouble in getting their ICT Pedagogical Licences. (See http://education.qld.gov. au/smartclassrooms/strategy/tsdev_pd-licence.html for elements of Queensland's ICT Pedagogical Licence).

Learning also occurred during teachers' everyday work with children in developing ePortfolios and in their personal use of ICTs. This highlighted a major benefit of ePortfolios in connecting schools and the real world of home and work. For example, teachers learned to use Photo Story by creating video clips from holiday photos, and then applied those skills in their teaching. The state education authority encourages the personal use of ICTs by providing teachers with laptops, and the use of Microsoft software at school and at home is permitted through an agreement involving an annual fee paid by the school. This simplified the task of enhancing the skills of teachers because everyone was using the same basic software.

## Other learning projects

The Professional Development Framework (see Table 4.1) that emerged from the ePortfolio Project was applied and refined in two other projects. The Success for Boys project received federal government funding of A$70,000 (approximately US$57,500), which paid for 300 participants to attend one introductory and four elective sessions and for each school to develop a response to the "issue" of the underachievement of boys. Administrators were encouraged to use the Professional Development Framework as a guide to develop a CLE for the analysis of the issue and the generation, evaluation, and sustaining of intervention strategies in specific contexts. The framework was ideally suited as a systematic approach to the problem of the underachievement of boys and the recording of cases of success stories for others to access. Teachers may have sought instant solutions to problems with boys, but this project involved an issue that could not be addressed by a single professional development event. Intervention strategies had to respond to each context; be applied consistently across the whole school; and be evaluated, monitored, and refined.

The ICTs in Mathematics project received A$25,000 (approximately US$20,500) of state government funding and involved a group of 25 motivated self-selected teachers. The group was immersed in the application of ICTs to support learning in mathematics at whole-day workshops, with further interactive learning through an online site. The Professional Development Framework (see Table 4.1) was applied in the design and evaluation of the project. An online site was organized around the five elements of a CLE, similar to the Web site designed for the ePortfolio Project. A facilitator was employed one day each week to develop and monitor the site and to collaborate with and support participants.

## Conclusions

Change cannot be hurried. Teachers required more than two years to experiment with ePortfolios and to be comfortable with ICTs. Professional development projects have to be sustained if support is to be provided over such extended periods of time. By persevering with early adopters until they become confident with the new processes, a critical mass of learners can be developed who will take a good idea through to accepted practice in a school or district.

The theme of ePortfolios was powerful and no doubt contributed to the success of the project. It is a simple concept and, once it was explained, teachers immediately saw how ePortfolios could be a focal point for all activity in their classrooms and provide a purpose for their involvement with ICTs. The simplicity of the concept reduced feelings of being overwhelmed, and allowed professional development to focus systematically on the associated information and skills that together realize the vision that each teacher had for ePortfolios.

Even with a highly motivating topic, the challenge for the project planning committee was to maintain teacher engagement when initial enthusiasm had to be translated into the hard work of implementation. Teachers will persevere to overcome obstacles if they are engaged in an issue important to them and their early enthusiasm is nurtured and supported. This was achieved by demonstrating that everyone had the capacity to learn ICT skills and that ePortfolios can be implemented in stages. Skill development was linked to a teacher's personal use of ICTs and care was taken not to overwhelm teachers. For example, the simplicity of modern plug-and-play applications was demonstrated at workshops and elective sessions were arranged to ensure that something was gained by participants of all skill levels.

The project highlighted the potential effectiveness and efficiency of in-house professional development. Education authorities should recognize and value teachers and administrators who are self-motivated to initiate and support professional development projects within and outside their schools. Though the implementation of ePortfolios was not a systemic imperative, the project nevertheless met numerous systemic goals such as the classroom integration of ICTs. These goals were achieved effectively because relevance was at a high level. That is, the needs of teachers were being met and experienced practicing teachers provided expertise. The goals were achieved efficiently, because although more than A$25,000 (approximately US$20,500) was received in grants over three years, the project would have been equally as successful with far less or no funding at all. The funding did allow selected teachers to be reassigned from their normal teaching duties at the beginning of the project to plan the implementation of ePortfolios in their classrooms. However, the keys to success were the commitment to sustain learning and the use of local experts (teacher leaders accorded recognition for their efforts), facilities, and resources in a systematic approach. The library of cases contributed to organizational memory, which other learners can access to solve issues. There is also a record for future professional development projects to improve what has been achieved, rather than beginning all over again.

The elements and principles of a CLE proved to be versatile in the design of learning experiences. A CLE can be designed, implemented, and sustained over a number of years, as was the case with the ePortfolio Project. On the other hand, I was able to apply the same elements and principles in a 60–90 minute presentation. Most importantly, teachers were taught in the same way they should teach. That is, teachers were continually reminded about the principles involved in their own learning, and were able to apply those principles in designing learning experiences for children working on classroom projects.

# GETTING STARTED RESOURCES

Aamodt, A., & Plaza, E. (1994). Case-based reasoning: Foundational issues, methodological variations, and system approaches. *Artificial Intelligence Communications, 7*(1), 39–59.

> The principles of case-based reasoning (CBR) are explained, including a model of the CBR cycle.

Commonwealth Department of Education, Science and Training (2001). *Making better connections.* Canberra: Commonwealth of Australia.

> Funded by the Australian federal government, this report focuses on professional development for the integration of ICT in education. The report investigates how the effectiveness of professional development may be measured, identifies professional development models, lists factors that are barriers or critical to the success of professional development, and makes recommendations for professional development projects.

Jonassen, D. H. (1999). Designing constructivist learning environments. In C. M. Reigeluth (Ed.), *Instructional-design theories and models: A new paradigm of instructional theory (vol. 2)* (pp. 215–239). Mahwah, NJ: Lawrence Erlbaum.

> Jonassen describes a model for designing constructivist learning environments. An adaptation of the model applied in the ePortfolio Project has five elements: the issue, information resources, case library, tools, and social and contextual support.

Jonassen, D. H., & Hernandez-Serrano, J. (2002). Case-based reasoning and instructional design: Using stories to support problem solving. *Educational Technology Research and Development, 50*(2), 65–77.

> The authors highlight the role of stories or cases in solving problems and recommend four activities to collect stories from practitioners.

Williams, M. (2005). Case Studies and Research into Planning Models of Professional Learning Programs. Retrieved October 24, 2007, from www.learningplace.com.au/deliver/content.asp?pid=26999

> Williams focuses on action learning in her report on models for professional development applied in Queensland, Australia. Besides analyzing strategies currently in use, Williams makes recommendations that apply to any professional development project.

## chapter 5

# Technology Apprentices, SWAT Teams, and Using Students for Professional Development

*Rae Niles*
*Sedgwick (Kansas) Public Schools*

## abstract

 THIS CHAPTER CHRONICLES the support of Student Technology Apprentices and Students Willing to Assist with Technology (SWAT) Teams in helping teachers and students in a rural, technology-rich Midwest high school. The initial use of students as part of a teacher professional development model helped lay the foundation for support of a one-to-one laptop computer initiative. The chapter also illustrates how the resulting relationship between teachers and students helped foster change in the teaching and learning environment. Suggestions are provided for educational leaders considering the use of K–12 students in the role of technology assistants.

# Worst case scenario

Welcome to a technology director's worst nightmare. It is mid-June and your school board has just approved funding for a one-to-one laptop computer initiative. You are a lone technology director in a small school with no support staff. You are not only charged with maintaining the hardware and installing the software, but are also responsible for offering the professional development necessary to ready your staff for teaching and learning in a laptop computer learning environment. There will be no additional staff hired for the task. What do you do?

Whether they are called Student Tech Teams, Nerd Squads, Computer Kids, Advanced Tech Tools Teams (AT[3]), or Students Willing to Assist with Technology (SWAT) Team, their goals are similar: to provide technical support and one-on-one professional staff development for their peers, community businesses and organizations, and—more importantly—for their teachers. This chapter describes one Midwest school district that has chosen to embrace its students as technology experts and then summarizes the changes in the teaching and learning environment that have occurred as a result.

# Background

Students who attend Sedgwick Public Schools, Unified School District 439 in Sedgwick, Kansas, enjoy a rich relationship with technology, one that includes serving as mentors and technology specialists for their peers, teachers, and community, too. Sedgwick USD 439 has a student enrollment nearing 550 students in kindergarten through twelfth grade. The district's schools are housed on one campus, and beginning with the 1999–2000 school year have benefited from a wireless computer network extending throughout the entire site. The 2007–2008 school year began the sixth year of the one-to-one laptop computer initiative involving students in the 10th, 11th, and 12th grades.

In 1998, USD 439 received a Technology Literacy Challenge Fund (TLCF) Grant and chose to use the funds to begin a seventh grade GenWHY Program modeled after the work done by Dennis Harper (Harper, 2006). The goal of GenWHY was to increase student technology skills and to create a collaborative partnership between students and teachers to help teachers more easily infuse technology into their classrooms. Students were to serve as the technology experts, working in conjunction with the teachers who were the content experts, to create lessons or projects using technology. The intent was to offer one-on-one technology training for teachers and, at the same time, to relieve teacher stress during the infusion of new technology.

Students involved in GenWHY met before school two mornings each week and learned about the ethical use of technology, how to use software programs, basic technology troubleshooting, how to improve higher-level critical thinking and problem solving skills by using the Internet to gather and evaluate information about a topic of their choice, and how to work cooperatively in a collaborative setting.

## GenWHY and GenYES

Using students to train teachers may seem like a novel approach to professional staff development; however, the GenWHY Program, originally funded through a 1996 U. S. Department of Education (USDOE) grant, offers a model for using students to train teachers to impact technology instruction (Harper 2007). The grant focused on training students to work with teachers by having students collaborate with teachers to create technology-rich lessons. The USDOE recognized the GenWHY Program as an exemplary program model (Carroll, 2000). Following the conclusion of the five-year grant, the GenWHY Program evolved into the GenYES Program and now publishes educational content for schools focused on empowering students to advance the use of technology in their own school (Harper, 2007).

Throughout the course of the school year, students used their newly acquired technology skills and worked with selected teachers of kindergarten through twelfth grade to develop a technology lesson or idea the teachers could use in one or several of their lessons. The students were to help their cooperating teachers by meeting with them on a regular basis and sharing technology expertise in a low-risk setting while strengthening the GenWHY students' own technology skills. The grant money for GenWHY lasted through three semesters.

## Technology apprentices continue without grant money

With the advent of decreased federal funding for support of the efforts begun by GenWHY, the district turned to locally funded opportunities for students to continue to work as technology experts. Initially, two high school students each enrolled as a technology apprentice to the district's technology director, who held an administrative role and was not a regular classroom teacher. It was decided each of the two students would work for one class period as a technology apprentice with the technology director. Their responsibilities included helping to troubleshoot common networking problems, helping to create and maintain the district's Web site, and occasionally assuming simple duties in the absence of the technology director. The apprentices provided ongoing technology support for faculty and students, including one-on-one tutorial lessons for teachers.

## A student teaches a teacher

When a technology apprentice worked with a teacher to help the teacher learn software needed for a lesson, the apprentice also offered additional ways the technology could be used to enhance current practice. A fictional example of the dialogue between a technology apprentice and a junior high school social studies teacher illustrates the ways in which the apprentice helped the teacher understand other alternatives for how to use the software.

**Teacher:** By learning PowerPoint I can lecture and not have to use an overhead projector or the chalkboard, right?

**Apprentice:** Well, yes, that is correct, but more importantly you can also consider ways your students could use the same software to not only present their ideas in front of their classmates, but for other types of assignments, too.

**Teacher:** What do you mean? I thought PowerPoint was basically used for lecture or giving speeches or presentations.

**Apprentice:** Yes, that is true, PowerPoint can be used for lectures, presentations, or speeches, but it can also be used to make story books, do outlines, or used as a graphic design tool. Your students could use PowerPoint as a graphic design tool to make brochures, posters, or signs. PowerPoint allows your students the ability to lay out their type and their graphics. It's easy to move the graphics and the text around using PowerPoint.

**Teacher:** I sure didn't know you could use PowerPoint for so many different types of assignments. I think I may want to try some of those ideas myself.

A year later, five high school students enrolled to work as a technology apprentice with the district's technology director. To expand the number of periods technology support was available throughout the district, each apprentice enrolled in one of five class periods. The second year, they expanded their responsibilities by offering their technology services to the businesses, churches, clubs, and organizations within the community. The technology apprentices were able to create Web sites for businesses within the community and to create logos, banners, and signs using graphic design software for the school's clubs and community organizations. Their outreach helped to establish credibility within the community for the technology efforts of the school.

# SWAT team evolves with one-to-one laptop computer initiative

With the advent of the 2002–2003 school year, efforts were in place for the one-to-one Apple laptop computer initiative. Recognizing the technology director had no support staff other than student technology apprentices to help prepare the laptops, the decision was made to use In-House Training—the capstone course in the career and technical education classes in the high school's business and computer department—as fertile ground to develop a cadre of students for the technology apprentice program. Seven 11th- and 12th-grade students were enrolled in In-House Training. Interestingly, six of the seven students had participated in GenWHY as seventh graders. Their technology skills were already solid.

## LITERATURE ESSENTIALS

### One-to-one laptop initiatives

Schools, districts, and states embarking on one-to-one laptop computer initiatives or other types of technology hardware and software infusion into the learning environment are faced with many challenges, and the range and scope of each entity's challenges vary widely (Apple Inc., 2005). Research indicates teacher training and professional staff development in a one-to-one laptop computer initiative affect the overall success of the initiative. Teacher attitudes and beliefs affect program implementation and success.

Regardless of the size of the one-to-one laptop computer initiative or the number of students and teachers involved, one thing is universal—the need for teachers to increase their personal technology skills and for them to offer quality teaching instruction enhanced by technology integration (Bonifaz & Zucker, 2004). Professional development for teachers is critical to help ease the transition from non-technology-based instruction to ubiquitous computing learning environments.

The cadre of seven soon named themselves Sedgwick High School's Students Willing to Assist with Technology (SWAT) Team. They were responsible for unpacking, configuring, testing, and supporting each computer during the deployment that was to occur six weeks after the start of school. They were also placed in charge of developing training and technology tutorials for their peers. The technology tutorials the SWAT Team members created ranged from elaborate QuickTime movies demonstrating how to add a printer to the printer menu to a concise step-by-step guide to creating a table using Microsoft Word. They also helped create step-guides for the care and handling of the laptop.

Using the collaboration skills they had initially learned as part of GenWHY and the expertise they had continued to hone during their high-school computer courses, SWAT members created the professional development necessary for their peers and their teachers to effectively use the newly acquired laptop computers.

The school year began the second week of August and the laptop computers were not distributed to the student body until the last week of September. Members of the SWAT team strategically identified the skills their peers would need to operate the laptop computers and, using presentation software, designed step-guides to be used on the day the laptops were distributed. The SWAT members would be teaching their classmates about the laptop computers during the initial training session when the laptops were distributed. It would be student led, not teacher led.

The SWAT team members also created print material with specific instructions and how-to guides for teachers to use, too. SWAT Team members worked during an assigned class period and also before and after school. Collaboration occurred during the lunch period and also in other classes throughout the day.

The day the laptops were distributed to each of the 85 11th- and 12th-grade students, the members of the SWAT Team served as the day's event organizers. The initial laptop roll-out included a large-group, student-led overview of simple computer operation and the proper care of the laptop. Different members of the SWAT Team highlighted one specific piece of software or technology tip. The training concluded with more one-on-one instruction as needed or informal small-group sessions organized by the students. The SWAT Team members were celebrities in the school. Students and teachers readily recognized the critical role the SWAT Team had played in making the one-to-one laptop computer initiative come to fruition. Being a computer nerd became cool.

During the first year of the SWAT effort, two other students changed their class schedules at the beginning of second semester to join the In-House Training class because they wanted to be a part of the SWAT Team. The following year the number of SWAT Team members doubled to fourteen. SWAT Team members assumed more roles within the school and functioned in the capacity of teacher in many specific situations, including whole-class instruction on how to use specific software on the laptop, Internet research strategies, and ways to use technology for classroom assignments. Students who were part of the SWAT Team were admired by their peers and appreciated by the teachers.

The In-House Training teacher, a business and computer vocational teacher, provided leadership for the SWAT Team. He worked in conjunction with the district's technology director to ensure the SWAT Team's success. His students were responsible for unpacking and labeling the laptop computers and computer backpacks with asset tags, recording the computer serial numbers in a spreadsheet, installing software, testing the student accounts created on the laptops to ensure software would launch, and tweaking settings on the student accounts for a more seamless technology experience.

Under the guidance of the In-House Training teacher, members of the SWAT Team bookmarked URLs in the Web browser, placed software shortcuts on the computer's desktop, and offered constructive criticism of the basic student account setup. They set up machines for their fellow students the way students would want them, not the way the adults might configure the laptop settings.

## Research reveals changes in teaching and learning

Research investigating teacher and student perceptions of the impact of one-to-one laptop computer access at Sedgwick High School revealed changes in teaching and learning (Niles, 2006). Research was conducted via an appreciative inquiry perspective to concentrate on the optimistic nature of an organization and the positive core by focusing on what works within the organization (Cooperrider & Srivastva, 1987). Appreciative inquiry is asset-based, rather than deficit-based, and allowed the researcher to focus on what was working within the one-to-one laptop computer initiative, rather than what was not working. Both student and teacher participation in the study was voluntary.

Data were collected through the use of student focus groups representing a cross-section by gender, socioeconomic status, academics, and grade level. Eighteen students, three boys and three girls each from the 10th, 11th, and 12th grades, participated in one of three grade-level focus groups conducted during the school day. Each of the focus groups responded to the same questions crafted by the district's technology director, the researcher for the study. The guiding questions for the student focus groups included:

1. Can you remember a time when you were using technology in class and it all came together for you and your classmates? What was happening? What did it feel like? How did the teacher respond? How did you respond?

2. How has the way teachers teach changed because of the use of laptops in the classroom? Can you share a personal story as an example?

3. Describe a situation where you used your laptop to complete a project. What was the project? What did you learn? How did having a laptop make learning more meaningful?

4. How has the use of your laptop in the classroom influenced the way your teacher interacts with you? Can you illustrate what you mean with an example?

5. How has the access to emerging technology influenced the dreams you have for your future?

Thirteen of the fifteen teachers at the high school also participated in focus groups. The guiding questions asked of the teacher focus group participants included:

1. Can you remember a classroom teaching event when you were using technology and it all came together for you and the students? What was happening? What did it feel like? How did the students respond? How did you respond?

2. What makes Sedgwick High School unique when compared to other high schools? Why is it different?

3. How has your teaching changed as a result of access to emerging technology?

4. Can you describe how using emerging technology has changed how you view teaching?

5. Can you describe how access to emerging technology influenced how you interact with students?

6. If you had the opportunity to talk with parents who were thinking of enrolling their children at Sedgwick High School, what would you tell them about the use of technology?

7. What dreams do you hold for the students you teach as they relate to applying technology to their learning?

Data were also collected through administration of the Left-Hand Right-Hand Column Case Method (Argyris, 1999). This method is used to gather data that members of an organization may be reluctant to discuss. Fourteen teacher participants responded in writing to a specific situation—in this case, their feelings about the use of laptop computers in the high school—using a constructed conversation crafted from a fictional scenario. On the left-hand side of the paper, teachers wrote what they might *actually say* to others in the conversation; the right-hand side was for the same conversation, but was for teachers to record what they would *really like to say*, but for whatever reasons, did not. The Left-Hand Right-Hand Column Case Method was distributed to the teachers following their participation in the focus group.

Data were analyzed using the comparative analysis matrix method (Miles & Huberman, 1994). The comparative analysis matrix method allows the researcher to be able to constantly compare and analyze data while identifying patterns, coding data, and categorizing findings. Data were cross-referenced with the study's three theoretical perspectives: organizational change, paradigm shift, and appreciative inquiry.

## Students function in capacity of teacher

Even though no specific questions were asked about the role of SWAT members, data revealed students often functioned in the capacity of teacher. Both teachers and students described experiences where the students served as the source of instruction. The experiences were not limited to one specific subject or classroom, but rather occurred in various situations and multiple classrooms. Teachers and students described occurrences when the teacher waived control and the student functioned in the capacity of teacher. Teachers and students articulated that the teacher no longer assumed the role of the sole instructor within the classroom; now students were instructors, too. One teacher described how students introduced him to new communication technology tools. He said, "I know I was pretty excited when the students showed me how they could instant-message their homework to me."

The research revealed students felt important when they taught teachers new technology skills. Learning from one another resulted in the interaction between the teachers and students affirming the "assets" (per appreciative inquiry) of the organization. The affirmation of this relationship helped strengthen teacher and student relationships within Sedgwick High School. Teachers were learning from students, not just students learning from the classroom teacher.

## Teachers relinquish control in the teaching process

Teachers and students reported that when students functioned in the capacity of teacher, the teacher had to relinquish control of the teaching and learning process. The paradigm shift of relinquishing control was not easy for some teachers. One teacher explained, "I hate to use this word, but it has forced you to give up some of the power and control in the classroom." She went on to explain, "I don't want to say they [students] are running the show, but they are driving more of the instruction these days."

Students who assumed the role of teacher were not limited to SWAT Team members. Many students assumed the role of teacher at different times in different classes. One teacher said, "It isn't always easy, but it definitely is wonderful when everything clicks into place. Students take control and enjoy teaching others and being able to accomplish more than ever before." One teacher explained how difficult it was to change:

> The scariest thing [for me] is not knowing how to do this. Once you start learning how to do it, it is a heck of a lot easier to say, "all right." When you give it up to the computers [have faith that the technology will work and that it is OK not to have all of the technology answers as a teacher], that's a pretty scary thing [for me].

Another teacher's description summarized what other teachers felt regarding the relinquishing of control of the teaching and learning process, "We have to relinquish power [in the classroom] to allow students to teach us how to use the software." Students also recognized their role in the learning process when the teacher gave up their control in the classroom. One student said, "I noticed that the students are becoming teachers."

## Students describe their teaching experience

Many high school students, not just SWAT Team members, described their experiences of teaching new technology skills to high school teachers. Student experiences ranged from setting up instant messaging software for a classroom teacher to helping a teacher configure the instant messaging software "at least a half a dozen times." Students described their sense of importance when teaching teachers how to use technology. A student shared, "It feels good." Another student said, "It makes you feel like you have more power." The sense of feeling important was related to the students' sense of accomplishment. "It makes us feel smarter," offered another student. Another student said, "[when teaching others] you're cool."

One student shared how teaching teachers to use the technology presented a win–win opportunity for teachers and students. Another student reflected on the advantages of teachers' understanding technology and knowing how to use the specific pieces of software, "It makes them [the teacher] want us to teach them how to do stuff. It opens their eyes to new projects that we can use [for future assignments]."

## Teacher roles morph from classroom experts to facilitators

Teachers and students acknowledged that the teacher's role changed from expert to facilitator and co-learner, and they described additional changes in instructional practices. Several students shared that they felt teachers talked less with the use of technology. Two students from two separate focus groups articulated identical comments when they both said, "They [teachers] don't talk as much." Two other students also offered similar responses when they said, "They don't explain it to us" and "It's like when it's on the computers, they [teachers] don't really have to explain it."

---

### LITERATURE ESSENTIALS

## *eMINTS model*

Missouri's Instructional Networked Teaching Strategies Program (eMINTS), beginning as a statewide initiative in 2004 and rapidly increasing nationwide, focuses on supporting teachers "as they integrate multimedia technology into inquiry-based, student-centered, interdisciplinary collaborative teaching practices that result in improved student performance, increased parent involvement [and] enriched instructional effectiveness" (eMINTS, 2004).

The eMINTS program provides teachers with ongoing professional development emphasizing effective technology integration and curriculum enhancement and practice of newly learned technology and teaching skills in a minimal risk environment. Participants have a minimum ratio of two children per computer and ongoing teacher training focused on successfully using technology such as digital cameras, presentation software, SMART Boards, LCD projectors, and external hardware adapters such as probeware. Classroom teachers work with a paid adult technology mentor during the school week and then gather monthly or quarterly with other eMints teachers. The success of the eMints model is tied to the strong ongoing professional development afforded the teachers involved in the eMints classrooms (Pitler, Flynn, & Gaddy, 2004).

---

Teachers recognized the shift of the learning and teaching paradigm. A teacher stated, "I think we have to be ahead of the game and adapt." Research also revealed teachers and students understood that the use of technology-supported instruction transformed the teacher's role from imparter of knowledge to facilitator of instruction. One teacher said, "It [technology] has changed what we teach." Another teacher offered, "I try to find new ways to use the technology that we have."

The influences of technology on teacher instructional practices were explained by teachers who pointed out the importance of adaptation. One teacher described the need for adaptation of instructional practices, "We need to be able to adapt to [technology] because [students] are not growing up the way we used to."

Research uncovered that students also believed technology made the teachers better teachers. A student described a transformation in one of his teachers, "I remember in [teacher's class], it totally changed when we got our laptops. I mean it went from 'Sit down and read!' to just being able to get on the computer and work things out on there."

## Changes in teaching practice result in student choice

The change in the traditional teacher role of expert to facilitator created a paradigm shift in the accepted practice of assigning homework or projects. Students were presented with choices of how to demonstrate their knowledge of content or key concepts. They were allowed to choose the tool that best exemplified their understanding of content. One teacher said, "I think the technology gives the kids other avenues to express their knowledge." Another teacher commented, "Every student learns differently, and if used correctly, the computers can help teachers find a way for every student."

Research also revealed that students were cognizant of the opportunity for choice when demonstrating concepts or content specific information. One student made a connection between a mandatory way of doing an assignment and wanting to do an assignment, "If kids want to do it, if they have a choice of what they are going to do, they are going to do it, and they are going to want to make it good because it's theirs."

The following dialogue between two students illustrates their belief that the novelty of knowing how to use technology and the fun associated with it was a dominant feeling among students.

> **Student A:** You look at some people that know a lot about computers like before we actually had this [laptops]. And I'm like, "Wow! What a geek!" Then you actually get into what it is all about and it is actually kind of cool.
>
> **Student B:** We are all geeks.
>
> **Student A:** Heck yeah, it is [cool].

## Technology-rich learning environment offers students post–high school advantages

Teachers and students believed immersion in a technology-rich learning environment created opportunities for preparing students for success following high school graduation. One teacher described his belief that by providing technology for students in

USD 439, he was preparing them for life after graduation, "How better to prepare your kids for the future than putting the technology that they are going to need after they get out of school in their hands now." Articulating similar beliefs, another teacher said, "What we have tried to provide, you can't get in a textbook." Another teacher said, "We want productive members of society … It [technology] makes them more productive." Teachers echoed similar sentiments by sharing that technology makes students more well-rounded individuals, too.

Students described the advantage of a technology-rich learning environment following high school graduation. One student said, "I think it [technology] just helps prepare you for life." Another student commented, "It [technology] … makes you think that you can achieve more than you thought you could." One student said, "You're definitely going to have an advantage if you know more than the people that don't [know technology] and have to get [computer] training."

## One student's success: Todd's story

Todd (not his real name), a graduating senior and a SWAT Team member, grew up with three brothers and came from a family that was part of the working poor. No one in his family or extended family had ever attended college. The idea that Todd could attend college started as a seed and was fertilized as he progressed through high school.

Todd worked with one of the coaches to help the coach create a Web site; he worked with three of the elementary teachers to strengthen the teachers' Web page creation skills; he began to help his peers with assignments requiring more and more technical expertise. By the time Todd was a senior, his peers and the teachers viewed him as an expert and came to Todd for technology help and advice. During the spring of his senior year Todd began to dream that he could attend college. He believed he could be successful. The expertise he had honed during high school working with his peers and the teachers led to a strong belief that he could attend college in the fall.

Using the skills he had gained, Todd crafted a digital portfolio showcasing his technology expertise and talent. He worked hard to include examples of when and how he had worked with teachers to improve their technology skills and also included examples of several of the many technology projects he had helped create. Todd submitted his digital portfolio for scholarship consideration and was soon rewarded for his efforts. A small Midwest community college believed Todd would be a good scholarship candidate and offered to have him not only attend the college on scholarship, but also offered him a chance to become part of the technology help desk at the college. Todd's high school teachers had benefited from the professional development he shared with them and now professors and instructors at the college level would, too. Additionally, Todd was working to break the cycle of poverty. He would attend college, do well, and ultimately graduate.

To directly correlate Todd's success with his involvement as a member of the SWAT Team or simply with his experience in a high school with a one-to-one laptop computer initiative is difficult at best, and most likely impossible. Factors influencing his success are interrelated and difficult to separate. Personal desire, access to social and cultural capital, and the opportunities afforded him in a technology-rich learning environment all played into his success. Regardless of what caused Todd to be successful, it is certain that Todd was successful. His teachers are proud of Todd and still believe the foundation of his success is tied to his experiences while attending Sedgwick High School.

## Application for student technology helpers in elementary schools

Although the efforts described in this chapter focus on students in high school, specifically Grades 9–12, elementary schools may also benefit from the use of student technology helpers to train teachers. Whether they are called technology helpers, Mouse Squads, or SWAT Teams makes no difference.

More and more students at younger ages are exposed to technology in their homes. They arrive at school with technology skills that their elementary teachers may not have or may be hesitant to explore. The use of student technology helpers in the elementary school should not be overlooked. Building leadership in an elementary school that supports the use of student technology helpers could mirror success similar to that experienced by Sedgwick High School. Elementary students could be used to help teachers understand how to use specific pieces of software and also to leverage specific Web-based solutions, such as blogs, wikis, or interactive age- and grade-level appropriate Web sites. Under Dennis Harper's direction, the GenWHY Program started initially with upper elementary students and has a proven track record with research that supports the use of students using technology to help classroom teachers (Harper, 2006).

## Epilogue

Over a period of ten years, a TLCF grant supported a GenWHY program (stage 1) that then evolved into technology apprentices (stage 2), a SWAT Team (stage 3), and finally into a teaching and learning environment where students function in the capacity of teacher (stage 4). The community, teachers, and students of USD 439 have crafted a relationship that positively affects teaching and learning. The strong teaching and learning relationship students share with their teachers and the community as a result of those initial technology opportunities is still felt. Students continue to work with teachers and to do real-world technology work for members of the community.

In this specific school, the SWAT Team model helped open a door to a new way of doing professional development and added to efforts already in place involving teacher training through workshops and inservice days. The SWAT Team model for teacher professional development allowed teachers to take risks and to try new things, and ultimately to impact student learning. The data collected via the appreciative inquiry research perspective gave educators at this school a clearer view of the assets within the one-to-one laptop computer initiative and helped to validate what had been occurring in relation to teaching and learning within the school. Additionally, the asset-based focus of appreciative inquiry allowed the challenges teachers were facing to surface, making explicit the pros and the cons of such an endeavor.

Regardless of whether they are called SWAT Teams, Student Tech Teams, Nerd Squads, or Computer Kids, their impact is similar. Schools that encourage students to support technology efforts and openly advocate the use of students as technology experts help to strengthen relationships between their teachers and students, and between the school and community, resulting in a win–win learning environment.

---

**LITERATURE ESSENTIALS**

### *Laptops for learning task force*

In March 2004, Florida's Laptops for Learning Task Force presented a comprehensive report to the Florida Commission of Education regarding the success of laptop learning initiatives across the United States (Florida Laptops for Learning Task Force, 2004). The task force was charged with identifying and describing best practices for laptop learning initiatives, offering a cost analysis of the benefits of mobile technology, and examining the equity of educational opportunities that could help guarantee Florida students would gain 21st-century learning skills. Based on a synthesis of prior research, the task force noted that successful professional development in a laptop learning initiative relies on ongoing teacher performance feedback, focuses on best practices, and holds teachers accountable for implementing instructional practices. The report further recommended classroom-based mentor or peer coaching to model technology integration strategies.

---

## Welcome to the present: Best case scenario

Welcome to the present. It is mid-June and your school board has just approved funding for a one-to-one laptop computer initiative. You are a lone technology director in a small school with no support staff who is not only charged with maintaining the hardware and installing the software, but also for offering the professional development necessary to ready your staff for teaching and learning in a laptop computer learning environment. There will be no additional staff hired for the task. What do you do? You organize a SWAT Team of student technology helpers and capitalize on the expertise available from the students in your school to help the classroom teachers!

## GETTING STARTED RESOURCES

Apple Inc. (2005). *Research: What it says about 1 to 1 learning.* Cupertino, CA: Author.

> Helping educators understand the potential of one-to-one laptop computer initiatives, as well as the research to support it, is critical when implementing change. This report offers insights into the types of ubiquitous technology initiatives, trends in mobile computing, professional development needs, and the research to support change.

Florida Laptop for Learning Task Force. (2004). *Laptops for learning: Final report and recommendations of the Laptops for Learning Task Force.* Tallahassee: Florida State Department of Education.

> The Florida State Department of Education's report offers an overview of the need for ubiquitous computing and the challenges associated with professional staff development needs in a one-to-one laptop computer initiative. The report also provides a compelling look at the needs related to closing the digital divide and preparing students and teachers for learning in the 21st century.

Harper, D. (2007). *Generation YES: Youth and educators succeeding.* GenYES. Retrieved September 15, 2007, from www.genyes.org/about/express/express8

> Dennis Harper, founder and CEO of the GenWHY Program, offers a Web site rich with content and online links for educators interested in beginning a student technology apprentice program. The GenWHY Program, originally a federally funded grant program, has evolved into the GenYES Program and provides a model for students to work with teachers to improve education in their own schools through the use of technology.

Maine Center for Meaningful Engaged Learning. (2007). *Maine center for meaningful engaged learning.* Retrieved September 2, 2007, from www.mcmel.org

> This Web site offers an extensive collection of one-to-one laptop computer initiative links, including links to research, best practices, workshops, resources, and step-guides for beginning a one-to-one laptop computer initiative. Additional links also include professional development resources for schools involved in a one-to-one laptop computer initiative.

Pitler, H., Flynn, K., & Gaddy, B. (2004). *Is a laptop initiative in your future?* Mid-Continent Research for Education and Learning. Retrieved January 14, 2008, from www.mcrel.org/PDF/PolicyBriefs/5042PI_PBLaptopInitiative.pdf

> This article offers a concise policy brief for schools beginning the process of a one-to-one laptop initiative with emphasis on common issues including effects on student achievement, professional development, funding, and benefits of ubiquitous computing.

**chapter 6**

# Sustaining an Innovative Professional Development Initiative

Key characteristics to consider

*George D. Warriner II*
*Sheboygan (Wisconsin) Area School District*

## abstract

SCHOOL DISTRICTS STRUGGLE to sustain professional development programs, resulting in an inability to make lasting changes in the learning community's culture. Further effects include a loss of creative energy by the community as initiatives repeatedly fall by the wayside, and skepticism by the educators regarding new initiatives. This chapter provides a roadmap for educational leaders to establish and sustain new initiatives in an educational community. The focus of the chapter is to show educational leaders how to identify and address characteristics to sustain effective professional development programs and to provide an example of how this was accomplished in one district.

Schools and school districts recognize the critical needs facing them as we move into a new century of educating children. There is no argument from educational leaders about the need to expand the use of instructional best practices into classrooms at every grade level and to increase the effectiveness of the educational organization. However, even in light of the research indicating such best practices, public school districts have had difficulty sustaining innovative ideas that benefit student learning.

## LITERATURE ESSENTIALS

### Sustaining innovations

Innovations have a set of perceived attributes that affect the willingness of a community to become adopters. Rogers (2003) and Cuban (1998) describe many of these attributes, such as: relative advantage, adaptability, observability, resource availability, and an available niche. Tatnall and Davey (2003) call this the "ecology" of the innovation. In addition, Hargreaves and Fink (2003) found sustainable educational innovations must improve student learning and be supported with existing resources.

A social system is changed by the introduction of an innovation, resulting in either adoption or rejection of the innovation (Rogers, 2003). One key to the sustainability of an innovation over time is ensuring that the goals of the innovation are met and other initiatives in the organization are not compromised or otherwise negatively affected (Hargreaves & Fink, 2003).

Fullan (2001) describes an implementation dip (a decline in interest or participation) as one of the most consistent findings limiting successful sustaining of innovation. A lack of a succession of leadership causes the failure of many educational innovations. Hargreaves and Fink (2003) state, "In general, planned succession is one of the most neglected aspects of leadership theory and practice in our schools. Indeed, it is one of the most persistently missing pieces in the effort to secure the sustainability of school improvement" (p. 699).

Whatever the reason for the failure of new programs to last over time, there is little doubt that schools and school districts have had a difficult time sustaining innovative programming. Rogers (2003) found that with every attempt at innovation, the social system is changed by the introduction of an innovation in some way, resulting in either adoption or rejection of the innovation. Rejection reinforces the status quo, making future attempts at innovation even more difficult. Faced with the challenging educational needs of students, public schools must find a way to provide and sustain innovative professional development opportunities that empower teachers to become better equipped to help every student learn.

## Structuring time for collaboration

When teachers do not work in a school culture that allows and encourages interaction among colleagues, they tend to withdraw from collaborative work, creating a silo effect, potentially stifling professional growth and student achievement. The tendency for teachers to become isolated is, in part, encouraged by the lack of structured opportunities for collaboration with their colleagues (Burney, 2004). School schedules most often do not allow common planning time for teachers who do not happen to share conference or planning periods. Opportunities for sustained teacher collaboration must be established if schools are to become places where student achievement is not only encouraged, but flows naturally from the learning environment (DuFour & Eaker, 1998).

Networking among teachers requires creating a community in which collaboration, experimentation, and sharing of experiences are structured to be part of the daily experience. This community will result in teachers actively creating and sharing a common vocabulary and educational philosophy. Teachers will begin to understand and value each other's perspectives and develop common expectations for what they are trying to accomplish (Sabelli & Dede, 2001).

The Instructional Technology Mentor Program (ITMP) described in this chapter is a comprehensive and systematic approach toward creating a collaborative and creative culture of professional support among educators. There are certain characteristics on which schools or districts can focus that may influence the success of implementation. These characteristics are found in literature on sustaining innovation through professional development. The key to success is attending to these characteristics so the process can have a fighting chance to have an impact on the learning and teaching environment in a school or district. The mentoring model presented here is supported by research familiar to educators and others who have an interest in sustaining innovations. According to a study by Joyce and Showers (2002), many of the activities utilized in mentoring promote constructivism which engages students in classroom learning. (Chapter 7 expands on the effectiveness of a coaching and mentoring model of professional development.)

## Overview of the instructional technology mentor program

The Sheboygan Area School District's Instructional Technology Mentor Program began in 1998 and has continued as a yearlong staff development program for 10 years. The district includes 26 schools (6 high schools, 3 middle schools, 17 elementary schools) and one early learning center, attended by a total of 10,400 students. Four of the high schools and five of the elementary schools are charter schools; all of the charter schools have been established since 2005. The district employs 800 teachers.

Structurally, ITMP has two components. One component focuses on the growth of K–12 teachers as lesson designers and instructional technology integrators. This part of the program helps teachers come to an understanding of who they are as teachers, who their students are as learners, and what tools they have available as teachers that can assist their efforts to meet the needs of their students. During a full week in the early summer, teachers are trained in how to adapt or create a lesson or unit using the district's unit-design strategy, Understanding by Design (UbD). Many of the mentors are already familiar with this framework, because the district has been emphasizing its use for the last several years. The UbD strategy focuses first on what the teacher wants the student to know and be able to do, and then addresses the instructional strategies (such as differentiated instruction) that would be most effective for the students (Wiggins & McTighe, 2001).

An additional week of training, and continuing activities throughout the school year, address the second component of the program. In the second week of training, teachers learn critical aspects of peer mentoring and strategies for successful collaboration with their mentees. They have an opportunity to begin their mentoring experience during two semi-structured days with the mentees, whom they have self-selected. Continuing collaboration among mentors and between mentors and their mentees is structured after the school year begins, to help establish a collaborative culture, even during the hectic days in the school year. Mentor-mentee pairs develop a plan for the year, focusing on increasing technology skills, pedagogy for technology integration, and curriculum writing.

## ITMP program details

The ITMP program coordinator is a former mentor in the program who has a 20% assignment to administer this program. In February of each year, the program coordinator recruits potential mentors using district-wide communication, typically a brochure delivered via e-mail. All prospective mentors attend a preliminary meeting to hear the expectations of the program, ask questions, and apply if interested. The program coordinator evaluates the applicants relative to their experience as a teacher and whether they applied as a school team or as individuals. Teachers who apply as part of a school team have preference in the application process. The program coordinator selects mentors from the pool of applicants to maximize the potential impact on schools, teachers, and students.

Teachers accepted to the program are contacted in March and laptop computers are ordered and prepared for their initial meeting as a team in April. This spring meeting allows the program coordinator to meet with the group and establish a working relationship with them. During this first meeting, the laptops are distributed and teachers work together to get them set up for use. Distributing the laptops early allows the teachers to become comfortable with this new tool before they begin the curriculum design work in June.

# Graduate coursework

Instructional technology mentors are enrolled in a three-credit graduate course that spans the school year. The district pays for the graduate credits from a state university and a former mentor serves as the course instructor. At various times throughout the history of the program, selected district administrators have contributed to the planning and instruction of this university course, which was instituted in the fourth year of the program. This course begins right after school dismisses in June with a four-day workshop that focuses on differentiating instruction, creating a lesson or unit that utilizes technology, and improving technical skills related to software and online resources. The goal of each teacher is to create one lesson or unit that will be implemented with his or her students, revised as needed, and shared with colleagues. Mentors can select an existing unit or lesson that they feel needs revision, or they can choose to create a new unit from scratch. Mentors are quite familiar with the district's content and process benchmarks, and they utilize these, as well as the corresponding rubrics, to complete their units.

A major focus of the June work is to make sure the mentors are comfortable using the UbD framework for creating lessons and units. In addition, differentiated instruction is introduced and emphasized during the training as an integral component of effective classroom instruction. Other resources that the mentors are exposed to and utilize during this first week of coursework include the district's technology benchmarks for students, modeled after the ISTE National Educational Technology Standards for Students. Mentors are also introduced to strategies that help them identify what type of learners they are and how they can relate to others who have a different learning style.

Mentors select a colleague from their school who will commit to learning about differentiated instruction and integrating technology into classroom learning experiences. Mentors must select a mentee who works in the same building. It is also highly recommended that they select a mentee with whom they already have a good working relationship.

In late summer, the group reconvenes for their second week of the program. Activities of this week focus on mentoring strategies, modeling collaborative behaviors and setting goals for their work with their mentees. All the mentors create and post Web pages explaining who they are and listing their goals as a mentor.

On the fourth and fifth day of late summer, the entire mentor–mentee group meets together with the program coordinator and the course instructor to begin their work as a team. This allows the mentors an opportunity to meet with their mentees in a semi-structured format, with scaffolding provided by the coordinator or instructor as needed. The year-long goal for mentors is to bring their mentee through the process of developing a technology-rich lesson or unit using the UbD framework and differentiating learning opportunities for their students (an outcome similar to the mentors' own work during their first week of the summer program). Although mentees are not provided a laptop for their work, mentors are encouraged to share their laptops or find ways that mentees can have adequate access to technology and other resources that they need to implement their units. Mentors and mentees are compensated for a set number of hours to work together during the school year on curriculum development. One release day per year is also available for each mentor and mentee to work during the school day.

During the school year, the course instructor facilitates mentor work and communication. Mentors continue their work with monthly journal entries that are posted on a group Web site and by utilizing group e-mail to share resources and problem solve. Quarterly "mentor chats" are held at a local restaurant where mentors reconnect and discuss their progress with their mentees. Mentors are also given a book to read during the school year; the chats provide a time when they can discuss sections of the book assigned by the course instructor.

Typically, early in the second semester, mentors have implemented their lesson or unit with their students and have had the chance to make revisions. At this point, each mentor is required to present their work at some type of showcase for their colleagues. Most often, this showcase is a regional conference that attracts several hundred educators from the area. Mentors create a booth that showcases their work and how the changes they have made changed student outcomes. The timing of this showcase coincides with the recruitment of mentors for the next year of the program.

Near the end of the school year, the program participants, all previous mentors, the program coordinator, the course instructor, and other district administrators are invited to a celebration dinner to recognize the accomplishments of the mentors and their mentees. New mentors and their mentees are the guests of honor at this banquet and are publicly recognized and awarded certificates of participation. In addition, mentors are given a lapel pin that designates their successful completion of the program.

## Participant feedback

Data were collected and evaluated using information from electronic communication among program participants (journal entries and e-mail); an online survey of all mentors; and structured interviews of the program coordinator, the course instructor, and several mentors. Although the requirements of the program are quite rigorous, most of the approximately 130 teachers who have completed the program indicated they are very appreciative of the positive changes they have made in creating learning opportunities for their students. Cited most often are the opportunities presented to the teachers to change what they are doing, along with the support needed to get it done. One mentor stated:

> After I went through the program, I discovered the richness in collaboration in talking with each other and helping teachers or staff and students do more self-discovery and how much more meaningful that was—being more collaborative in nature and reflective.

Engaging students in their learning was another benefit of the program that was often cited; as one mentor stated:

> For me personally, it was "Wow, here is all this technology!" Our kids could latch on. Kids who are having difficulty with other things, this could raise their level up. This could give them a level of expertise in some form that would be useful for them in their life.

Each mentor created an integrated instructional unit, using UbD, differentiated instruction, and technology. Often, mentors revised other lessons or units they had used in the past. There were even changes in the district culture, at least as far as the mentors were concerned. A typical comment came from one of the mentors:

> We do all of our planning together. If I am doing something in technology, that gets passed on to the other people on my team. Throughout the district, people are passing forms back and forth. We would send them back and forth as attachments. So they had the same things I had.

Although each mentor received a laptop to use as long as they were in the district, how these laptops were used differed widely from teacher to teacher. Many teachers were in schools where technology access for students was difficult to come by on a regular basis; in other schools, students had much better access. Access was one of the most significant issues in determining how much the technology-rich units impacted student learning. Where access was adequate, student learning opportunities were positively affected. In a fifth-grade classroom, for example, one result of a mentor's redesign of her data collection unit in math was that students were able to effectively use a spreadsheet program to accurately identify data trends and predict likely future data points using a line of best fit. This was in comparison to the lesson before the mentor program, in which students did not even get a chance to learn about the concepts of statistical predictions.

## Timeline of events

The following section outlines key events that occurred during the establishment of the ITMP. These events relate to the key characteristics for sustaining the program. (See Figure 6.1 for timeline.)

## Program begins

In 1998, the Instructional Technology Coordinator reviewed the existing professional development activities and worked with staff to create the Instructional Technology Mentor Program. In addition to the training, teachers were provided with a desktop computer and a $50 software allowance. Each teacher determined how to utilize the hardware and software with his or her students and mentor.

## Mentor feedback leads to changes

After the first year (and every year) of the ITMP, the mentors and mentees were asked to provide feedback on the successes and shortcomings of the program. The initial feedback was overwhelmingly positive, but the one change every mentor recommended was restricting each mentor to a single mentee. In the first year, mentors were encouraged to work with two or more other teachers during the school year. This one change made a major difference in the workload of the mentors and improved the quality of mentoring experience.

## Separate budget created

The first two years of the ITMP were funded by carryover funds in the instructional technology department and a Technology Literacy Challenge Fund grant. The instructional technology coordinator created new budget accounts in the third year to ensure that funds were specifically earmarked for this program.

## The refresher year

As the focus of the training moved away from technology skill acquisition and toward utilizing technology to engage students by differentiating instruction, mentors from the first three years were offered the opportunity to take an additional week of training to establish these practices in their classrooms. This meant that there were no new mentors trained in 2001–2002.

## ITMP coordinator position established and an implementation dip

A major step in the establishment of the program was the Board of Education's approval of a new, part-time (20%) administrative position to coordinate the ITMP. This formalized the program and separated the program from the instructional technology coordinator's direct responsibility. A consequence of the refresher year was that the momentum that had been building around the program was weakened, because there were no new teachers involved in the program and, therefore, no new lessons, no sharing at the regional conference, and no end of the year celebration. The numbers went from 15 mentors per year to 8 in 2002–2003 and 12 in 2003–2004.

## Momentum regained

In 2005, the ITMP had become established as a useful and popular program. Each year since 2005, there has been a waiting list of 5–15 teachers.

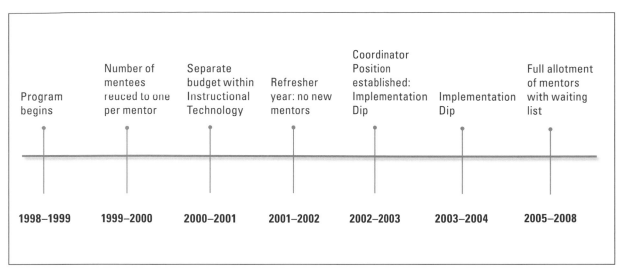

FIGURE 6.1. Timeline of important events in the Instructional Technology Mentor Program

## Critical events in establishing the instructional technology mentor program

There were at least three critical events during the implementation of the Instructional Technology Mentor Program that help identify the characteristics that existed in the district and within the program as it became part of the normal operations of the instructional technology department: program initiation, retraining early mentors, and ITMP administrative position and budget.

### Critical event 1: Program initiation

The first critical stage was at the beginning of the program, when it was being conceived and initiated. There were gaps in the instructional technology professional development program of the district that prompted the instructional technology coordinator to look for opportunities that would address the needs of the teachers and the district with respect to the use of technology in the teaching and learning process. Teachers had been participating in after-school technology workshops and conferences that were not having an effect on their instructional strategies. Much of the training, while well attended, was not effective in making an improvement in student learning. Teachers were looking for a way to help them make sense of the new technologies and had shown, by their consistent participation in after-school technology workshops and conferences, that they were willing to put some time and energy into this effort. Surveys and interviews of staff clearly indicated that the school community had a deep concern for the welfare and education of their students. This caring environment provided a foundation for the success of the mentoring program that came to be established.

## Critical event 2: Retraining early mentors

The second critical moment in the process of the ITMP becoming sustained in the district was at the point where the program coordinator decided to forgo one year of training a new group of mentors in favor of retraining mentors from the first three years. The decision was motivated by the evolution of the training toward utilizing UbD and differentiated instruction during the initial three years. The program coordinator decided to make sure the vanguard—the early adopters—were kept current with the new training. Although this seemed to put the momentum of the program in jeopardy, the reinforcing of the early adopters added to the program's credibility by being responsive and adapting to the mentors' needs. This additional year helped solidify their sense of personal identity with the ITMP, and allowed the program coordinator to adapt and further refine the training with a group that recognized how the program offered an opportunity to help them and others become better teachers. The additional trust and communication that this year fostered also added to the mentors' sense that the program coordinator was responsive to their needs.

## Critical event 3: Establishing ITMP administrative position and budget

The risk that the instructional technology coordinator took with retraining the first three years of mentors could have been a factor in the small implementation dip that the program experienced in the fifth and sixth years. During those two years, only 12 of the available 15 spots were filled. In every other year, there have been more applicants than available spots. The apparent decline of teacher interest in the program was preceded by two important benchmarks in the Instructional ITMP: a formalization of the program coordinator's role and the segregating of the ITMP budget into its own budget location. In the fall of the fourth year, the board of education approved an administrative position to oversee the program. The addition of this position solidified the program's standing within the organizational structure of the district, making a new position within the activity system. Without the creation and approval of the administrative position and the budget, the institutionalization of the program would not have occurred, because the reduced numbers of teachers who volunteered to be mentors indicated that interest was waning.

## ITMP as an activity system

One of the key premises of activity theory is that the tensions that exist between different elements of an activity system cause the system to transform and expand the system to address the needs exposed by the tensions (Dobson, LeBlanc, & Burgoyne, 2004). The ITMP activity system functioned in such a way that the mediation between the school community and the other components of the activity system served to reduce tensions that emerged as the program progressed. Tensions such as the selection of mentees, working with too many mentees, difficulty utilizing the plethora of tools (each mentor had a stipend for peripherals and/or software), and presenting lessons to colleagues both within and outside the district were mediated with interplay between those in the community. This interaction reoccurred every year and at each gathering of the community, either face-to-face or online.

## LITERATURE ESSENTIALS

### *Activity theory*

Activity theory is a conceptual framework, built on Vygotsky's (1978) concept of the Zone of Proximal Development (ZPD), that is useful in studying how subjects move toward reaching outcomes with the help of certain psychosocial contexts and technologies. The outcome of an activity system is a product of all the interdependent components of the system: the subject, community, division of labor, tools, and rules (Table 6.1). These components act together to move the entire system toward an outcome or goal.

A. N. Leont'ev analyzed activity at three levels: operations, actions, and activities. This hierarchy classified *operations* as the basic level of activity, while *actions* are directed at achieving goals. Systems that function at an action level merely accomplish a set goal (Kuutti & Arvonen, 1992), while an activity system meets the needs of the community with longer-lasting and more meaningful effects. Actions by individuals can be considered more linear and one-way, while activities of groups are iterative and expansive (Engeström, 1999). The table below (Warriner, 2005) outlines some possibilities for different relationships of a teacher as participant—the "subject" in an activity system—from operations to actions to activities.

**Table 6.1** | An example of an activity system with a teacher as subject

|  | **Goal of Operation** | **Goal of Action** | **Goal of Activity** |
|---|---|---|---|
| **Teacher as Subject** | Teaches same as always | Looks for new ways to teach | Seeks to understand students' learning |
| **Tool** | Proven lesson plan materials | Uses technology to teach same lesson | Uses all resources to negotiate with students how and what to teach |
| **Community** | Classroom as community | Shares with colleagues to improve | Develops and expands new relationships that influence practice |
| **Rules** | Teacher as knowledge dispenser | Includes standards as guidelines for teaching | Collaborates with teachers and students to determine operating and learning principles |
| **Division of Labor** | Teacher as worker, student as learner | Team teaching, cooperative learning | Teacher as co-learner with students |
| **Object** | Completed lesson | Meet standards | Co-create learning expectations with students |

As the program evolved in the first three years, improving instruction with the effective use of technology became more of a shared outcome of the program coordinator, the mentors, and the district. After the fourth year, the year when early adopters were invited to a second year of training in the program, improving instruction with technology became formalized in the syllabus of the university graduate course, now a part of the program. The convergence of the community on a common outcome gave the ITMP an identity and a sense of cohesion that promoted the sustainability of the program.

The interconnectedness of the community of mentors, mentees, and program coordinators helped mentors and mentees utilize the abundance of tools during the year of formal training and beyond. E-mail groups, new software, presenting at conferences, and creating new lessons could have been intimidating for the teachers, which would have diminished the impact of the new tools and strategies. Many new mentors initially expressed the feeling that they were overwhelmed by the technology or dwarfed by their colleagues' expertise, but these feelings were mitigated by the support that the community provided and the sense of responsibility mentors developed toward the program and their colleagues.

The community also had a profound impact on how the mentors responded to the expectations associated with the program. With the requirement that each mentor create a technology-rich lesson or unit came the support from a community that helped them be successful. Perhaps the most daunting task before the mentors was working one-on-one with their selected mentees. In this instance, the tools—including the chats and e-mail—along with the strong interconnectedness of the community helped them through the process. The number of mentees that have continued on to become mentors (25) provides more evidence that this process was successful.

## Planning for the implementation of an innovative professional development program

The Sheboygan Area School District was the site of an innovative program that has become acculturated into the professional development environment. Districts looking to initiate and sustain an innovative program need to look at two activity systems: the larger district activity system and the activity system that will be created with the implementation of the innovation. If each of these activity systems indicates a need and available support for the long-term implementation of the innovation, and if the innovation is structured to be responsive to the needs of the school community, the likelihood of sustaining the innovation is increased.

A district should first look at its culture and do an objective assessment of whether teachers and administrators in the district are committed to improving student learning and to fostering an environment that promotes support and involvement of the school district. In addition, a serious commitment to the innovation requires the district to commit adequate resources over time to sustain the program through an eventual, and likely, implementation dip. Without this long-term commitment, the program's credibility with the adopters will suffer, putting future adoption rates in jeopardy. Even with those characteristics in place, any innovation that is being considered must be able to fill a need in the district that is not being addressed by some other program.

A district is likely to be prepared to sustain an innovative professional development program if it has certain characteristics:

- The staff is committed to improving the culture of learning

- There are adequate funds to sustain the innovation for at least 3–5 years

- The innovation fills a long-term need of the district

The innovative program's activity system must utilize the school or district community to address the adopters' needs for improvement and support, and at the same time must be structured as an open process that creates value for the adopters (mentors) and the district. Innovative program leaders need to be assigned to the program for a prolonged period of time (at least 3–5 years) and have the ability to be flexible while maintaining the focus of the program.

If the district is not prepared to sustain an innovative program for an extended period of time as outlined above, all is not lost. Changing the preparedness of the district is a lengthy process that will provide many obstacles to be overcome. To make initial inroads, identify and address areas of the district's culture that need improvement. Start with modest goals, keeping the end in mind. For instance, if staff is not committed to improving the culture of learning, begin to work in small groups that explore innovations in education. As these ideas begin to permeate the small groups' philosophy, a gap analysis will indicate what is missing from their practice and what is needed to attain their new goals.

## Predictors for sustainability of an innovative program

As the professional development program is designed, there are several characteristics a program planner should consider that will help ensure its sustainability (Warriner, 2005):

- The results of the innovative program will add capacity (or value) to the adopters.

- Adopters easily understand the goals and procedures of the innovation.

- A process is in place that will ensure the adopters and program leaders will form a vibrant community of support that is also available to others (potential future adopters).

- A process is in place that will ensure the adopters have the ability to choose to continue involvement in the innovative program in a variety of capacities, including leadership.

- A long-term plan is in place that will ensure that program leaders will be assigned to the innovation for at least 3–5 years.

- Program leaders are committed and empowered to make changes to the innovation as the program evaluations indicate.

- Program leaders will ensure that the educational community is aware of the innovative program.

It is not likely that all of these characteristics will be present in every school district looking to implement and sustain an innovation. Many of the characteristics are not even controllable by school districts. The key is to focus the most effort on the characteristics of the activity system that can have the most impact on how the adopters will be affected, such as the interconnectedness of the community, an outcome that is shared by the community, and a commitment to the long-term success of the program. This structure of support will provide resources to maintain the program through the likely implementation dip. Changes in the program must be in response to feedback gathered and embraced as the next step in the process of acculturation of the program.

If the district appears ready to support a long-term innovative program, there are a few keys (Warriner, 2005) to designing a professional development program framework:

1. Identify an area of long-term needs that could be addressed with a professional development program.

    a. Conduct a formal needs assessment of the educational community.

    b. Evaluate district and/or state assessment results to identify existing learning needs of students.

2. Develop a professional development program (or modify an existing program) that addresses the predictors of sustainability as indicated above.

3. Ensure leadership of the program includes membership for all stakeholder groups affected by the program.

4. Focus on addressing explicit district needs.

5. Incorporate feedback loops to ensure the program addresses the continuing needs of the educational community.

6. Create a plan that allows for growth based on success.

## Final thoughts

There is very little research documenting the processes of successful school innovations. It is not because of a lack of innovative programming. It may be because so many innovations fail to become acculturated into the school or district that conducting research would be too resource-intensive. The Instructional Technology Mentor Program became a long-standing program in the district because it met the needs of the teachers as individuals and as a part of a larger activity system. The mentors in this program felt that they were supported, connected with their colleagues, becoming better teachers, and that the results were worth all the effort. In addition to these personal characteristics, the entire community in the Instructional Technology Mentor Program converged on a common goal on which the activity system focused. They recognized that the program was credible and that it would be supported over time. Also helpful was that there were others (in the district and in the regional conferences) who were able to see and appreciate what the mentors and the mentor program were doing. When the predictors for sustainability of an innovative program are present, professional developers can proceed with greater confidence!

## GETTING STARTED RESOURCES

Engeström, Y. (1999). Activity theory and individual and social transformation. In Y. Engeström, R. Miettinen, & R.-L. Punamèaki-Gitai (Eds.), *Perspectives on activity theory* (pp. 19–38). Cambridge; New York: Cambridge University Press.

Engeström takes Vygotsky's concept of a mediating artifact and the Zone of Proximal Development and expands it to a more comprehensive and explanatory model for community activities. This is his foundational work with Activity Theory.

Fullan, M. (2001). *Leading in a culture of change*. San Francisco: Jossey-Bass.

Fullan looks at five core competencies that can enable leaders to successfully guide their community through a sustainable change process. He describes the implementation dip as a major obstacle to sustaining an innovation.

Hargreaves, A., & Fink, D. (2003). Sustaining leadership. *Phi Delta Kappan, 84*(9), 693–700.

This is a brief outline of their book entitled *Sustainable Leadership*. Hargreaves and Fink describe common principles for successfully leading schools through change.

Rogers, E. M. (2003). *Diffusion of innovations* (5th ed.). New York: Free Press.

In this classic work, Rogers details many characteristics that enable innovations to become part of a larger culture. This book is useful to schools, businesses, and any organization looking to have innovative ideas received well and eventually acculturated into the community.

Tatnall, A., & Davey, B. (2003). ICT and training: A proposal for an ecological model of innovation. *Educational Technology & Society, 6*(1), 14–17.

Tatnall and Davey describe four aspects of a community's ecology that can enable or prevent change. Considering the available time and resources, ability to compete with existing programs, cooperation within the culture, and an available niche are keys to a successful implementation of an innovation.

**chapter 7**

# Peer Coaching and Technology Integration

Insights from three projects

*Kara Dawson*
University of Florida

*Judy T. DiLeo*
Altoona School District (Penn.)

*Mary Lane-Kelso*
Northern Arizona University

*Ann Barron*
University of South Florida

*Maryanne Fazio-Fox*
Northern Arizona University

*Diane Yendol-Hoppey*
University of Florida

## abstract

THIS CHAPTER SHARES three peer coaching models designed to support teachers as they learn to integrate technology—Model 1: the Microsoft Peer Coaching program, which is a national model supported by Microsoft's Partners in Learning initiative; Model 2: the Raising the Bar model, which is a statewide model led by a state university; and Model 3: the Peer Mentor model, which began with federal Enhancing Education Through Technology funding and operates at the district level. The chapter concludes with key recommendations the authors believe must be considered so that peer-coaching efforts can most effectively support teachers as they learn to use technology in teaching and learning.

Teachers need ongoing support in the form of job-embedded professional development to integrate new teaching practices into their existing instructional repertoire (Lieberman & Miller, 1991; Richardson, 1999). With the onset of technology resources in schools today, enhancing teachers' integration of technology into their daily teaching practices requires this same type of job-embedded support (Christensen, 2002; Margerum-Leys & Marx, 2004). One form of job-embedded professional development often used to support teacher growth within the classroom context is peer coaching. Peer coaching is a generic model of professional development that may be adapted to diverse disciplines and can only be successful if exemplary practices related to the subject area are embedded within the exemplary practices of peer coaching. The goal of peer coaching is to provide collegial support to teachers as they make changes in or implement new instructional practices (Valencia & Killion, 1988).

This chapter shares three peer coaching models designed to support teachers as they learn to integrate technology into teaching and learning: (1) the Microsoft Peer Coaching program, which is a national model supported by Microsoft's Partners in Learning initiative; (2) the Raising the Bar Model, which is a statewide model led by a state university; and (3) the Peer Mentor Model, which began with federal Enhancing Education Through Technology (EETT) funding and operates at the district level. Each model is introduced in Table 7.1 and is more fully described in the following sections. The chapter concludes with key recommendations, drawn from the results of the three projects, that the authors believe must be considered so that peer coaching efforts can most effectively support teachers as they learn to use technology in teaching and learning.

---

### LITERATURE ESSENTIALS

#### *Essential characteristics*

Peer coaching involves a *collaborative* coaching cycle around an innovation (Joyce & Showers, 1980). The process requires a *foundation of rapport, trust*, and a *shared desire to learn* (Grimmett, 1987). In many ways, peer coaching formalizes the concept of peer support for exemplary technology integration identified over a decade ago (Becker, 1994).

*Prolonged engagement* is important when peer coaching is used to support technology integration (Bradshaw, 2002; Margerum-Leys & Marx, 2004). Likewise, reflection is important (Brookfield, 1986; Zeichner & Liston, 1996). *Reflection* is key to helping teachers become critical evaluators of their technology integration practices and promoting changes in technology-enhanced teaching practices (Orr, 2001; Dexter, Anderson, & Becker, 1999).

*(Continued)*

## LITERATURE ESSENTIALS

*(Continued)*

### Essential contextual facilitators

Peer coaching must be perceived as a *job-embedded* tool (Lieberman, 1988; Lieberman & Miller, L., 1991; Richardson, 1999) for professional growth *focused on changes in practice* within a *school's culture* (Cochran-Smith & Lytle, 1993). The school culture must be assessed in terms of its openness to change, teacher readiness, and support structures (Mouza, 2003; Schofield & Davidson, 2002). Professional development leaders should consider the social environment and teachers' willingness to learn, rather than the technical tools, as the central catalysts for change (Dexter et al., 1999).

*An inquiry stance* to teachers' daily work is also essential (Dana & Yendol-Silva, 2003). That is, peer coaching should involve the systematic, intentional study of technology's classroom impact. Although some studies have shown improved student outcomes related to technology integration (Fouts, 2000; Schacter, 2001; Waxman, Connell, & Gray, 2002), educational technologists recognize the need for more consistent, classroom-based results (Bull, Knezek, Roblyer, Schrum, & Thompson, 2005).

*School administrator support* is also critical (Garmston, 1987; Mouza, 2003; Dawson & Rakes, 2003) as are opportunities to *monitor progress* toward shared goals (Stein & Wang, 1988). Technology integration professional development is most successful when proximal goals designed to promote efficacy are used to reach larger goals (Orr, 2001; Bradshaw, 2002).

### Essential conditions

Teachers must engage in *quality training* and *preparation* (Joyce & Showers, 1980). The literature related to technology integration preparation is immense and encompasses many of the traits previously discussed. In addition, it should focus on constructivist uses of technology, student-centered learning, and learning with, rather than from, technology (Brooks & Brooks, 1999; Jonassen, 2000; Poole, 2003).

*Development of pedagogical content knowledge* (Shulman, 1986, 1987) is also critical. Technical pedagogical content knowledge is essential to peer coaching for technology integration and requires developing a working knowledge of how technology can be used to support subject matter learning and instruction in a classroom (Hughes, 2004; Mishra & Koehler, in press).

Finally, *teacher beliefs* (Pajaras, 1992; Richardson, 1999) are critical to address in the peer coaching process. Teachers' beliefs highly influence their classroom practices, yet they are often ignored in technology integration professional development (Ertmer, 1999).

**Table 7.1** | Overview of peer coaching models

| | Microsoft Peer Coaching—MPC *(FL)* | Raising the Bar: A Personal Trainer Model for Teacher Technology Integration Training *(AZ)* | The Peer Mentor Model for Promoting Expertise with Technology Among Teachers *(PA)* |
|---|---|---|---|
| **Type of Peer Coaching** | Expert Peer Coaching | Team Coaching | Reciprocal Coaching; Co-Teaching; Train-the-Trainer |
| **Context** | This case study presents a statewide evaluation of the MPC effort in Florida. This initiative is part of Microsoft's Partners in Learning program and aims to enhance standards-based academic achievement through the integration of technology. | This peer coaching strategy uses a two-tiered mentoring model that uses personal trainers and on-site mentors. This case study involves 15 teachers in one school. | The district in this case study had on-site Apple trainers available to a limited number of teachers for one year. The teachers involved in that training became the mentors for others who had had no training, thus magnifying the effect of the original Apple trainer. |
| **Goals** | To determine how well the MPC materials aligned with literature on exemplary peer coaching and to determine the perceptions and attitudes of the facilitators and coaches. | To provide professional development opportunities that enable Arizona teachers to meet state standards and increase their use of Internet-based resources. | To take advantage of available assets (personnel, available training, etc.) in order to increase the strength and effect of technology integration among teaching staff. |
| **Evaluation** | • Checklist matrix of the processes, contextual facilitators and essential conditions of peer coaching.<br>• Survey and interviews. | • NCREL Learning with Technology Tool.<br>• Pre-post teacher feedback.<br>• Review of teacher-designed materials. | Comparison between participating and nonparticipating teachers and students in terms of teacher attitude/usage and student achievement. |
| **Outcomes** | • The MPC materials aligned with literature on exemplary peer coaching. However, the process of peer coaching frequently took precedence over technology integration.<br>• Program success was dependent on the local context.<br>• Facilitators and coaches differed in their attitudes about the digital divide and technology and about how technology changes the role of the classroom teacher. | • Mentoring facilitated the uses of technology that were multidisciplinary, standards-based, focused on higher-level thinking, and authentic.<br>• Mentoring improved teacher-student interactions and home-school communication.<br>• Mentoring in the use of technology reignited teachers' passions about their profession and resulted to many new instructional strategies. | • Peer-mentor participants showed measurable improvement in teacher attitude and usage levels and student achievement compared to non–peer mentor participants.<br>• Non–peer-mentor participants became interested in the coaching and mentoring process.<br>• Participants in experimental and control groups sought to continue the peer mentor model beyond the life of the funded initiative. |

*(Continued)*

**Table 7.1**  |  *(Continued)*

| | Microsoft Peer Coaching—MPC *(FL)* | Raising the Bar: A Personal Trainer Model for Teacher Technology Integration Training *(AZ)* | The Peer Mentor Model for Promoting Expertise with Technology Among Teachers *(PA)* |
|---|---|---|---|
| **Lessons Learned** | • Peer coaching efforts must combine exemplary peer coaching strategies and research-based technology-integration practices.<br><br>• A strong focus on creating a school culture ready and willing to support peer coaching for technology integration is essential.<br><br>• Funding for evaluation of peer coaching programs should include strategies to explicitly explore student achievement. | • One-on-one mentoring was the most important factor contributing to teachers' success.<br><br>• Online and face-to-face interactions are recommended to maximize success.<br><br>• Focus on academic content and the added value of technology is essential.<br><br>• Peer mentoring is most successful when there is a combination of well-designed materials, sound pedagogical strategies, and powerful relationships between mentor and mentees. | • Considering the local context is essential when planning any kind of coaching or mentoring plan.<br><br>• Mentored teachers must have a voice in the process and feel they have permission to take risks.<br><br>• The mentor-mentee relationship is critical to success.<br><br>• Compatibility of personalities is more important than similar grade level or subject matter pairings. |

## MODEL 1

# Microsoft Peer Coaching: Expertise with technology among teachers

*Ann Barron*
  *University of South Florida*

*Diane Yendol-Hoppey*
  *University of Florida*

## The context of the Microsoft Peer Coaching model (MPC)

The MPC program was inspired by the Teaching+Technology Coaching Initiative, which was created by the Puget Sound Center for Teaching, Learning, and Technology (PSCTLT), a nonprofit organization that is committed to improving teacher preparation and professional development (Peterson, n.d.). In 2004, Microsoft announced their Partners in Learning program to "establish an ed-tech framework to help educators foster 21st century information skills and raise student achievement and graduation rates among at-risk kids" (Ishizuka, 2004, p. 30). As a portion of Partners in Learning, Microsoft collaborated with PSCTLT to create a national blueprint for the Peer Coaching program. The Microsoft Peer Coaching (MPC) program was designed to "work with select states during the next five years to develop sustainable plans for digital learning, which can then be replicated in schools across the country" (Ishizuka, 2004, p. 30).

## Goals of the MPC model

The primary goal of MPC is "to enhance standards-based academic achievement through the integration of technology" (Microsoft, 2005, p. 1). To achieve this goal, the program emphasizes a systemic integration of technology throughout a school, implements a professional development model wherein teachers are trained to serve as coaches and mentors for colleagues at their school, and actively works with the school administration and teachers to promote sustainability of the peer coaching model (Microsoft, 2005).

## Participants in the MPC model

The MPC model involves several participants (including state/district facilitators, school administrators, teacher coaches, and collaborating teachers) to ensure success.

### State/District facilitators

The state/district facilitators serve as coordinators, ensuring that the coaches have the resources, time, and materials necessary to mentor their peers. In addition, the state/district facilitators play an active role in providing observations and feedback to the coaches.

### School administrators

Many of the characteristics on which the MPC program is built are context-specific. Therefore, school culture and administrative support are essential. To ensure support from the principal and other administration, a School Support Agreement is recommended, which outlines the roles and responsibilities of the school administration as well as the teacher coaches.

### Teacher coaches

Coaches may be identified based on their expertise with technology, their willingness to mentor colleagues, or recommendation of the school administration. In all cases, the coaches should be motivated to implement, support, and sustain the program by actively mentoring a collaborating teacher.

### Collaborating teachers

The MPC program recommends that a teacher coach serve as a mentor to one individual—preferably another teacher who is working in the same school building. Because the coaching process includes both formal and informal mentoring, it is best to maintain a close relationship between the teacher coach and the collaborating teacher.

## The process for implementing the MPC model

The Microsoft Corporation, through its Partners in Learning National Program, provides a wealth of instructional and support materials. For example, training sessions for facilitators and coaches are available, as well as print materials (Student Handbook,

Coaching Guide, and Facilitator Guide), and electronic materials (CD with resource materials and a Microsoft Peer Coaching Web site) that are "designed to advance 21st century skills and classroom application of these skills, and build school system leadership capacity to support these skills" (Microsoft, 2006, p.1).

## Case study: Implementation of training for MPC in Florida

The Florida Chancellor of K–12 Public Schools invited several school districts in Florida to participate in the MPC pilot program. Each district appointed a facilitator (generally district-level personnel) to be trained to facilitate the program throughout his or her district. In addition, districts selected 12 practicing teachers to mentor at least one collaborating teacher during the upcoming year. In conjunction with the MPC program, a series of workshops for facilitators and coaches took place in Florida during the spring and summer of 2005. The trainers and the materials (student manuals, trainer's guide, and Microsoft Peer Coaching Web site) for the workshops were sponsored by Microsoft, in conjunction with the Puget Sound Center for Teaching, Learning, and Technology. Following the training, each district implemented the MPC program in ways most appropriate for their local context. Budgetary constraints prevented evaluators from conducting research within each local context. Thus, researchers focused on evaluating the design and implementation of the MPC training program and the associated material.

## Evaluating the effectiveness of MPC training and materials: Data collection and analysis

The evaluation of the design and implementation of the MPC training program and materials in Florida included the review of the training materials and resources provided by Microsoft and the Partners in Learning program, as well as an investigation of the perceptions of the coaches and facilitators who attended the training sessions.

The design of the MPC materials was analyzed using characteristics of exemplary peer coaching and technology integration models. Based on this review of relevant literature, a checklist matrix (Miles & Huberman, 1994) was developed. The major areas of the checklist reflect the elements of peer coaching that evolved from the literature review: processes, contextual facilitators, and essential conditions. (See Table 7.2 for the checklist matrix.)

Findings suggest that the program design is in close alignment with the literature on exemplary peer coaching; however, the process of peer coaching frequently takes precedence over technology integration. Participants were neither encouraged to stretch their knowledge about how technology can be used to support subject matter learning and instruction in a classroom (i.e., pedagogical content knowledge) nor given the opportunity to consider how technology integration can help promote higher levels of thinking, multiple intelligences, learning styles, and differentiated instruction. In most cases the technology integration ideas presented within the program represented status quo rather than transformative uses of technology.

**Table 7.2** | Technology integration peer coaching matrix

| PROCESS OF PEER COACHING FOR TECHNOLOGY INTEGRATION | | | | | | |
|---|---|---|---|---|---|---|
| **Characteristic** | **Implementation** | | | | | **Evidence** |
| | 0 | 1 | 2 | 3 | 4 | |
| Collaborative coaching cycle | | | | | | |
| Rapport/trust/shared desire to learn | | | | | | |
| Voluntary | | | | | | |
| Immediacy/prolonged engagement | | | | | | |
| Shared goal | | | | | | |
| Non-evaluative | | | | | | |
| Communication | | | | | | |
| Reflection | | | | | | |
| Deep understanding | | | | | | |
| **CONTEXTUAL FACILITATORS OF PEER COACHING FOR TECHNOLOGY INTEGRATION** | | | | | | |
| **Characteristic** | **Implementation** | | | | | **Evidence** |
| | 0 | 1 | 2 | 3 | 4 | |
| Embedded in school culture | | | | | | |
| School culture focused on inquiry and change | | | | | | |
| Job-embedded | | | | | | |
| Administrative support | | | | | | |
| Monitor progress | | | | | | |
| External forces | | | | | | |
| Incentives | | | | | | |
| **ESSENTIAL CONDITIONS OF PEER COACHING FOR TECHNOLOGY INTEGRATION** | | | | | | |
| **Characteristics** | **Implementation** | | | | | **Evidence** |
| | 0 | 1 | 2 | 3 | 4 | |
| Quality training | | | | | | |
| Student learning focus | | | | | | |
| Pedagogical content knowledge | | | | | | |
| Teacher beliefs | | | | | | |

**0:** *No evidence of this characteristic in the peer coaching effort*
**1:** *Little evidence of this characteristic in the peer coaching effort*
**2:** *Some evidence of this characteristic in the peer coaching effort*
**3:** *Substantial evidence of this characteristic in the peer coaching effort*
**4:** *Consistent evidence of this characteristic in the peer coaching effort*

The facilitators (N=14) and coaches (N=46) who participated in MPC workshops were surveyed relative to their attitudes towards technology and perceptions of professional development. Overall, both sets of participants agreed with the positive statements in the "Attitudes towards Computer Use" section and disagreed with the negative statements. There were two noteworthy differences between the responses of the coaches and facilitators. Significantly more facilitators than coaches disagreed with the statement, "Computers further the gap between students along socioeconomic lines." The mean for the facilitators was 3.33, and the mean for the coaches was 2.33 (p<.01). The majority of the coaches are classroom teachers; perhaps they have a "better" view of the digital divide as it impacts their students. The other item that differed was, "Computers change the role of classroom teachers." In this case, the facilitators were more likely to agree (M=4.36, SD=.74) than the coaches (M=3.37, SD=1.31), and the difference was significant (p<.01). It is interesting to note that the facilitators perceived that computers changed the role of the teachers more than the teachers (coaches) themselves.

In the "Perceptions of Professional Development," all of the participants were positive about the peer coaching program. The majority of the respondents enjoyed participating in the Peer Coaching program, felt competent to serve as a peer coach, and thought that the program would enhance collaboration and result in higher student achievement.

The participants at the training workshops were also interviewed relative to perceived benefits and limitations of the program. Although most of the participants were very enthusiastic about the program, some concerns were expressed about the time and resources that would be required. In addition, there were some frustrations with the Web tools that were provided as an integral part of the MPC model. In particular, some districts (especially those that use Macintosh computers) were concerned with a few of the tools that did not function well on Mac computers.

## Conclusions From MPC

Peer coaching has an excellent track record in education as a powerful tool for professional development. Implementing peer coaching to enhance the integration of technology (as advocated by the MPC program) may indeed prove to be an effective and efficient approach. However, additional research should be conducted to ascertain the power of the approach and to identify techniques, conditions, and contextual facilitators that should be in place when applying peer coaching to technology integration.

MODEL 2

# Raising the Bar: A personal trainer model for technology integration training

*Maryanne Fazio-Fox and Mary Lane-Kelso*
*Northern Arizona University*

## Context

Over the past decade, the authors created, tested, piloted, and retrofit a professional development model for working with teachers beginning to use technology. The model was used in teacher training programs at K–12, professional, and university levels in Arizona. Referred to as the Raising the Bar model, it involves a two-tiered mentoring schema that uses personal trainers and on-site teacher mentors. The program is uniquely effective largely due to the use of personal trainers; that is, technology integration experts who serve as one-on-one guides for teachers grappling with technology integration in their classrooms. The personal trainer model partners technology integration experts with on-site teachers at a variety of levels, from kindergarten to university. The linchpin metaphor of the personal trainer is borrowed from the fitness world. The personal trainer in this context is a professional educational technologist who works with teachers individually to assess their current level of skills, both in using computer-based applications and in creating curricular activities that incorporate technology. This helps them personally advance the level of their technological skills and practices. Over the course of applying the model, with and without the personal assistance, we have come to fully appreciate the powerful nature of including this tier in the professional development structure.

## Goals

The goals and objectives of the professional development program are:

- To provide professional development opportunities for teachers to enable them to more adequately address both the Arizona State Technology Standards and the Arizona Academic Standards.

- To provide an opportunity for teachers to incorporate Web-based resources into content curricula using best practices as recognized by educational technology policy makers.

- To provide opportunities for teachers to potentially enhance teaching and learning, and concomitantly improve student outcomes through the use of technology-integrated curricula.

## Participants

In this case study we demonstrate how the model worked with faculty at Northland Preparatory Academy (NPA) in Flagstaff, Arizona during the 2004–2005 school year. A total of 15 faculty members joined the project at the outset. Three cohorts of NPA teachers took part in online and face-to-face workshops, and in one-on-one mentoring, as well as completing online curricular projects.

## The personal trainer process

Training was delivered using a combination of face-to-face workshops, one-to-one collaboration with a personal trainer, and Web-delivered instruction via the World Wide Web. The overarching mission of the professional training program was to provide teachers with a means of integrating technology in their classrooms. Technology-integrated modules were delivered through, and made extensive use of, the World Wide Web. The capstone goal of the training for each teacher was the design and implementation of at least one curricular piece, a module which exhibited exemplary technology integration practices. An introductory workshop for all NPA faculty members planted a vision of best practices for integrating technology in the classroom through examples and models.

Teachers were then scheduled into one of the eight-week training blocks that were held during the academic year. NPA faculty members participated in an intensive eight-week program with a cohort of a minimum of four other teachers, during which they completed online activities and communicated with their cohort, met with the personal trainers in person to conceptualize their module, mined the Web for resources for their projects, and—with the personal trainer—completed the module and a plan for implementing the module. (The Web address for a sample outline and timeline is http://jan. ucc.nau.edu/~mel8/outlineandtimeline.pdf). The final step was for teachers to develop Web-editing skills to maintain and update their Web-based projects. (To view the teacher-created modules, please go to http://jan.ucc.nau.edu/~mel8/npa/samples.htm).

## Evaluating effectiveness

The purpose of this training program was to provide participant teachers with a means of producing, using, and editing technology-integrated curricular modules for their classrooms. The data collected aimed to measure growth in the development of skills related to using technology in teaching and learning. This included technical skills, pedagogical practices, and perceived changes in student performance with the integration of technology into their curriculum. The rate of change was relative to the individual participant's baseline skills and knowledge measured at the start of the training program.

### Data collection

Several instruments were used to measure the success of this model. The NPA faculty completed an online self-reporting tool (www.ncrtec.org/capacity/profile/profeng.htm) at the beginning of the training and toward the end of the program. The data collected was used to gauge change within the group of NPA participants. Workshop Evaluation and End-of-Project Evaluation forms were collected to elicit teachers' feedback on the training and gauge perceived changes in student performance. In addition, teacher-designed curricular materials were showcased and evaluated with peer responses at the final Web-editing workshop.

## Data analysis

Conclusions drawn from the data demonstrate that all respondents to the pre- and post-survey showed growth in the development of skills related to using technology in teaching and learning, by comparing the baseline pre-survey results with post-survey results. The rate of growth was variable, with some teachers making quite significant strides. NPA teachers with more technology knowledge and skills already in place tended toward a slower growth rate. These results may be accounted for by the high skill level and technology experience with which they began the project. In addition, workshops, end-of-project evaluations, and peer responses were analyzed to measure training effectiveness and gauge perceived changes in student performance. Discussion of the patterns and themes emerging from the feedback follows.

## Outcomes

Based on data collected, several themes emerged that can be described best as connectedness, motivation, and relationships.

### Connectedness

Data suggested that this training experience facilitated the use of technology and established new avenues of communication and interaction for the teachers and the students. The faculty reported more access to resources and curricular materials using the Web, as well as more interest from their students using the developed curricular materials. Moreover, teachers observed an increased feeling of connectedness to the world outside the classroom for the students. Teachers reported that use of the Web encouraged extensions from home, adapting and extending activities to challenge and embrace a larger number of learners, and observed students more involved in group work. One teacher commented, "It seems to be designed for individual students, but there are in-class components that are more collaborative." Teachers reported that they, too, felt less isolated and had tools with which to reach out to other professionals in the field and expand the communication to students. One teacher commented, "creating and maintaining my Web site will help me in introducing more resources to my students and will help me to communicate to my students more than what I normally could because of the time constraint in the classroom."

### Motivation

When asked to provide feedback for each other's projects, teachers consistently responded positively that projects were aligned to state standards, demonstrated higher-order thinking skills, were multidisciplinary, gave clear directions, had a demonstrable outcome, were visibly appealing, and were free of cultural and gender bias. However, the primary commentary from teachers spoke to how the Web curricular materials that were developed during the training program allowed them to take on the roles of facilitator and motivator for their students. Teachers observed that the technology tools appealed to the students' sense of natural curiosity. Using online materials developed to examine the issue of the death penalty for example, one teacher commented, "Students who participated in death penalty debates were fascinated by it. I even heard about it from kids during Math!!" Repeatedly, teachers expressed their own thrill of learning how to use the Web to both develop online materials for their students and utilize the Internet for research.

### Relationships

Though the role of the personal trainer was recognized at the very inception of the model as a key factor, the significance of the role became fully appreciated as the training unfolded. Teachers reported that having that person guiding their learning is the most important factor for making this training work. Having that personal relationship allowed the personal trainer to be a bridge for the participating teacher in crossing over into the practice of technology integration. These relationships between personal trainers appeared to be extremely important to the participating teachers as a method to learn new skills and bring these skills into the classroom activities. The teachers reported that having that trainer on-site increased their chances for making this training work.

## Conclusions from the Raising the Bar model

The success of the Raising the Bar model over the years has been demonstrated through its various iterations. Several key factors are required to ensure its success. This model's scalable quality rests on the efficient use of both online and face-to-face interactions. Providing teachers the opportunities to develop their skills in technology integration requires that program leaders recognize the added value of technology integration. Academic outcomes are clearly evident in technology-rich learning environments. The digital divide exists both among and between teachers and students. Customized training attuned to individual needs addresses the spectrum of skill levels and at the same time, provides all students technology-supported curriculum to help level the digital playing field. Finally, to implement this program the recipe for success is a combination of well-thought-out training materials and pedagogical strategies, coupled with a structure that builds in powerful relationships with technology mentors. Highlighting the personal aspect of training builds those bridges of trust for educators as they develop their skills and changes the paradigm to include those personal relationships. The confidence and ownership teachers feel from their curricular products helps to reinvest them for future endeavors so the process can continue beyond the training. The key factors in the successes seen in the model, therefore, stem from the relationships created and nurtured by the very structure of the model.

MODEL 3

# The Peer Mentor model for promoting expertise with technology among teachers

*Judy T. DiLeo*
*ESL Teacher and EETT Coordinator: Altoona School District (Pennsylvannia)*

According to Jenson, Lewis, and Savage (2002), there is great "diversity of teachers' and administrators' own stated preferences for 'what works' and 'what doesn't work,' as they attempt to make more and/or better use of computers in their classes and schools" (p. 482). The Peer Mentor model is a blended implementation of "train-the-trainer," peer coaching, and co-teaching models of professional development that can forestall the problems that typify professional development: poor retention after short-term training sessions, time limitations, and scheduling issues (National Center for Educational Statistics, 2000; Polselli, 2002). Initiated in Altoona, Pennsylvania to solve particular problems related to the cost of technology training for teachers, the process proved to be adaptable across settings.

## The Context of the Peer Mentor Model

Districts' unique assets form the framework of individual Peer Mentor programs. For this reason, the Peer Mentor model used in one district can—*should*—differ from that of another. In Altoona, for example, the district had on-site Apple trainers available to a limited number of teachers for one year. The teachers involved in that training became the mentors for others who had had no training, thus magnifying the effect of the original Apple trainer. This was an effective way to extend the impact of finite professional development resources. By using available resources (personnel, time, flexibility, etc.), a Peer Mentor program will meet needs more specifically than would other formulaic plans.

## Goals of the Peer Mentor Model

The primary goal of Altoona's Peer Mentor model was to increase teacher proficiency with technology and teacher willingness to use it to enhance student achievement while simultaneously taking advantage of available assets (personnel, available training, etc.). Key to this venture was a willingness to exercise flexibility in the use of these assets to maximize the effect of finite resources for professional development.

## Participants in the Peer Mentor Model

In Altoona, the district's Peer Mentor model used inservice time with the Apple trainer to train several key teachers. Teachers in two other schools were targeted for training by the new "experts" during successive cycles of staff development. Thus, although intervention by the Apple trainer ended after the first year, growth continued among an increasing numbers of teachers.

To identify the "experts" who were best equipped to serve as peer mentors, program developers looked at three areas: (1) prior participation in technology integration training; (2) evidence of daily integration of technology with daily instruction; and (3) a positive, supportive relationship with peers. In addition to teachers, Peer Mentor programs may include administrators, community members, district tech support staff, and others. The next section discusses how the Altoona district built a team of individuals who successfully implemented, supported, or participated in the Peer Mentor program.

## Case Study: Altoona school district (PA)

Altoona's Peer Mentor model made use of available resources: inservice time with an Apple trainer (until available days were depleted), a group of four tech-savvy teachers, and support from a technology coordinator. Goals included increasing teacher proficiency with technology and willingness to use it to enhance student achievement.

Prior to the start of the program, teachers in one school had received training from Apple personnel; at the same time, they implemented their knowledge within their classrooms. During the first year, four teachers whose skills were exemplary became mentors for eight teachers spread between two other schools. During Year One, these 12 teachers attended inservice sessions together and visited each other's classrooms to practice integration and implementation of technology with instruction. In Year Two, the original eight learners became mentors for grade-level partners in their schools while the original mentors offered resource support as needed. The coordinator provided inservice training specific to the needs of participants and monitored progress and outcomes.

## Evaluating effectiveness

At the end of the program, a comparison between participating and nonparticipating teachers and students showed measurable differences. Teacher attitude and usage levels among the Peer Mentor group improved, while those of the control group remained at constant levels throughout the program. Table 7.3 demonstrates these gains through direct quotes reflective of changed teacher attitudes toward technology from the start to the end of the EETT intervention.

The time teachers spent using laptops and related tools was logged to determine if the Peer Mentor model enhanced teacher acceptance of technology as an instructional tool. By the end of the first marking period, time with technology increased among all users in the Peer Mentor–supported group, while usage levels remained constant for members of the control groups. Although some of this increase can be explained by the fact that teachers knew that their time with technology was being monitored, other measured behaviors, prevalent among members of the experimental group and only incidental among members of control groups, indicate that growth in use was attributable to the Peer Mentor program (See Table 7.4).

**Table 7.3** | Teachers' voices on technology over time

| | In the beginning... | Later... |
|---|---|---|
| **Teacher A** | "Do they really expect us to use computers *every day*?" | "How can I accomplish my goals if the cart goes to two additional teachers next year?" |
| **Teacher B** | "Don't expect me to use the computers after January; I have to get the kids ready for the PSSA." | "Can we share PSSA practice Web sites at the next meeting?" |
| **Teacher C** | "My students are too needy! It'll be impossible to get around to them with the iBooks." | (To an incoming EETT teacher): "You'll see, they're pretty good at helping each other; just help them to help each other." |
| **Teacher D** | "I was drafted into this; I have no computer skills; I shouldn't be here." | "Do my kids still get the laptops next year when the grant is over? I want to expand this year's social studies project." |
| **Teacher E** | (To another teacher): "If I can't get them (laptops) to work, you can take my turn with them." | "Two of my kids' laptops are down; can't we have a direct line to the tech department for help when we need it?" |

**Table 7.4** | Comparison of average weekly technology-related behaviors between control and experimental groups of teachers from the first semester to the last semester of the project

| Behavior | Control Groups # times/week | | | |
|---|---|---|---|---|
| | Semester One Year One | Semester Two Year One | Semester One Year Two | Semester Two Year Two |
| Search online for materials to complement instruction | 0 | 1 | 0 | 2 |
| Create online assignments* | 0 | 2 | 2 | 3 |
| E-mail peers for collaboration | 0 | 0 | 0 | 2 |
| | Experimental (Peer Mentor) Groups # times/week | | | |
| Search online for materials to complement instruction | 1 | 4 | 7 | 11 |
| Create online assignments* | 3 | 6 | 7 | 10 |
| E-mail peers for collaboration | 5 | 9 | 12 | 8 |

*Unrelated to the learning software through which teachers were required to develop student lessons

Even the less tech-savvy teachers, some of whom had had only one year of mentor training before the EETT project ended, expressed interest in continuing the EETT process even without the formal support of peer mentors or coordinator. Collaborative teams that grew out of the project continue to flourish. One teacher declined a transfer offer to a less needy school, even though she had previously requested the transfer, simply because she did not want to forfeit daily access to computers for herself and her students.

Student achievement gains, measured by examining the Grade 3–5 scores of participants on the Pennsylvania System of School Assessment (PSSA), were more significant among children in the classrooms of Peer Mentor participants than they were among members of control groups (See Table 7.5). Comparisons between students in classrooms with zero, one, or two years in a technology-rich environment revealed thought-provoking outcomes. When comparing groups, students with zero years in a Peer Mentor–supported classroom actually fared better than students with just one year in such a classroom: 62.5% of these students showed gains while 42.86% of students with one year in a Peer Mentor–supported classroom showed gains. However, 85% of students who participated in classes with tech-savvy teachers for two years were markedly better than those of their counterparts in either the zero- or one-year exposure groups. This outcome suggests that consistency in effective delivery adds substantially to the impact of technology on student achievement; it also indicates that effective use of technology does indeed enhance student learning.

**Table 7.5** │ Comparison of PSSA scores between students who participated in Peer Mentor–supported classrooms for one, two, or three years

| Years in a Peer Mentor–supported class | PSSA Gain | | PSSA Loss | | PSSA No Change | |
|---|---|---|---|---|---|---|
| | Number of Students | Percent of Students | Number of Students | Percent of Students | Number of Students | Percent of Students |
| 0 years (40 students) | 25 | 62.50 | 3 | 7.50 | 12 | 30.00 |
| 1 year (28 students) | 12 | 42.86 | 7 | 25.00 | 9 | 32.14 |
| 2 years (20 students) | 17 | 85.00 | 2 | 10.00 | 1 | 5.00 |
| Total | 53 | ** | 12 | ** | 22 | ** |

## Conclusions from the Peer Mentor Model

In the Altoona case study, the Peer Mentor model of support for technology integration was successful. Teachers gained critical skills and maintained their ability and willingness to use technology. Especially gratifying was the fact that additional teachers in the targeted schools expressed interest in using computers in their classrooms.

As the teaching profession becomes increasingly rigorous, it is necessary to support educators as they begin their careers, when new programs are being implemented, and when the expectations of their schools and communities change. Though no single method of support is the universal remedy for helping teachers, the Peer Mentor model can effectively capitalize on the talents and tools available within a school district to support the professional development needs of teachers.

## Key recommendations for peer coaching and technology integration

As evidenced in the preceding descriptions, peer coaching takes a variety of different forms depending on the context of the coaching. However, we believe that, regardless of the format, most successful peer coaching efforts share a number of attributes. The following recommendations are based on our experiences and are provided for district and building-level professional developers; administrators, teacher-leaders, and technology committees responsible for planning professional development activities; and private, government, university, and agency consultants and researchers who design, implement, and assess the process and outcomes of professional development.

### Recommendation 1: Peer coaching for technology integration must foster a deep understanding of technology's potential in classrooms.

Teachers need to be provided with examples of how technology can transform teaching and learning. Cutting-edge tools of the Web 2.0 variety require little to no technical skill but have the potential to substantially alter what happens in classrooms. Peer coaches may benefit from using a research-based continuum of technology integration such as those developed during the Apple Classrooms of Tomorrow (ACOT) project (Sandholtz, Ringstaff, & Dwyer, 1997) or Levels of Technology Integration (LoTi) (Moersch, 1999) to informally assess both their beliefs and practices and those of their mentees.

Peer coaches may benefit from using (and subsequently sharing) a variety of online support networks such as Ning's Teacher 2.0 social networking community (teachers20.ning.com) or Web 2.0 for Educators (cpitwebtwoinfo.pbwiki.com), a teacher-made wiki that provides great resources and examples. Likewise, Web sites like the George Lucas Foundation's Edutopia provide video-based examples of transformational technology uses. Peer coaches (and their mentees) can subscribe to its Spiral Notebook blog via RSS feeds.

As teachers and their coaches are considering all of these new possibilities for classrooms, peer coaches must help to ensure that they have opportunities to consider the variety of roles students can play in technology integration. For example, students may be consumers of technology (e.g., gathering information from a Web page) or producers of technology (e.g., creating a digital video about community history). They may also use technology as individuals, within a collaborative group, and to communicate with those outside classroom walls. In addition, teachers should consider a variety of assessment strategies to gauge student learning and how technology can help promote higher levels of Bloom's taxonomy, multiple intelligences, learning styles, and differentiated instruction.

### Recommendation 2: The peer coaching process is based on relationships.

Peer mentoring is most successful when there is a combination of well-designed materials, sound pedagogical strategies and powerful relationships between mentor and mentees. It is critical that a peer (as opposed to a novice–expert) relationship be established early in the peer coaching process. Mentees must be given a voice in the process, be encouraged to take risks, and completely trust the intentions and actions of the peer mentor. In fact, we believe that the compatibility of the mentor and mentee on a personal level is more important than similarities in grade levels or subject areas.

### Recommendation 3: A focus on student achievement is essential throughout the peer coaching process.

Peer coaching must include evidence-based documentation of student achievement. If technology does not support student learning, its use is questionable.

Teacher inquiry is a powerful tool to support this need. In addition to providing multiple, evidence-based accounts of student learning, it can support participants in moving toward a deeper understanding of technology integration, enable them to reflect on their teaching in systematic ways, help monitor progress over a period of time, and promote a culture of school change through increased feelings of professionalism. One outstanding reference for teacher inquiry is, "The reflective educator's guide to classroom practice: Learning to teach and teaching to learn through practitioner inquiry" (Dana & Yendol-Silva, 2003).

## Concluding comments

Peer coaching is a generic professional development model that is adaptable to any discipline. Consequently, the success of peer coaching for technology integration is predicated on both exemplary research-based peer coaching strategies and exemplary research-based technology integration professional development strategies. This chapter highlighted three different models of peer coaching for technology integration in three geographically diverse regions of the United States. Those wishing to undertake similar peer coaching efforts should ensure that design and development includes a focus on transformational uses of technology, strong interpersonal relationships between mentors and mentees, and a focus on how technology affects student achievement.

## GETTING STARTED RESOURCES

Holland, P. E. (2002). Professional development in technology: Catalyst for school reform. *Journal of Technology and Teacher Education, 9*(2), 245–267.

The author offers insight into three skill levels of technology use among public school teachers. This article can help mentors gain insight into the varying needs of the teachers with whom they will work.

Jenson, J., Lewis, B., & Savage, R. (2002). No one way: Working models for teachers' professional development. *Journal of Technology and Teacher Education, 10*(4), 481–496.

This article formed the springboard from which the Peer Mentor model was developed in the district described in this section. Because teacher input formed the foundation for some of the discussion, the methods described are based on practical "what works" evidence from the field. Information in the article allows the reader to tailor suggestions to meet a district's particular needs.

Mullinix, B. B. (2002). *Selecting and retaining teacher mentors.* Washington, DC: ERIC Clearinghouse on Teaching and Teacher Education. (ERIC Document Reproduction Service No. ED477728). Retrieved April 6, 2008 from www.ericdigests.org/2004-1/mentors.htm

As important as selecting and pairing mentors and learner teachers, staff developers must devise strategies for retaining and fostering relationships with mentor trainers. This article describes various means of accomplishing this goal.

Polselli, R. (2002). Combining Web-based training and mentorship to improve technology integration in the K–12 classroom. *Journal of Technology and Teacher Education, 10*(2), 247–272.

The use of mentor-supported Web-based technology training for teachers is the subject of this study. For districts interested in duplicating this process, the article includes a concise outline of implementation procedures.

Trautman, S. (2006). *Teach what you know: A practical leader's guide to knowledge transfer using peer mentoring.* Upper Saddle River, NJ: Prentice Hall.

Although the emphasis of this text is on technology in the business arena, the author successfully describes the implementation of peer mentoring systems from a variety of perspectives. The attention given to in-house and distance mentoring is of particular value to educators as they develop peer mentor programs among teachers within and between school buildings.

## chapter 8

# Digital Storytelling Promotes Technology Integration

*Sally Brewer*
*David R. Erickson*
University of Montana

## abstract

IN NEED OF an innovative approach to change teaching practice related to the use of instructional technology in a rural state, a group of educators merged components of a cohort model, storytelling, and multimedia technology to assist teachers in using technology to share Montana's history and traditions. Essential to the success of this model are an on-site coordinator, a learning circle of teachers, supportive school administration, and access to equipment and software. Not only do teachers learn to use technologies, but more importantly, they reflect upon how what they are learning can enhance their teaching and their students' learning. The outcomes include increased teacher comfort with technology and a constructivist classroom in which students are involved in shaping their learning.

Challenged by the need for an innovative approach to change teaching practice related to the use of educational technology in a rural and remote state, a group of educators came together and discussed ways to proceed. Not only did these educators want to help teachers better integrate educational technology into their classrooms; they also wanted to involve students, families, and community members. Reaching out to Native American and other students living in poverty was one of the major goals of the Montana Technology And Learning in Every School (TALES) grant. It was determined that these goals might be accomplished with an integrated thematic multimedia storytelling approach, that is, digital storytelling. Using this approach, students would acquire language and literacy skills as they participated with teachers, parents, and community members (a learning circle) in designing interdisciplinary multimedia products built around the traditions and legends of Montana's diverse cultures and communities. Teachers would become more comfortable using and integrating technology into their classrooms.

This combination of storytelling and technology resulted in the model for professional development (see Figure 8.1) that is described in this chapter. This model was piloted during the Montana TALES Technology Innovation Challenge Grant project (funded by OERI of the US Department of Education, Grant #R303A980187). The purpose of the Montana TALES project was to design and implement an exemplary model of professional development in which teachers became thoughtful, innovative learners infusing multimedia technology into the school curriculum.

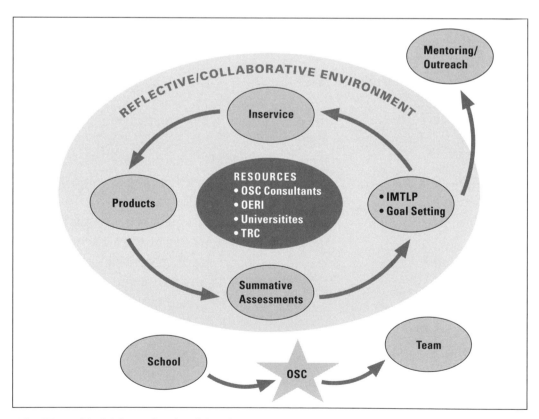

**FIGURE 8.1.** Model for professional development

# Planning aspects

Prior to developing this model, the TALES team reviewed the literature to determine barriers to using technology and approaches that have and have not worked in the past. The team wanted this model to overcome as many of the barriers identified by Willis (1993) as possible, including lack of faculty awareness and comfort with technology, time for faculty to learn to use and integrate technology, technical and administrative support, access to equipment, and faculty development.

## Identification of personnel and resources

After an interested school's administrators decide to adopt this model, which includes not only purchasing technology resources, such as computers, software, and other digital tools, but also time to learn and practice using these technologies, the next step is to identify or hire an On-site Coordinator (OSC). The OSC is a critical element of this model because he or she not only provides staff development but also support for the teachers involved in the project. The OSC needs to be technology savvy, and more importantly, able to teach the teachers in the learning circle how to use the technology. Because the OSCs are involved in every step of the model, they need to have good interpersonal skills. They assist members of the learning circle in the first step as they set their goals and objectives for the coming year. They mentor learning circle members when necessary. The OSC frequently acts as the spokesperson for the learning circle and as an advocate for the project.

The members of the learning circle need to be identified next. The members may be teachers, staff, or community members. They have to be interested in learning about technology and willing to work together. The learning circle members make important contributions to this project. First they bring enthusiasm for learning and doing. The interest and excitement that the first learning circle shares about their projects and the integration of technology into their classrooms provide an impetus for other teachers in the school to want to learn more about using technology and creating multimedia tales. Each year, a new learning circle is started until the entire faculty and staff in a school has been trained. Frequently one member of a learning circle will become an expert on a particular piece of equipment or software application. This is important as the use of the different technologies spreads throughout the school. Because the school library media specialist can be a valuable resource in gathering information for the stories, it is recommended that he or she also be a part of the learning circle. However, whether or not he or she is part of the learning circle, the library media specialist is a resource. Resources fall into four categories: (1) print and nonprint primary resources, (2) people resources, (3) equipment and software, and (4) inservice providers. Print and nonprint resources may be available through the school library or via interlibrary loan. People resources, particularly community members who have lived in the community a long time, are particularly helpful because they bring the history of the community to life through interviews. These oral histories can be audiotaped and transcribed, or videotaped.

## LITERATURE ESSENTIALS

### *Essential conditions*

Researchers have found that *support from a school's administrators* is an important component for effective staff development. Administrators not only can provide monetary support for new equipment, but also release time and/or incentives for faculty who are learning new technologies (Wizer & McPherson, 2005; McGrath & Sands, 2004). Lack of access to equipment is one of the primary barriers to teachers' use of instructional technology. Teachers need access to technology not only during the school day but also after it (Meltzer & Sherman, 1997).

*Technical support* is a key component because when computers and other digital equipment are not functioning properly, most teachers have neither the time nor the knowledge to repair it. Thus, a trained technician is essential both to technology training activities and integration into the classroom (Lim & Khine, 2006; Wells, 2007).

### *Essential characteristics*

The *On-site Coordinator (OSC)* is a combination of a mentor, facilitator, and advocate. This person works with a learning circle of teachers, parents, and community members to help them learn new technologies and plan their projects and implement them. Other responsibilities include advocating for the use of technology and keeping the administration informed about technology projects. The OSC is a critical person not only in this model but any technology-enriched school (Cole, Simkins, & Penuel, 2002).

By participating in a *learning circle*, teachers no longer feel isolated as they try new technologies or teaching strategies (Lovett & Gilmore, 2003; Zorfass & Rivero, 2005). Although the members of learning circles are primarily teachers, parents or administrators may also be involved. The learning circle provides a safe, comfortable environment in which the members can learn (King, 2003). It also provides teachers an opportunity to share what they have learned and talk about how they might incorporate it into their teaching.

The members of learning circles learn to use a variety of digital technologies as they create their *digital stories*. A digital story consists of a collection of still images and video clips that are combined with either music or narration or both to tell a story (Kajder, Bull, & Albaugh, 2005). The individual tale provides not only a vehicle for staff development but also a way for teachers to personalize what they learn (Salpeter, 2005; Jakes & Brennan, 2005; Thibeault, 2004).

Because the format of the finished tale depends upon the equipment and software being used to bring it to life, an inventory of available equipment and software needs to be conducted early in the school year. Once the learning circle members have determined how they want to tell both their personal and their group tales, the equipment and software needs may change. Therefore, the OSC also needs to identify vendors who can provide not only these tools at the lowest prices but also the best technical support for the purchased items. The final resource to be identified is potential inservice providers. Certainly, the OSC will provide much of the training and technical support. However, as technologies change, it is useful to have outside resources to draw upon. These resources may include faculty at a local university who conduct workshops on various technology topics or private organizations that offer training. If the funding is available, state and national technology conferences provide excellent training opportunities. They also provide a venue for the teachers involved in the process to share what they have learned. Then, another group of teachers in another school can begin the seven-step process that will be delineated in the following paragraphs.

## Implementation of the model

### Getting ready

Once the learning circle members have been identified, the faculty development process begins. In this step, the teachers become learners. The first item, then, is to determine what the teachers need to learn. This is accomplished by having them complete a technology competency self-assessment instrument such as Doug Johnson's Code 77 rubrics or the Taking a Good Look at Instructional Technology (TAGLIT) teacher survey. These instruments help the teachers assess their technology knowledge, skills, and comfort implementing interdisciplinary curriculum that uses technology to support student learning. Then the learning circle members complete an Individualized Multimedia Technology Learning Plan (IMTLP). This plan helps them identify their individual goals and objectives for the year and the activities that might help them accomplish their goals. As the teachers complete their IMTLPs, they decide what questions they want to answer in their personal tale. Not only should they identify the primary question, which might be, "How did skateboarding evolve into a major sport," they also should identify subtopics. These might include questions about the chronological history, the people involved in this sport, and information about the equipment needed. From there, the learner needs to decide what will be the content outcomes and what will be their learner outcomes. Based on the answers to these questions, the learner, usually with the help of the OSC, determines what technologies will support these outcomes. During the second and third years of the grant project, some learning circles planned both their personal tales and their group tales at the start of the year. Other learning circles planned their group tales after they had finished their personal tales.

The OSC and the members of the learning circle decide how frequently they will meet, typically weekly during the first semester. The second semester, the meetings are determined by the progress of the group tale. These decisions about which technologies to use will impact the next phase of the model.

In this initial step, the OSC acts as a facilitator. The OSC provides the self-assessment tools. The assessment already may be constructed, like the TAGLIT survey, or the OSC may tailor an assessment tool so that it focuses on technologies available in their school district. Then the OSC helps members of the learning circle complete their IMTLPs. After the technology surveys and the IMTLPs are completed, the OSC reviews them to determine what technologies need to be acquired and taught that year.

## Inservice: Learning about technology

Although the goal of this staff development model is to help teachers become comfortable using and integrating technology into their classrooms, the first workshop is usually about storytelling. In this workshop, learning circle members learn how to use a concept mapping program like Inspiration to clarify the key elements of their stories. They learn how to organize their information, plan their projects, and create storyboards.

Then the faculty, staff, administrators, and community learners attend technology workshops, which might be demonstrations or hands-on sessions, to learn about available software and digital tools. These workshops provide a vision of what can be done with various tools. Frequently these workshops provide attendees with enough information that they can continue learning on their own, and these inservice activities may occur on a weekly or a monthly basis.

Frequently, there is no one best method to learn how to use a new software application or a new digital device. It might take several different approaches before the student understands and becomes comfortable with a new tool. Follow-up activities may include video tutorials, print tutorials, or mentoring by the OSC.

Although the OSC may have conducted some workshops about a range of technologies, at this point, mentoring becomes an even more important piece of the model. As a mentor, the OSC may review a software program that the learning circle member learned in a workshop or provide some continued training that allows the learner to move to an enhanced level of expertise with that program.

## Products: Learning by doing

By this point, the learning circle members have assessed their knowledge of technology, set goals for themselves, and been exposed during workshops to the technologies they might use in creating their tales. Now they gather the resources they need to create their tales and get to work. If the teachers need to use online databases and other Internet resources for their research, they might work with the their school library media specialist or a librarian at a public or academic library. In the libraries, the teachers might find pictures in books that they wish to scan to include in their multimedia presentations.

These tales range from autobiographical tales to stories about their ancestors or communities in which they have lived. These tales incorporate many of the technologies they have learned: software applications like PowerPoint, Photoshop or iMovie, and digital tools, such as digital camcorders or scanners.

During this phase, the OSC becomes the guide on the side. He or she may provide just-in-time instruction on a software program or digital device, or could help people find the resources they need to "tell" their tales. The OSC's role is to facilitate the entire production process of the individual tales.

## Assessment of personal tales: Product sharing and reflection

The learning circle members gather in late November or early December (about four months after they formed the learning circle) to share their personal tales. Although the actual creation of these tales is important, it should be noted that the sharing of their efforts contributes to the learning process. The learning circle members can proudly share what they have learned. Then other learning circle members can ask questions about how certain parts of a tale were created and learn from their colleagues. Everyone can take time to reflect not only on *what* they learned, but also *how* they learned. For example, they might ask learning circle members, "Did having a demonstration of a particular program and then time to play with it provide enough learning support, or did they need to have a print tutorial to refer to after the demonstration?"

During this meeting, the OSC facilitates both the sharing of the personal tales and reflection process. During the reflection process, the teachers reflect not only on what they have learned but also how they can incorporate what they have learned into their classrooms. This summative assessment, sharing and reflecting on the personal tales, serves as a formative assessment for the next step.

## Creating the group tale

The members of the learning circle now have to plan to create their group tale, which is an interdisciplinary project that may also be taught across multiple grade levels. They need to plan not only how the tale will unfold but also what technologies will be used to tell it. They must decide who will be involved in the creation of this tale. Sometimes, only the learning circle members are involved in the project, but many times their students and community members are also involved. For example, the learning circle that created the movie titled "Mary Fields" engaged the entire community. This movie, created in Adobe Premiere, told the story of a pioneer woman instrumental in the development of a Montana community on the Missouri river in the 1880s. The school planned an open house where elementary students explained how to make homemade soap, much the way Mary Fields would have done. Other students shared a cut-out face of Old West characters where one could have photos taken; here students had learned to take digital photos and print those. And still other students described the medical tools and medicines of the day. Over 70% of the community attended this important open house event and watched the professional-quality movie that the learning circle of teachers created to document the history of their small town. Today, the movie is available in the community library–museum, a testimony to this unique community and school collaboration.

After the plan has been outlined, the members of the learning circle begin the creation process, gathering information and resources they need to complete their projects. Then, they draft their tales. As they work collectively on their project, they may ask the OSC for help with the technology or they may have learned enough during the previous semester to be able to complete it on their own. This process usually encompasses most of the second semester, and the group tales are subsequently shared at a meeting of all of the TALES teachers at the end of the school year.

The OSC at this point serves the roles of both project facilitator and trainer. The learning circle members decide not only on the topic of the tale but also what technologies they need to present the tale. The OSC facilitates weekly meetings of the team, helps identify resources, and provides just-in-time training on the technologies that the team is using to present its tale.

## Sharing group TALES and reflection

Annually in June, TALES teams comprised of the OSC and the learning circle members, past and future, from across the state gather in a central location to share the group tales created by the learning circle members and their students. These tales illustrated both the collaboration among teachers and the teachers' technology proficiency. All of the tales showed creativity of one form or another, in the song that the music teacher wrote for the group tale, or the work of the art majors in a high school, or the story of the tale itself. Groups of teachers from each school took turns viewing each other's final tale for the school year and reflecting on what they had learned. The feedback from other schools' teams regarding the products is extremely valuable and helps guide the new teams to ever better group tales.

The end of the conference marked the beginning of some time to recoup after an extensive year of story-telling and technology applications. Many teachers enthusiastically enlisted to help the next year's team during summer inservice opportunities and upcoming opportunities for additional learning. August would bring a new school year, new students, and new learning circles.

## Ongoing support via TALES network

The network of schools engaged in the TALES model serves multiple purposes. First, it provides OSCs with opportunities to meet with each other monthly, learning new technology, sharing what works and what is not working, and returning with new ideas for their respective teams. Second, it provides opportunities for those having previously completed the district inservice to volunteer to mentor and reach out to others within their own school or district or across districts around the state. One teacher may become the expert in using iMovie or Premiere and be willing to share that expertise with program teachers. This approach of providing expertise and mentorship from within the various schools is critical for the ongoing success of the model.

## Methods of evaluation

The model was evaluated through direct observation, journals, and interviews. The OSCs met weekly with participants and constantly learned what was and was not working in relation to learning new technologies and integrating those into individual teachers' practices. They made constant adjustments and shared those modifications and findings through journal entries and ongoing discussions with other OSCs across the state. Monthly, the OSCs gathered to learn new technologies themselves and delighted to be able to visit with each other about their own teams' learning and frustrations they were encountering.

More formal interviews were conducted in Years Three and Four, documenting these learning experiences, assisting in revision of the model. Team members from schools eagerly shared their excitement about learning new technology and applying their expertise to their own classrooms. One kindergarten teacher used a large screen TV connected to her computer to share the digital versions of the stories her students wrote with the help of seventh-grade students who paired with her students. Once each story was scanned, all the students would gather in front of the TV and carefully listen as their teacher would begin to read the words on the page, and then ask for others to complete the sentence. Not only could the students speak the words, they were learning them visually. This innovative teacher also used the computer-TV connection to anchor mathematics lessons and counting, always moving from physical representations that students made to the digital photos of those lessons. Her classroom was alive with activities and references to those activities for days and weeks after, so that students were reinforcing learning through actually seeing the same situations repeated.

## Impact on learning environments

Participating in a learning circle for a year had a considerable effect on the teachers. One of the primary goals of the project was to develop teachers who were comfortable using and integrating technology into their classrooms. We also wanted them to work collaboratively across disciplines and grade levels, as well as with members of the community. The group tales accomplished these goals and much more.

The teachers did indeed become comfortable using technology and began to integrate it into their classrooms. Many of them became technology leaders and mentors in their schools. Members of the learning circles became close as they worked through their personal and group tales. One group created its own identity, "The Pink Ladies." They wore pink satin jackets and carried pink bowling ball purses to all the TALES meetings. Their Group Tale, a type of interactive "Where's Waldo" adventure, was actually a history of their hometown. As the students tried to find their teachers, they learned about their local history. The project not only created a sense of belonging but also pride in what teachers were creating and students were learning.

Another group tale reflected nearly the entire K–8 school's efforts to anchor learning around a theme for the year: fire. The theme was both relevant and timely, as smoke from a devastating summer forest fire continued to fill the valley weeks into the school year. Each grade level identified content related to the fire theme. Mathematics students looked at data from fires; science students investigated the speed at which vertical pines burned compared to horizontal pines through hands-on simulations and buzzing smoke detectors; music students composed and performed a song. And the Group Tale, "We Weren't Here to See It" summarized the history of Montana events over the past 150 years, the last verse of the song changing to "Now we are here to see it." The still images in the PowerPoint slide show summarized the students' and teachers' efforts over the past year, with images included from the community evening where firefighters brought in their equipment for the students to learn more about fire fighting, as well as those of a large tree cross-section showing growth rings from more than 150 years with multiple fire damage from previous years.

TALES schools reached out to their communities in a variety of ways. In order to be able to tell tales about their communities, many learning circle members interviewed members of their communities to learn about a particular event or period in history. Many of these interviews were audiotaped. Others were videotaped so that key quotations could be included in the Tale. Some schools opened their computer labs to the community two or three nights a week. During these open lab times, basic technology classes were frequently offered to community members. Other schools held "Technology nights," which showcased their students' work.

The results from these outreach activities were vast. One outcome was that the community members felt a closer connection to the schools. Also of interest during this project was that almost every technology bond that was presented to the voters of that community was passed, because the community members could see the impact that this investment made. The community support for the technology expenditures had a major effect on student learning. It provided a technology-enriched environment, full of digital tools in which students could learn.

## Impact on student learning

The integration of these new technologies is an important final step in the model. First, it demonstrates that the teachers have really learned how to use these technologies and have become comfortable using them. If teachers know how to use instructional technology but are not comfortable using it, then they will not use it in their classroom because it is too much work. However, when teachers are comfortable using different technologies, then they integrate them into their classroom instruction. The use of these technologies becomes as seamless as using paper and pencil. Students benefit from the integration of educational technology into the curriculum in several ways. First, they learn how to use the technology tools, which may help them become more engaged in learning. It provides them with new ways of communicating, collaborating, and sharing what they have learned. In this technology-enriched student-centered environment, students learn to construct their own knowledge. They work with their teachers to find information, evaluate it, and use it in their multimedia projects. Ultimately, all of this may help the students be more successful.

# Recommendations

In order for schools to replicate this model, several elements are essential. First and foremost, it is critical to have an OSC who has both strong technology skills and strong communications skills. The OSC must be able to train teachers and students how to use the technologies necessary for their tales, but also promote the integration of technology into the curriculum and the staff development necessary to use the technology to both administrators and the community.

The next essential element is the learning circle, which includes teachers, staff, and community members who are dedicated to this project. They must be able to create a team that can collaborate. These people must be enthusiastic about learning new technologies and incorporating them into their classroom instruction. This enthusiasm not only will carry them through their year of learning-by-doing, but also will spread to other teachers. The team members should plan to meet approximately two hours every week to learn new technologies and to work together on their tales.

We found that both the personal and group tales are essential. The personal tale promotes buy-in by the members of the learning circle. The group tale helps the teachers become more comfortable using technology and finding ways to incorporate it into their classrooms.

Support is the last key ingredient, both in the form of technical support and support from the school's administration. Teachers cannot use technology, as a personal tool or classroom tool, if it does not work. Therefore, adequate consistent technical support is absolutely essential. They need to have someone available on a regularly scheduled basis to help with computer problems, software questions, and other technology-related challenges. Administrative support is key for a number of reasons. Administrators can ensure that adequate financial resources are available for technology expenditures. They can show their commitment to technology use by providing time for workshops, modeling technology use in their own work, and supporting the technology leaders in the school.

This model was designed to overcome barriers often cited to technology integration. It was designed as a vehicle to involve the community in school activities and to capture the unique stories of the community. The teachers learned about technology in learner-centered environments from facilitators who used a constructivist approach. This model promoted support for the use of technology not only by the teachers and students, but also by the school's administrators and community members. Although it has been several years since the grant ended, many technology-using teachers across the state are still proudly proclaiming that they were a TALES teacher.

## GETTING STARTED RESOURCES

Center for Digital Storytelling. (2007). Retrieved October 15, 2007, from
www.storycenter.org

The Center for Digital Storytelling is dedicated to helping people of all ages tell stories
digitally. This site provides information about workshops. It also provides examples and
resources.

Hannan, M. and Kicenko, J. (Eds.) (2002). *Facilitator's guide to running a learning circle.* (ERIC
Document Reproduction Service No. ED475005)

This guide describes what a learning circle is and what it isn't. It provides information
about managing learning groups. Guidelines and tips for facilitators are provided.

MacArthur, C. and others. (1993). *Mentoring: An approach to technology education for teachers,
executive overview. Computer mentoring: A case book. Computer mentoring course guide.*
(ERIC Document Reproduction Service No. ED364187)

These documents are designed to help schools develop a technology staff development
model based on the computer mentor model. In this model, a mentor teacher mentors
one to five teachers on the use of the computer in the classroom.

Porter, B. (2004). Digitales: The art of telling digital stories. Retrieved October 15, 2007 from
www.digitalstories.org

This site, created by a long-time technology trainer, provides information about how to
create digital stories, resources to create them, and different ways to assess the finished
projects.

Wizer, D. R. & McPherson, S. J. (2005). The administrator's role: Strategies for fostering
staff development. *Learning & Leading with Technology, 32*(5), 14–17.

In this article, the researchers provide recommendations for administrators who wish
to support technology use in their schools. The types of administrative support that are
needed to promote technology integration are clearly defined.

## chapter 9

# Teachers Doing IT for Themselves

## Action research as professional development

*Vince Ham*
*Derek Wenmoth*
*CORE Education*

*Ronnie Davey*
*University of Canterbury*

## abstract

THIS CHAPTER DESCRIBES three teacher professional development initiatives in New Zealand that were based on mentoring groups of teachers through supported action research projects. It outlines a rationale for action research as a useful model of professional development in the context of the integration of new technologies, and it analyses the main challenges posed by these programmes for the teacher educators who acted in the role of action research mentors during them. It finishes by proposing six teacher preoccupations that professional developers need to be responsive to when mentoring action research as professional development for teachers.

# Models and modes of teacher professional development

Teaching is at heart an ethical activity. It is an attempt to do good for others. And so it is too with teacher professional development (PD). Its goal is to improve teaching practice, and increase teachers' understandings of the social practice we call teaching, thereby enhancing that fundamentally ethical purpose of teaching, which is to foster learning. Teaching therefore, either the teaching of children in a classroom or the teaching of other teachers in professional development contexts, is about people interacting with and empowering other people. So it should hardly be surprising, though it is often ignored or skirted around in the Information and Communication Technologies (ICT) literature, to find that the key factors in providing effective professional development programmes are felt by participants to revolve more than anything else around the nature of the developmental processes involved, and the nature of the socio-professional relationships established between mentors and mentees during the programme.

The raft of new, digital technologies used in education is usually collectively referred to as 'Technology" in the US literature. In other parts of the world they are more commonly called 'IT' (Information Technologies) or 'ICT' (Information and Communication Technologies). The latter is the term used in the authors' jurisdiction.

Hargreaves and Fullan (1992, 1996), Brookfield (1995), and others have argued for some time that the keys to teacher change lie in the deeper cultural, discursive, and institutional contexts within which PD occurs, and in the progress of professional learning programmes as socio-professional events and processes. Thus they argue that we should be implementing PD models defined not as the short term-transfer of information, handy hints, or skills to individual teachers, but as the long-term facilitation of cultures of self-enquiry, critical reflection, and self-renewal in whole school communities.

There has thus been a long-standing need, not least in PD programmes on the integration of new technologies, to distinguish more clearly than we do between modes of inservice provision, meaning the particular tactics, forms, and formats of implementation and delivery used, and models of in-service provision, meaning the overall culture or strategic nature of the PD experience, its purposes and focus, how teachers experience it over time, and the sociocultural nature of the development process. In short, when evaluating teacher PD programmes in new technologies, we need to pay less attention to how they are organised by those who provide them, and more to how they are experienced by those who participate in them.

# Three examples of action research as a model of professional development

One PD model that *does* take the process and experience of the participant as its epicentre of interest, that *does* focus the process and experience of PD on the situated concerns, needs, and puzzles of practice (Munby & Russell, 1995) of the individual teacher, and that *does* position that individual teacher as a professional "learner" enquiring onto his or her own practice in a broader cultural context, is that of action research. In the narratives that follow we outline three examples of the action research model in action, and the variations in mode that they employed.

## Example 1: Teachers as test pilots

For over 80 years, The New Zealand Correspondence School has provided a traditional correspondence education to students living in remote parts of New Zealand. Throughout this time, the fundamental form of provision had remained the same. Instruction was embedded in printed resources, with exercises and assignments for the students being exchanged by post.

The failure of the school to embrace the opportunities provided by online technologies to challenge the pedagogy inherent in this process was highlighted in a 1998 report of the Education Review Office, which found that the school had not moved sufficiently with the times, and that a more individualised, responsive, and flexible approach was required. A major restructuring of the School thus began in 2000, focused on how technologies might foster a rethinking of the pedagogy of distance teaching inherent in the paper-based modes of delivery. This started with the creation of a two-year research and development pilot within the school known as the *eSection*.

Run as a separate unit within the School, eSection's role was to act as a centre of innovation whose goals were to identify the pedagogical implications of moving distance education from a print to an online base, to challenge the pedagogical assumptions and practices encouraged by a print-based mode of distance schooling, and to recommend technical and systems infrastructures most appropriate to these new pedagogies. As a PD model, eSection was an example of action research for organisational change (Carr & Kemmis, 1986).

There was no established best practice in online learning operating at the School, and it was eSection's job over a period of 2–3 years to experimentally test what this best practice could become. Each of the 15 eSection staff was engaged in an action research project focused on an aspect of e-learning specific to their particular teaching context. The teachers were to disseminate their findings within the School during the project, and after the pilot period were to return to their various Departments as change agents to enculturate e-learning more broadly across the School. External facilitation of the research by an experienced action research facilitator provided methodological support, workshops, and regular reviews of key findings in each cycle of the process.

LITERATURE ESSENTIALS

## *Defining principles of action research*

Internationally, approaches to teacher action research have rather different geneses in different jurisdictions. In the UK, for example, action research originated primarily as a method for situated curriculum development (Stenhouse, 1981; Elliot, 1991; Somekh, 2005). In Australasia, it is most often characterised as a practical tool that individual teachers and teacher communities use to solve problems of their daily pedagogical practice (Kemmis & McTaggart, 1988; Robinson, 1993; Ham & Kane 2004; Zuber-Skerritt, 1996). In the US the term is more closely associated with the general reflective practice movement encapsulated in the work of Brookfield (1995), Argyris and Schön (1974), and others.

Whatever flavour of action research one prefers, there is an emerging consensus around a common core of defining principles that characterize teacher action research. In education, at least, *action research* usually refers to iterative empirical enquiry in which practitioners investigate some aspects of their own professional practice in order to improve that practice. Within this, common principles or characteristics define action research as a model for teacher professional learning:

- Action research is a form of *reflective practitioner enquiry*. It involves a commitment to practitioner reflection and enquiry as being all of the mode, the purpose, and the culture of professional development in an organisation.

- Action research is highly *situated*. Research questions derive from the daily practice of teachers, and consist of the questions puzzling the teacher practitioner rather than the research preoccupations of any outside researchers.

- Action research is a form of *self-study*. An action research enquiry may involve the collection and analysis of data about and from others, but only insofar as it has relevance for the practice of the actor-researcher. One does not *action research* others.

- Action research is *problem-based*. The impetus to undertake it derives from a perceived need in the researcher to solve a particular problem or puzzle of their practice, and not merely a generalised *desire to know*.

- Action research is a form of *empirical investigation*. It involves the ongoing, planned gathering and analysis of data by practitioners about their own teaching practices.

- Action research is *cyclical and iterative*. The research process is based on recurring cycles of action, observation, reflection/analysis, and further action.

*(Continued)*

## LITERATURE ESSENTIALS

*(Continued)*

- Action research is *empowering*. It provides teachers with the reflective enquiry processes and tools by which they can identify, reveal, and resolve institutional and other constraints on effective practice that they will be able to apply to other puzzles of practice in the future.

- Many also argue that the process should be *collaborative*, either being a collaboration among colleagues investigating the same basic phenomenon together, or being a collaboration between a teacher and a mentor knowledgeable in the process and the field of investigation.

- Many, though not all, argue that the findings of action research are typically *shared* or *published* with a wider teacher community through various forms of publication or presentation.

*(For a range of perspectives on the nature and role of action research in education see Stenhouse, 1981; Elliot, 1991; Somekh, 2005; Carr & Kemmis, 1986; McNiff, Lomax, & Whitehead, 1996; Mills, 2003; Zuber-Skerrit, 1996; Ham & Kane, 2004; Robinson, 1993.)*

---

OE is an acronym for 'Overseas Experience,' very common in Australasia. It refers to the tendency for young people after graduating high school or university to go on an extended period of overseas travel and work before they settle down.

The explorations of their online teaching led to a noticeable shift in the teachers' pedagogics, from a highly instructivist style in their dealings with paper-based lesson resources to a much more constructivist one in the online environment. They universally reported a far greater degree of participation by students in their learning in the latter, and a much greater sense of student-centeredness. Moreover, through the process of reflecting on the experiences of the teachers and learners in the pilot, the eSection team worked together to develop a common pedagogical philosophy to underpin their activities and to inform their work with colleagues in other areas of the school. The result was the "Learner-centred, digitally minded" vision statement that has now become the Correspondence School's strap line. After the two year pilot, the role of the original eSection staff evolved within a large-scale professional development programme known as the BigOE, in which the eSection members contributed their expertise in a PD programme for all 350 teachers at the School.

### Ken, secondary school teacher

*Year 10–11 science students*

**Investigation:** How can I best create and apply the use of reusable learning objects in secondary science teaching?

**Findings:** My initial idea of using HTML files for building online Reusable Learning Objects (RLOs) proved to be the most successful one. The modular nature of the RLO makes its incorporation into learning programs a very simple process. My next question is how can I design online RLOs so that students can use them most effectively?

### Pauline, kindergarten teacher

*Pre-school students*

**Investigation:** How can I use ICT to foster a community of learning for the parent families that I work with?

**Findings:** I found parents were very keen to use the online environment as a place to share and exchange ideas and resources to support the learning with their students. The shared document areas and frequently asked questions were more popular than the open forums, although the forums were used by a core of parents which were in turn read by a much wider group.

### Suzanne, secondary school teacher

*Year 10–11 English students*

**Investigation:** How can I use mixed media to enable a more personalised approach to working with distance students?

**Findings:** While I initially focused on using ICT to create invidivualised work-sheets for my students, my findings identified the immediacy of contact and response to students in the online environment as being of most value. I then went on to look at developing ICT-based templates that could be easily populated to suit individual needs.

# Example 2: Teachers as self-developers

Since 1999, New Zealand has implemented a national programme of funded professional development for teachers on integrating ICTs known as the Information and Communications Technologies Professional Development (ICTPD) School Clusters programme. Under this initiative, central funding for teacher technology professional development is devolved to small groups of schools, as both producers and consumers of their own PD programmes, which have committed to a cluster model of working together for the benefit of teachers in all of the schools. The funds may be spent only on teacher professional development, not to defray schools' hardware, software, or infrastructure costs. Teachers are involved in the programmes for up to three years. No particular delivery mode, or model, is mandated for the cluster's PD programme, and applicants for ICTPD funds develop and propose their own forms of delivery.

In one of the recent programmes, a range of action research or self-study projects was undertaken by teachers from various clusters as their chosen form of professional development. About 40 teachers or cluster facilitators initially volunteered to investigate their own best practice in relation to some aspect of ICT use in the teaching and learning process. The teacher-researchers were given one day's release from teaching duties per term for up to three years, and were supported with resources on research methodology and once-per-term school visits from a research mentor from a College of Education. About 20 of the teachers completed their extended action research project into their own integration of ICTs with students, and of these 12 were subsequently published (Ham, Moeau, Williamson-Leadley, Toubat, and Winter, 2005).

Taken as a group, the action researchers' reports provide rich case study evidence which exemplifies, personalises, and puts into a variety of contexts how technology integration actually played out in individual teachers' professional lives during the PD programmes, and therefore the impact of the action research process itself on their own classroom practice. In this sense, their research reports can be read not so much as stories about teachers' growing technical ability with ICTs, or their growing confidence as ICT users, nor indeed their more frequent classroom use of ICTs. Rather they are best read as self-reflective stories of individual teachers coming to grips with what constitutes quality and value in teaching, and what it is that might constitute productive learning when students use ICTs in classes. The ICT-based activities investigated provide the context for these reflections, but they are not the *substance*. The substance is denoted by the much more pedagogically oriented phenomena than the studies addressed. They are, at essence, studies of things like equity, integration, quality teaching, information literacy, peer tutoring, narrative, whole school development, and so on, not studies of ICTs. Moreover, in critically investigating such phenomena in the context of their own practices, the teachers themselves found they moved beyond a preoccupation with ICTs, per se, to a preoccupation with more fundamental aspects of what for them constitutes quality teaching and learning in general.

## Paula, primary school teacher
### Year 3–4 students

**Investigation:** Am I optimising computer use in my classroom to support our school's PD focus on what is powerful learning and what is powerful to learn? I defined optimising as meaning what I could do to increase the frequency, variety, and quality of computer use in my classroom.

**Findings:** I have decided that using computers in my classroom needs to become much more part of my regular planning to have the most effect. Increasing the *quality* of computer use in my classroom was more problematic than increasing its frequency and variety. Optimising quality in my students' ICT use involved fostering active participation and motivation among learners; deliberately developing social and cooperative skills; allowing learners to create, interpret, and organise knowledge; and encouraging visual forms of presentation. For me as the teacher, moreover, *powerful learning* was seen in my using conscious reflective practice to improve my teaching.

## Pip, primary school teacher
### Year 1 (new entrant) students

**Investigation:** Most of my colleagues and I were still building units around the computer programs rather than using the computer as a tool to enhance learning opportunities for our pupils. I therefore investigated how I could truly integrate ICTs by looking at how I could use one single software package (Kid Pix) in a variety of units of work over the year.

**Findings:** What I learned as a result of the research went well beyond pragmatic considerations of teaching strategies and management techniques. My own belief now is that for ICTs to be truly integrated they must be a planned part of everyday teaching and learning, and must be embedded in teaching that fosters creativity and higher order thinking. I also believe that the keys to successful integration are not just the use of a wide range of teaching strategies, systematic inclusion of ICT in planning, and careful consideration of management and routines, but also the use of ICTs for different purposes: as an information source, as a means of communication and presentation, and as a context for thinking. Indeed, all the things that made the integration of ICTs effective for me were in fact also the keys to good practice in any teaching and learning activity.

## Jill, secondary school teacher
### Year 11 English students

**Investigation:** What are the specific information skills that my students acquire when using ICTs for research? What do my colleagues and students see as the value added by using ICT based information resources, and how do ICTs compare as sources of information with print and other media in my own and my students' minds?

**Findings:** We were surprised at the relatively low level of literacy skills, strategies, and information literacy demonstrated by both classes, especially when using online resources. To this extent the study confirmed a suspicion that students may have been allowed to "run before they learned to walk" with ICTs, and our belief that information skills are not yet well taught at all levels or subject areas in our school. The main learning for me was that unless there is shared knowledge and understanding among staff of the need for an information literate school community, and unless information literacy skills are actually taught and practised as part of whole school process, learning with ICTs may still be shallow learning.

## Example 3: The collaborative sabbatical

The E-Learning Fellowship was a study award scheme funded by the New Zealand Ministry of Education in which a group of up to 10 pre-school, primary, and secondary teachers across the country were released for a school year to undertake practitioner research into some aspect of their students' use of ICTs for learning. Begun in 2004, the scheme originated in a desire to recognise the innovative work of teachers at the forefront of using ICTs for better learning in schools, a desire to give those teachers the time and space to push the boundaries of their own experience and understandings of e-learning, and a desire to involve them in practitioner research projects that might be of interest and use to their teacher peers. Research, as it were, by teachers, for teachers.

Under the scheme, the selected Fellows were brought together as a professional community, intensively mentored by experienced research mentors, and supported by business or other academic partners. The e-Fellows define and conduct a research or innovation project of interest to themselves, and in the year following the Fellowship, share their findings with the wider teaching community. The teachers conduct studies in their own schools with their own students, but they also meet together for up to eight weeks over the year in facilitated professional learning workshops, working together as a collaborative community and assisting each other with their respective enquiries. Thus its description here as the collaborative sabbatical.

As was also the case for the other action research models outlined above, the focus of the e-Fellows' self-studies was not essentially about teaching with or through ICTs. They were about whether, and what, and how, their students might learn with or through ICTs, and they are about how they as teacher-researchers went about identifying the nature and worth of that learning.

This identification of student learning outcomes in the context of ICT-mediated student activities was one central goal of the E-Learning Fellowship programme, and was a common theme across all of their research questions. It was the concept and shared purpose that bound what might otherwise have been seen as a rather eclectic or even disconnected set of projects, undertaken by teachers from different school sectors, and with a wide range of specific research interests. What would a teacher of senior secondary school physics from the top of the country (having a long and meaningful professional collaboration) have in common with a New Entrant teacher from the bottom? Not physics, of course, nor handwriting; not high stakes assessment nor pre-writing skills, not quantum theory nor basic number recognition; but learning. In this case, it is the learning that occurs when students use ICTs.

The second goal of the Fellowship programme was to provide a formative professional learning experience for the e-Fellows themselves, stretching and challenging their knowledge and understanding of e-learning and providing the opportunity for them to reflect deeply on their own and their colleagues' e-learning practices. In this sense the stories they published can be read not just as a set of findings from e-learning research, but also as a window into what the Fellows learned about themselves and their own e-learning practices as a result of trying to isolate the learning that might or might not have been a feature of e-learning for their students.

## Indira, intermediate school teacher
### Year 7–8 gifted underachieving students

**Investigation:** How can the use of high-end multimedia production tools foster creativity in my underachieving 10–12 year old students?

**Findings:** High-end multimedia production software may be best described as a significant enabler in respect of the creative process. There was very little by way of teacher intervention or teaching about creativity in these lessons, and yet the students still used the tools to express themselves and to be creative in ways that it is difficult to claim would have been possible in other, more traditional media. The specific enablers inherent in the software were found to be the range and choice of functions available, the visual accuracy offered, the automation of menial tasks, its judgemental neutrality, the fostering of multimodality in expression, the inherent provisionality of any product, and, above all perhaps, its inherent interactivity. Using the software, the students demonstrated all of the key characteristics of creativity outlined in the literature, most notably: producing original ideas and products; not being afraid to be different or wrong; a keen sense of humour and seeing humour in the unusual; and displaying intellectual playfulness, imagination, and fantasy.

## *Jo, kindergarten teacher*
*Pre-school students*

**Investigation:** How might my Kindergarten students use ICTs to foster complexity, connections, and continuity in their storytelling?

**Findings:** I found that the desire to literally tell their stories through multimedia, and to communicate their ideas independently of text conventions, led these children into greater experimentation and exploration in their storytelling, and also stimulated an enthusiasm for experimenting with a range of other ICTs. It was hard to tell in my research whether the desire to tell more complex stories led to more complex uses of ICT or whether the desire to use the ICTs led to complexity of children's stories. Possibly both occurred.

## *Keri, primary school teacher*
*Year 1–2 students*

**Investigation:** How could I use ICTs to get more focus when my students were engaged in the forming intentions talk part of their writing process?

**Findings:** In my research the computer provided the environment, excuse, direction, and opportunity for most of the students to talk about their writing. As teachers we: scaffolded a learning environment, fostered social and collaborative skills, and modelled verbal forming intentions and the writing process. We supported with time, space, direction, permission to talk, and the application of the ICT tool to the learning experience. I felt the major key to the success of the ICT in enhancing the children's talk was in fact their own perception of the computer activity. They viewed the computer activity as fun, remembered the learning experiences as not work, and knew it to be a context for collaboration. The students acknowledged the computer as a tool, which you engage in and talk about, at, and around.

# The three exemplars as professional development models

As organisational modes of PD, all three programmes used different tactics and outwardly looked different. They were differently resourced in terms of the funding and release time available to teachers. They differed in the amounts of time and frequency of contact with each other and their mentors. They varied in where the PD sessions took place, sometimes being held in teachers' schools, and sometimes in external live-in workshop venues. Sometimes the focus was on working together and sometimes it was on working as individuals. The groups of teacher-researchers were constituted from very different schooling sectors, and had widely varied subject specialisations. And, in two of the programmes, they were physically scattered across the country.

As models of PD, however, the only significant differences among the three initiatives related to the extent to which the action research component was embedded in the teachers' daily teaching lives. The eSection teachers merged action research into what they did; the ICTPD group added action research onto what they did; and for the e-Fellows, the action research was what they did. Beyond this, they shared more commonality as a PD model than difference. The overall purposes, broad methodology, and professional development cultures involved were the same. In all three, action research was seen as being the professional development. In all three, the teachers' individual studies were consciously framed within larger, common questions about effective e-learning pedagogies and about the identification of learning outcomes when students used new technologies. All involved a commitment to making the PD experience authentic and empowering for teachers. All based their enquiries in the situated problems of the teacher-researchers themselves. All were experienced as collaborations with at least one or two others. And all involved a significant level of active mentoring from internal and/or external mentors. All, in other words, exemplified the ecological, self-enquiry PD models that Fullan (1996) and others argue are most effective in bringing about teacher change.

This does not mean that the process was an easy one for the teachers. Many of the teachers found that the additional demands on their time and professional energy of simultaneously teaching and also researching teaching (or in Schön's [1983] terms, of simultaneously reflecting *on* action and reflecting *in* action), were excessive, and all found it challenging. However, for those who saw the process through, what the experience of action research facilitated, and what the teachers themselves commented on most in evaluation interviews across all three programmes, was not so much increased ICT skills, but increased pedagogical awareness in general. They universally reported that the experience had, above all else, given them a tool with which they could better investigate and understand, and even critique, the connection between students' use of ICTs and their learning. They felt, in short, that it had helped them become more self-critical and more autonomous as reflective ICT practitioners.

## Implications for professional developers

Traditionally, those who provided professional development to teachers were considered to be trainers. Now, their roles have broadened immensely … they have to be facilitators, assessors, resource brokers, mediators of learning, designers, and coaches, in addition to being trainers when appropriate. Practitioners of professional development, often teachers themselves, have a new and wider variety of practices to choose from in meeting the challenging learning needs of educators …
(Loucks-Horlsey, 1996, n.p.)

In this concluding discussion, we examine action research as professional development from the perspective of the teacher educators responsible for mentoring the action and the research, as opposed to that of the teachers responsible for conducting them.

One of the features of all three of our examples of action research as a model of professional learning was that they all involved a significant element of external mentoring, and it was perhaps no coincidence that the arguably least successful of the three models (the ICTPD cluster example) was also the least intensively mentored. Even though there was an emphasis in the designs on the teachers solving their own particular and situated problems, on teachers asking their own questions and gathering evidence about their own practices, and on action research as a form of self-improvement through self-study, that did not mean that it was a process undertaken in isolation or unsupported. In all three cases, the model of action research involved significant support from external mentors with experience as inservice teacher educators knowledgeable about the integration of new technologies, and experienced as action researchers themselves.

In the examples cited, two of the authors acted in this mentor role. Thus, at the same time as the teachers in these programmes were action researching their practice as teachers of children, we in turn were conducting our own action research into our process and practices as the teacher educators or professional developers facilitating their development. Our own action research was framed broadly around an emerging core principle of much current work on teacher change and teacher professional learning, especially where that change or learning is aimed at fostering reflective practice and self-enquiry in teachers or teacher educators. This principle may be expressed thus:

> That mentoring for change in teachers' professional practice is likely to be effective largely insofar as the process of that mentoring addresses the concerns, preoccupations, and needs of the participants in that change; and that those preoccupations, concerns, or needs themselves change as practice changes.

This notion, which is expressed in one meta-analysis of effective inservice teacher education as a principle of contextual responsiveness in facilitating teacher change (New Zealand Ministry of Education, 2006), is central in one way or another to most facilitation models relevant to inservice teacher education. It is manifest in Munby and Russell's (1995) injunction to frame reflective practice around teachers' own puzzles of practice; it is explicit in Bruner's notion of scaffolding and in Vygotsky's zone of proximal development; it is implicit in much of the literature on situated cognition and the co-construction of knowledge; and, of course, it is central to the literature on concerns-based adoption models of teacher learning (Hall & Hord, 2001).

As one of our mentees put it, mentoring action research, and indeed mentoring reflective practice in general, is more a matter of responding to the ever-changing needs of the mentee than it is a matter of transferring knowledge or expertise. Being an effective professional developer is about knowing your stuff; but it is even more about paying attention. The research question we as professional developers asked, therefore, was: in facilitating action research as professional learning, what should we as mentors be paying attention to, or be responsive about? What are the main challenges that our teacher mentees faced in conducting action research as a form of professional development, and, therefore, what challenges do these in turn create for us as professional developers?

After analysing the record of our many mentoring sessions with action researchers during these and other projects, our conclusion is that there are six interconnected but conceptually distinguishable puzzles of practice that preoccupy action researchers during this kind of professional development process, and to which those responsible for the professional learning of others need to be attentive. These six practitioner preoccupations may in turn be divided into those focused on the enquirer and/or process of enquiry, and those focused on the evolving relationship between mentor and mentee. These primary concerns and challenges, which we are calling the Six Ms of Mentoring Critically Reflective Practice, are listed below.

## Reflection—Inquiry-focused preoccupations

**Meaning.** Teachers expressed a range of concerns about how they could make sense of professional experience generally, and how they could make sense of the evidence-base gathered during reflective enquiries in particular. Much of this involved preoccupations with identifying a dilemma of practice that was worthy of investigation; with making connections between their personal experience and the body of literature and theory; and, especially, with how to identify the learning outcomes of one's own teaching actions. Typical questions in which teachers articulated these concerns included: What is it about my practice that I want to find out about? What data shall I gather and analyse? How should I analyse it? What big picture theories does my experience relate to? How do we know when we have enough data? What does this mean for my practice as a result? Why should anyone else be interested?

**Me-ness.** These preoccupations were about the conceptual difficulty and personal challenge of becoming the subject of one's own enquiry. They were about keeping the focus in critical reflection on the practitioner identifying and critiquing their own practice, and they were also about ensuring that the issues addressed and questions asked were authentic and owned by the teacher-learner. These concerns were often expressed in questions like: Is this about "me" or "them" (i.e., students)? How do I gather evidence about "me" while I am teaching "them"? How do I deal with challenges to my own (espoused) theories, thinking, and practice? Am I asking questions that are important to "me"?

**Manageability.** A further set of teacher preoccupations were centred on the practical manageability of conducting formalized self-study and self-enquiry at the same time as, and as an integral part of, doing their normal job. The concern here was about making it all seem doable and realistic, and was articulated in questions like: What should I focus on, and what can I leave out? How do I keep my research questions manageable? How do I deal with the expansion of workload issue? How do I manage my time?

## Relationship-focused preoccupations

**Momentum.** This preoccupation was about maintaining and sustaining a reflective enquiry over an extended period of time, through successive reflection-action cycles, and in the face of the continuous distractions of daily professional life. Key questions here included: What are my intrinsic motivations and levels of self-efficacy in this? How do I deal with constraints of time? What if my questions change over time? How do I deal with new dilemmas of practice that arise from, or while resolving, others?

**eMpathy.** Many studies have shown that the affective and cultural domains are a vital consideration in adult learning. This set of concerns was about feeling safe and secure— not so much about the teaching process as about the mentoring process itself. It was also about balancing the needs for both support and challenge in the mentor–mentee relationship, and, when the research is collaborative, about individual's roles and identities within the group. Related questions included: How do I fit and what are my roles within this group? How do I "feel" about my practice and how do I feel about the process of professional learning and self-critique? Am I safe doing this?

**eMpowerment.** These preoccupations were about managing the inevitable change in mentor and mentee roles over time, about managing the changing balance of authority in the relationship, and about moving the mentor mentee relationship forward in ways that decreased dependence and fostered autonomous, collaborative action over time. Typical puzzlings about power and authority were: What is my level of (in)dependence here? In relation to what? What professional status do I have/feel I have within the organization in relation to those with whom I am working? What professional status do I bring to the professional learning activity? What do I know already, what do I need in the way of new knowledge, and what does my mentor know that can help me?

# Conclusion

As we redefine the roles and functions of inservice teacher educators, moving such a definition from being trainers of teachers, or even teachers who teach teachers, toward being teachers' facilitators, mentors, or coaches, then mentoring critical reflection through self-study techniques such as action research increasingly becomes a focus of the enterprise. And when mentoring evidence-based reflective practice is the focus of the activity then there are certain preoccupations of professional learner practice that need attending to by the professional mentors more than others.

In our study we found that, in mentoring teachers' action research, we needed to give primacy of attention to their changing preoccupations and needs as professional learners rather than our preoccupations as professional educators. We also found that being contextually responsive as a professional developer is primarily about managing the enquiry process and about managing the professional relationship between professional developer and teacher, mentor, and mentee. It is not primarily about transferring what either they, or we, already know about curriculum content, or about ICTs, or even about teaching.

We conclude that teachers' predominant concerns when undertaking action research as a model of professional development in ICTs revolved around making that professional learning experience self-focused, contextually meaningful and manageable, and around managing the relationship between mentee and mentor in a way that is emotionally and culturally empathetic, sustained over time, and, ultimately, empowering for the teacher. It is these six preoccupations that we propose dominate mentee thinking when undertaking PD to develop their reflective practice, and that thus need in turn to become the preoccupations of mentors' practice in facilitating it.

## GETTING STARTED RESOURCES

eFellows. (n.d.). Retrieved October 30, 2007 from www.efellows.org.nz

Thirty or more e-Fellows' progress and New Zealand ICTPD teachers' action research reports are accessible at the e-Fellows Blog and Web site.

Mills, G. (2006) *Action research. A guide for the teacher researcher.* (3rd ed.). Upper Saddle River, NJ: Merrill Prentice Hall.

This textbook and its accompanying Web site provide a practical, common-sense introduction to action research as a professional enquiry method suitable for educational settings. There is also an instructor version for professors and professional learning mentors that is accessible on registration. The Web site is available at http://wps.prenhall.com/chet_mills_actionres_3

Senese, J. (n.d.). *The Action Research Laboratory.* Retrieved October 31, 2007 from Highland Park High School. Web site: www.d113.lake.k12.il.us/hphs/action/page1.htm

This Web site profiles a group of American high-school teachers who are taking charge of their own professional development by conducting action research projects on their own teaching.

Somekh, B. (2005). *Action Research: A Methodology for Change & Development.* Maidenhead, UK: Open University Press.

One of the few books that provides a rationale for action research as a model of professional learning that is derived largely from the experience of working with teachers involved in technology integration projects. An abstract may be accessed at http://eric.ed.gov/ERICWebPortal/Home.portal by searching for document number ED493196.

University of Kansas. (2005). *The Action Research Network.* Retrieved October 31, 2007 from http://actionresearch.altec.org/index.php3

At this site, professors and mentors can set up group sites and manage students' or mentees' action research papers through the network. There are tools for submitting and reviewing papers and draft reports, and for communicating about the work. The site can also be used to read any and all of the action research studies that have been submitted by teachers from across the U.S. Registration is required.

## chapter 10

# Higher Education Institutions as Partners for Technology Professional Development

*Craig A. Cunningham*
*Louanne Smolin*
  *National-Louis University*

*Sarah McPherson*
  *New York Institute*
  *of Technology*

*Kimberly A. Lawless*
*Josh Radinsky*
  *University of Illinois at Chicago*

*Scott W. Brown*
  *University of Connecticut*

*Nicole Zumpano*
  *Chicago Public Schools*

## abstract

THIS CHAPTER DESCRIBES three projects where collaborative planning and implementation of technology integration professional development activities involved partners and leaders from higher education and other agencies. The chapter includes reflections on program strategies, successes, and limitations, as well as comparisons between these and other programs for the development of inservice teachers. It additionally provides examples of strategies and products created, explores the issues inherent in developing evaluations for university–school partnerships, provides evaluation strategies, and offers lessons learned that support replication of the models.

The three model projects described in this chapter demonstrate the possibilities for professional development when K–12 teachers are supported systematically by collaborations with higher-education institutions and other partners. The projects all represent higher-education partnerships with K–12 schools; substantial, long-term funding; collaborative planning; a focus on curriculum (subject matter); a variety of incentives for participants; follow-up components; and outside evaluators. Briefly, the three projects described in this chapter are:

1. The Web Institute for Teachers (WIT), an intensive summer professional development program for urban inservice teachers, held at the University of Chicago from 1997 until 2004, earning mention as an exemplary project in ISTE's *Connecting Curriculum and Technology* (ISTE, 2000). WIT focused on helping teachers to access, use, and create Web-based learning materials such as WebQuests and curriculum webs.

2. Project TITUS (Teachers Integrating Technology in Urban Schools), received the 2004 American Association of Colleges for Teacher Education (AACTE) Best Practice Award for the Innovative Use of Technology. The project brought together K–12 teachers, teacher-education faculty from the University of Illinois at Chicago, and technology consultants to design technology-infused curriculum modules.

3. The Maryland Technology Academy (MTA) Program, an intensive professional development component of The Maryland Technology Consortium (MTC), was a collaboration of the Maryland State Department of Education, Johns Hopkins University Center for Technology in Education, and Towson University. The MTA was established to build technology integration leaders who could promote and support use of technology in schools throughout the state.

## The Web Institute for Teachers

The Web Institute for Teachers (WIT) was hosted by the Chicago Public Schools/ University of Chicago Internet Project (CUIP), and took place during the summers from 1997 through 2004, with a majority of its teacher-participants from the Chicago Public School (CPS) system. The seminar was four hours a day, five days a week, for four weeks, providing teachers with 80 hours of instruction in building Web-based lessons, WebQuests, and curriculum webs. More than 700 teachers participated in WIT during its eight years of existence. The program evolved from one homeroom—or section—with a total of 22 participants and two college professors as instructors in 1997 to its peak in 2003, when the program involved 16 homerooms, each homeroom consisting of 15–24 participants (for a total of 270 participants), a lab assistant, and two instructors (called mentors). The Institute took place for the most part on or near the University of Chicago campus, allowing teachers intense time to focus on the program rather than the interruptions that naturally occur when in their own school settings.

Originally focusing on one curriculum strand, over time different strands were developed to account for the variety of participant skill levels and needs (Cunningham, Dairyko, & Boxer, 2000). The emergence of diverse strands is an example of how ongoing reflection and a quest for continuous improvement influenced the program. The basic strand was intended for teachers who had emergent or limited technological skills (often including no experience using the Web for teaching), and focused on using existing Web resources and building new Web resources with simple, freely available Web-editing software. Teachers in the advanced strand spent more time engaged in curriculum planning and built more elaborate curriculum webs accompanied by in-depth teaching guides (Cunningham & Billingsley, 2006). Advanced members worked with more sophisticated Web-editing software, allowing members to create more complex and interactive Web sites. Each strand of WIT had a set of online learning modules created by program mentors and utilized in a sequence based on the needs of their homeroom participants.

Mentors were for the most part K–12 teachers and often former participants in the program, meaning that they were already skilled in the development of curriculum webs, teaching guides, and learning modules. The mentors could easily identify with what the participants were experiencing in the Institute and could help problem-solve how the curricula would play out in the classroom. Two mentors in every section allowed for one mentor to move about the room while the other was conducting whole-group activities. the personalities of the mentors to balance out, one mentor to handle technical or other problems while the other continued with the scheduled activities, and in general for the two to be able to support each other. This arrangement also allowed for some on-the-job training, as experienced Lead Mentors were paired with those who had less experience conducting teacher professional development. Weekly meetings of all mentors, together with the director, assistant director, technical coordinator, and lab assistants, proved to be key in contributing to a smoothly running and responsive program.

Another important component of the program was the weekly plenary sessions, in which everyone from all of the sections and strands came together for a lecture by various outside speakers and a catered lunch. Plenary speakers (including instructional technology leaders such as David Warlick [2002], Diana Joseph with Cunningham, [2004], and Vivi Lachs [2000]) addressed topics related to Web-based education, but often included extension topics, such as museum Web sites or relevant academic research like the future of the Internet or the importance of building motivation into curriculum webs. Audiences participated in question and answer segments, and during the final plenary session of each year, selected outstanding projects were showcased as "Director's Picks."

## Planning WIT

A program as intense and rigorous as WIT requires a great deal of planning. There are many details to decide upon: topics, software, schedule, prerequisites for participants, outcomes, and who will teach participants. During the spring prior to each Institute, potential mentors and other support personnel began planning the summer program. These spring trainings began by reviewing topics that were covered the previous year: what worked, what didn't, and what could be improved upon. At this point a general scope and sequence was formed. Although there was a lead developer for each learning module, there was also a critical friend—another mentor who would walk through the module, making sure the content was accurate, user friendly, and complete. The role of the mentor during spring training was not only curriculum creator but also decision maker, as they shaped their sections based on the needs of its participants and not around a set curriculum decided upon by someone else. Because of this approach, mentors became more vested in the quality of the program.

Planning continued throughout the summer institute. One day each week during the Institute, participants were given lab time to work on their projects while all of the mentors met for staff meetings and reflections on the logistics of the program. In some instances, aspects of the program were being changed up until the last two days.

Ongoing planning from year to year resulted in a number of improvements to WIT: a standardized template was developed for the curriculum plan for each Web-based lesson and unit; participants developed an implementation plan that took into account their local technology availability and other contextual factors; special how-to guides were developed for each task necessary for posting a home page, WebQuest, or curriculum Web; supplemental units were developed on the use of operating systems; relevant software was made available either directly on the WIT server or installed in each lab used by WIT; and a CD was provided with all of the software and learning modules for participants to use at home. The gradual accumulation of such improvements illustrates a perhaps obvious but important point: professional development usually gets better with subsequent implementations.

## WIT participant experience

Teachers interested in WIT submitted a paper application and an online supplemental application, in part to test the applicant's skills using the Web. CPS applicants were accepted to ensure that as many CPS schools as possible were represented, and then according to prior knowledge and experience. Participants received a stipend of $1,000, upon completion of the Institute, as well as T-shirts, books, catered lunches on selected days, and software.

Everything associated with the program can be accessed from WIT's Web site at webinstituteforteachers.org, which includes learning modules, homeroom schedules, mini-lessons, and other pertinent information. The benefit of putting learning modules online was twofold: to make users more comfortable with navigating the Web, and to allow participants to access learning modules at their leisure. An additional benefit was that participants could view any homeroom to see what was happening with members in sections that were not their own. All products produced in WIT are public domain, except those produced in 2003 by some participants funded through the Chicago Public Schools, when a contract between CUIP and CPS required some limitations on produced materials.

Each participant in WIT was given space on the Web server, with their own directory and private passwords to access their space. Teams were given a common directory to house projects, meaning that any member of the team could make changes, with or without the consent of team members (this created some problems, but nightly backups prevented most disasters). This server space remains available to all former participants, and over the years, former participants have used their space to create additional projects, modify personal home pages, and allow their students a chance to be showcased on the Web. The following site is one such example of how a French teacher has used her space with her students: http://webinstituteforteachers.org/~ddelaney/.

Along with Web-authoring tools, participants were exposed to other forms of technology including e-mail accounts with the training to successfully utilize them; homeroom e-mail lists; and a handouts book created by mentors so members had directions at their fingertips, relieving the stress some felt with using the technology.

WIT was comprised of more than just mentors and participants; there were multiple layers of support woven into the program. When participants had a problem, the first line of defense was the teaching assistants, followed by the mentors. This provided three people per section. Most problems were minor, involving uploading Web pages and forgotten steps in Web page design. When more significant problems arose, participants were able to contact the technology coordinator (who also served as server administrator), the assistant director (who prior to this position was a mentor), or the director. Challenges within the program, be they personal or curriculum issues, were addressed (when appropriate) by all the mentors at the weekly meetings, allowing for different points of view as well as differences in expertise.

Follow-up to the summer institute included meetings held during the subsequent school year; one-on-one and small-group trainings provided by the staff of CUIP (for those participants who worked in the CUIP-supported schools); homeroom e-mail lists; and direct e-mail support available from the mentors, director, and technical coordinator.

## WIT funding and evaluation

WIT was funded using a variety of mechanisms. The first two years were paid for by Eisenhower Math and Science grants from the U.S. Department of Education. During the third through eighth years, most members were sponsored by CPS, with additional funding received from the University of Chicago Women's Board, the Joyce Foundation, the participants' private and public schools, and tuition paid directly by some participants.

Internal evaluations of WIT were conducted each year through participant surveys, an online feedback form, and weekly reports from each mentor. Also, in 2001, WIT was evaluated by Rockman et al., as part of a larger evaluation of the Chicago Public Schools/ University of Chicago Internet Project. Data consistently showed that participants valued the program highly. For example, in 2002, in response to the statement "WIT 2002 is among the best professional development experiences I have ever had," 83 strongly agreed, 45 agreed, 0 were not sure, 2 disagreed, and 2 strongly disagreed, for an agreement rating of 97%.

However, the impact on the participants' teaching in their own classrooms is much less clear. Anecdotal evidence indicates that some WIT participants were transformed by their teaching and continue to use their server accounts to deliver new content in new ways. Many participants benefited enormously from the 80 hours of supported technology use. However, six months after the conclusion of WIT 2003, 201 of 285 participants had not logged into their server accounts to change their pages. This does not indicate whether they had *used* the pages they had created during WIT, but indicates that most participants did not modify their pages or create new ones after WIT was over.

A more comprehensive study of the impact of WIT on teaching and learning was never funded or completed. However, some final reflections can be made about the factors leading to a successful program and also about its limitations. Of chief importance to WIT's success was the continuous improvement of the program from year to year, fostered by the systematic involvement of the instructional support staff and a willingness to welcome and embrace participant feedback. Also important was attention paid to each participant's learning needs at every stage, and a multitiered system of support that extended beyond the individual homeroom. The constructivist instructional model, in which participants planned and built materials specifically designed for their schools and classrooms, resulted in high levels of engagement and persistence toward successful fulfillment of the program's high expectations. This intense engagement in technologically demanding work for 80 hours during the summer was perhaps WIT's greatest contribution to the professional development of its participants.

WIT's primary limitations were the lack of systematic day-to-day follow-up in those schools not included in CUIP, the inclusion of significant numbers of teacher-participants who were not necessarily ready to embed Web-page creation into their professional lives, and a lack of attention to the specific pedagogical demands of varying subject matter. The ready availability today of forms- and template-based teacher Web pages and WebQuests (through Edline.com, TeacherWeb.com, or Teachnology.com, for example), would allow participants to focus more on pedagogy and subject matter rather than the technical aspects of Web pages and servers.

## Teachers integrating technology in urban schools

The University of Illinois Project Teachers Integrating Technology in Urban Schools (TITUS), a US Department of Education PT[3] grant, incorporated collaborative curriculum design into professional development. Through a unique university–school partnership, K–12 teachers, teacher-education faculty, and technology consultants collaborated to design technology-infused curriculum units and lessons using the curriculum design process as the source of professional development. The design process helped teachers to use technology in ways that reflect domain-centered instruction grounded in effective classroom practices.

Project TITUS incorporated curriculum development into professional development with faculty in teacher education programs, Project TITUS facilitators, and Chicago

Public School teachers collaborating to design curriculum lessons and units of instruction that could be used across university and school contexts, including K–12 classrooms, university teacher preparation classes, and field-based experiences. The purpose of the collaborative was to seamlessly "tie" technology and content within instruction that could be implemented across university and school boundaries.

## Description of the collaborative design process

The TITUS approach was to engage university and school participants in curriculum design communities of practice, closely centered on the K–12 instructional context. Inherent in this design process was the notion that teachers learn by doing. Therefore, participants conjoined their respective areas of expertise, subject matter knowledge, and pedagogical knowledge of K–12 instruction. Focusing on learning standards and objectives within content areas, they engaged in a planning process with one another that integrated content objectives, pedagogical approaches, and the role of technology. This enabled participants to discuss technology tools in the context of helping their students achieve the identified learning objectives. Though the curriculum lessons produced were valuable products, it was the collaborative design process that offered the greatest potential for transforming instruction. The work of collaboratively designing curriculum activities with unfamiliar technology tools afforded reflection on the goals of instruction, and also provided an opportunity to communicate across university and school boundaries (Radinsky, Smolin, Lawless, & Newman, 2003). The participants developed lessons that used a technology tool (e.g., GIS software) to teach a mode of domain thinking, based on a set of core concepts, skills, and epistemic forms of the domain (Collins & Ferguson, 1993), with specified learning objectives to be taught using the selected technology tools. Therefore, participants learned to use technology in ways that were aligned with domain-centered instruction grounded in effective classroom practices. A key benefit was that the design process modeled thinking about technology as a tool for achieving instructional objectives, rather than an end in itself.

## Professional development structures

The power of merging professional development and curriculum design is that the process can be replicated within a variety of professional development formats or structures. As such, university and school collaborations can be more flexible and organic, based upon particular needs or desired outcomes. TITUS used three main structures: university–school collaborative design teams, academic year workshops, and week-long summer institutes. For the purposes of this chapter, we will discuss the annual professional development summer institute which blends both the traditional workshop format and the curriculum design team approach to professional development. (Please see Radinsky, Smolin, & Lawless, 2005, for information on the other structures.)

During the annual Project TITUS Summer Institute, public school K–12 teachers collaborated with university teacher-education faculty and public school technology consultants to design technology-infused lessons using the design process as a site of professional development. Each day of the institute, participants chose two hands-on workshops to attend from a series of choices. The final hour of each day was devoted to the lesson design process. Participants were organized into cohort groups loosely based on content area and grade level. Attendance in these groups remained consistent over the course of the week, enabling participants from different schools but working in similar disciplines or grade levels (including special education cohort groups) to create a community of practitioners with like interests and experiences. During this design hour, participants created their lessons using a Web-based template that reflects the lesson design approach. The Web-based template can be viewed at http://www2.ed.uic.edu/summer2006/moduledev/ModuleDevIndex.asp

Each day, a different aspect of the planning process, reflected in the template, was discussed. For example, during the first day of the institute, participants analyzed a lesson created by a previous participant. This analysis helped participants understand the alignment between objectives, technology use, step by step activities, and assessments. During days 2 and 3, participants identified the content area objectives around which they planned to develop a lesson and brainstormed assessment techniques relevant for these objectives. Days 4 and 5 were devoted to identifying resources, planning step-by-step activities that also included models of products that their students would be creating, and assessment strategies. All components of these lessons were uploaded to the Web-based database, so that on day 5 participants presented their completed lessons to their cohort peers, inviting commentary and suggestions.

Each step of this week-long process was scaffolded by the Web-based lesson development template and the help of an on-site technology facilitator who discussed the day-to-day activities and what needed to be accomplished by the end of the week. More importantly, the technology facilitator worked one-on-one with each participant providing just-in-time instruction, design suggestions, and resource identification.

Because lessons were shared through the Web, the community of learners who participated in the summer institute was not only sustained but expanded to other teachers. As participants implemented lessons, they were also modeling technology-rich instruction for teacher candidates placed in their classrooms.

## Outcomes

The following sample lesson was developed by a Chicago Public elementary school teacher during our annual Summer Institute. Entitled "The Middle East/India," it was designed to engage students in critical questions surrounding this region of the world, and to engage students in the research process.

Figure 10.1 shows the overview of the unit, identified during the first day of the Institute, and provides specific vital information, including the grade level and subject area, as well as how the unit will be introduced to the students. Participants then continue the design process over the course of the week, aligning objectives and standards to their unit idea; developing detailed activities and technology materials, including templates to be used within the lesson; and designing assessment strategies that are aligned to their objectives.

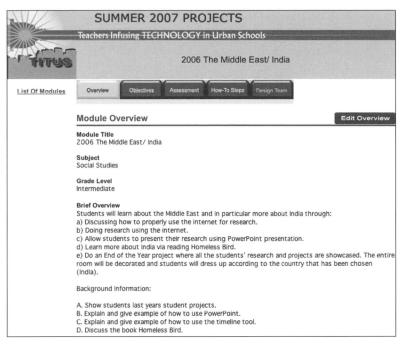

FIGURE 10.1. Unit Overview

Using a design process as the organizational foundation for professional development facilitated the integration of technology in multiple ways. It afforded the opportunity to focus on particular phases of the K–12 planning process, ensuring cohesive alignment between objectives, standards, activities, and assessments. As the focus of design was on content area instruction, it created a situated, authentic context in which participants could incorporate what they have learned in technology workshops to develop a standards-based lesson, rather than a decontextualized focus on a particular technology tool or application. Because workgroups remained intact over the course of the week, participants became a community of practitioners, gaining familiarity with one another's work and supporting each other by sharing ideas and resources, ultimately enhancing teachers' successes with technology integration.

## Project TITUS evaluation

Multiple and varied evaluation strategies were employed to triangulate the effects of our summer institute on teacher behaviors and practices. First, stakeholder evaluation was received through survey data, including a pre- and post-assessment examining the knowledge, attitudes, and behaviors (KAB) of participating teachers. Based on Bloom's taxonomy, the KAB approach examined the cognitive, affective, and behavior components involved in learning (Schrader & Lawless, 2004). If a given professional activity was successful, it increased learners' knowledge of the content, heightened the value or importance they placed upon integrating these new techniques, and increased the number of classroom behaviors related to these new practices. Results of the pre- and post-KAB surveys indicated strong benefits for inservice teachers, including significant gains in knowledge and skill with respect to technology usage (t=4.438, p<.01); attitude toward the importance of technology in the curriculum (t=2.5, p<.05); and behaviors consistent with effective technology integration (t=6.84, p<.01) as a result of participating in the multiple activities associated with the Project TITUS professional development model.

The second evaluation data stream came from a document analysis conducted on lessons developed by mentor teachers during the institute. Lesson plans were sorted into one of four categories of technology integration based upon the Technology Integration Teacher Survey (Smolin, Lawless, Newman, & Jullian, 2002): (1) technology nonuser, (2) technology adopter, (3) technology integrator, and (4) technology innovator. The analysis indicated substantial growth in the level of sophistication in the designs of lessons integrating technology into their classrooms. A Q-sort technique was performed by two independent raters, yielding 97% agreement in ratings; differences were resolved in conference. Results of the sorts indicate that in Year One, approximately 65% of submitted complete lessons were considered to be technology adoption plans (i.e., lessons in which a teacher appropriates a technology resource such as an Internet site or a software application as a supplement to existing curricula). By comparison, over 60% of the lesson plans submitted in Year Two were rated as technology integration plans, a higher level of infusion than technology adoption. These lesson plans use technology to innovate on the learning process, increasing student problem solving, interaction, and engagement.

Observation data obtained from a sample of participating teachers during classroom instruction served as the third data source. For this purpose, project faculty employed an observation protocol based upon the Technology Integration Teacher Survey discussed above (Smolin, Lawless, Newman, & Jullian, 2002). Analysis of the observation protocols indicated increases in teachers' use of both classroom and lab-based technology resources to integrate technology into their curriculum from Year One to Year Two. Of the teachers observed, all were using technology as an extension of their curriculum (technology adoption) rather than as a remediation resource (technology nonuse), which indicates a higher level of pedagogical practice. There was also an increase in the use of technology resources outside of their classroom. Teachers actively created lessons that utilized computer lab resources, frequently coordinating with computer lab teachers to convene class in the lab.

Finally, an online survey and a series of semi-structured focus groups were conducted three months after the institute to gauge long-term impact of the lesson design approach to professional development. Results of the online surveys indicated that a lesson design approach to professional development was having a lasting impact (Smolin, Lawless, & Radinsky, 2006). Not only did they indicate an increase in their sense of self-efficacy (83.4% of the participants considered themselves at least a competent user of educational technology), but the lesson approach also appeared to have an impact on teachers' collaborative efforts: 60.9% reported that they participated on a project team developing curriculum materials that infuse technology. Results of focus groups indicated that teachers viewed their summer institute experiences as very positive. Many reported that it met their needs and encouraged them to move beyond using technology for their own professional purposes, but for their students' learning as well. As one participant indicated, "The technology has opened up adventures of innovations for me as an educator by strengthening my basic computer skills and at the same time introducing me to new ways to infuse technology in the classrooms." Participants also reported increases in sensitivity to *opportunities* for using technology to further particular pedagogical objectives.

Overall, these results indicated that a design-based approach to professional development provided a powerful context and learning community in which teachers could learn certain facets of technology integration that are more difficult to learn in traditional workshop settings. The emphasis on lesson design helped participants develop a rationale for technology integration that was centered on learning objectives related to their particular students, meaning technology became more seamlessly infused in learning activities, rather than standing alone. The collaborative nature of the design process also changed the way in which participants accessed technology resources available to them in their schools. For example, results of the observations indicated that they were collaborating with school technology coordinators more readily and using technology resources outside of their classrooms, such as in computer labs. The database of lessons became a great source of seed ideas for the development of new lessons.

## Maryland Technology Academy (MTA) program

The Maryland Technology Academy (MTA) Program, an intensive professional development component of Maryland Technology Consortium (MTC) for educators across Maryland, was a collaboration of the Maryland State Department of Education (MSDE), the Johns Hopkins University Center for Technology in Education (JHU/CTE) and Towson University (TU). The purpose of the MTC was to build a system of professional development for teachers at all stages of their careers and all levels of technology integration proficiency. The project was funded by the U.S. Department of Education's Technology Innovation Challenge Grant (TICG) program and MSDE.

The goal of the MTA was to produce a statewide network of technology integration leaders who would provide technical support and professional development to other educators and contribute to strategic technology planning initiatives in their schools and districts. In a year-long experience, which included a three-week Summer Institute, periodic follow-up events, and a Web-based learning community, participants collaborated with colleagues, developed authentic instructional products, received systematic follow-up support, and engaged in reflection on their teaching. The MTA Leadership Program, along with the related Administrators' Symposium and Satellite Academies, served approximately 2,000 Maryland educators over a five-year period.

### Program attributes

A program logic map was used by the MTC partners to depict the attributes of an effective professional development model and to lay out the expected outcomes of high-quality professional development. Inputs of the logic map included model attributes such as intensive, ongoing, and systematic training; active community of learners; inquiry-based; incorporating action research and reflective teaching; authentic product development;

and alignment with National Staff Development Council (NSDC), ISTE and National Council for the Accreditation of Teacher Education (NCATE) standards. Intermediate outcomes in the logic map were improved skills with digital content, technology integration, and leadership, leading to increased technology integration. This in turn led to outcomes of improved instruction and ultimately increased student performance.

## MTA planning

Education leaders in Maryland recognized the importance of increasing students' technology use and determined that a program to build a network of leaders would be instrumental in putting the recently developed Maryland Technology Plan into action. Thus the concept of the MTA Leadership Program was born. The planning process involved close cooperation and collaboration among all three partners, Towson University, Johns Hopkins University, and the Maryland State Department of Education. Each institution took responsibility for major elements from facilities, to curriculum, to communication and project oversight.

The recruitment process involved inviting teachers and library media specialists from across the state to apply for the 120 slots allocated each year for the Academy. Applicants were encouraged to apply as a team so that they could work together collaboratively and share their new expertise in their schools and districts. Multiple intrinsic and extrinsic incentives were provided. Participants were selected to become MTA Fellows according to a competitive and stringent evaluation process. In addition, many of the leadership development activities involved team building with a team leader to act as coach during the instruction and reflection processes. Extrinsic incentives included monetary stipends, books by renowned technology experts such as Jaime McKenzie and Alan November, software, and membership in MICCA and ISTE. At no charge, participants received six MSDE continuing professional development credits and, with tuition payment, they could receive up to six graduate credits in instructional technology from one of the partner institutions of higher education.

## MTA leadership program curriculum

The MTA curriculum was aligned with the ISTE National Educational Technology Standards for Teachers (NETS•T), Maryland Content Standards and Voluntary State Curriculum, and National Staff Development Council (NSDC) standards. Curriculum goals were that participants acquired the skills needed to:

- Use technology in the context of constructivist classrooms and project-based learning

- Construct and design instructional activities that incorporated technology to support student learning

- Use technology to more effectively and efficiently assess student progress

- Provide professional development to other educators within their sphere of influence

The MTA curriculum addressed three basic themes: leadership, advanced technology skills, and curriculum integration, accomplished through four complementary curriculum strands: Leadership Skills, Digital Content, Curriculum Integration, and Connections. In the Leadership Skills strand, Fellows explored leadership roles and responsibilities related to the effective use of technology in instruction. They examined their school's needs and designed a change implementation plan (ChIP) which included goal-setting, instructional strategies, technology integration, and professional development, according to the Understanding by Design framework of Wiggins and McTighe (2001). The Digital Content strand provided hands-on learning experiences in computer labs allowing Fellows to design Web-based learning activities and multimedia applications for use in their classroom during the following school year. Classroom management techniques, copyright, and ethical use were also addressed. Projects and curriculum for this strand can be accessed at http://cte.jhu.edu/techacademy/. In the Curriculum Integration strand, Fellows researched, designed, and developed student learning activities using technology to support academic achievement. Topics included applying the constructivist approach to teaching and learning, authentic assessment strategies, and using appropriate technology tools to accommodate students with special needs. They also examined a range of assessment strategies used to developed assessments for their instructional units. Fellows explored ways to use technology for collaboration and data collection in the connections strand. Fellows further learned how to use a Web-based electronic learning community for communication, collaboration, and resource storage and retrieval.

The MTA project team additionally provided an Administrators' Symposium to assist school administrators (primarily building principals) in gaining the knowledge and skills needed to effectively plan for technology use and support the emerging technology integration leaders within their schools and districts. National leaders and Maryland State Department of Education administrators shared their vision for using technology in Maryland schools. Participants learned strategies for developing building level technology plans, acquiring and allocating resources, and designing professional development.

The MTA program was eventually expanded to 20 regional satellite academies throughout Maryland. The satellite academies focused primarily on the curriculum integration strand, allowing districts to customize the MTA program to support their specific needs for addressing state standards. The MTA satellite programs served an additional 600 participants each year over three years.

## Change implementation plans

The primary product of the MTA Fellows was a comprehensive ChIP tailored to each specific instructional setting. The ChIP was essentially a twofold instructional plan: (1) to integrate technology into instruction in the classroom or school, and (2) to use technology for professional development for colleagues in buildings or districts.

As a statewide program, the focus of the MTA was on increasing student achievement in core content areas, especially reading, writing, and other language skills, for which standards are set and on which students are regularly assessed through mandated state tests. All Fellows, regardless of the district in which they worked, could relate to the state standards and design instruction intended to prepare students for the state assessments. The initial step in developing the ChIP was to analyze school data to identify achievement gaps. Based on the identified needs, Fellows selected appropriate state content standards as the focus of the instructional unit they planned for students and the professional development experience they planned for educators. Required elements of the ChIP project included:

- An analysis of an important need based on student achievement data

- A vision statement about how to address the identified need

- Student learning goals based on state or national standards

- An instructional unit for students that addressed the identified needs and learning goals

- A related professional development plan for educators

Fellows systematically collected evidence on the effects of their instruction on student performance at both the classroom and school levels. They used a database to record information about their action research and reflective teaching activities. During the year, participants had several opportunities to report on successes and challenges implementing the ChIP at MTA follow-up sessions and state or regional conferences.

Building and sustaining a sense of community among the participants was an important aspect of the MTA Leadership Program. A proprietary electronic learning community (ELC) was developed by Johns Hopkins for collaboration and participation among MTA colleagues throughout the year. Its features were typical of Web-based communication tools including an announcements area, an online calendar, threaded discussions, instant messaging and chat features, and document sharing capabilities. Fellows used the ELC as a life-line for sustaining ongoing collaboration throughout the state.

## Outcomes

The evaluation of the Maryland Technology Academy was designed to provide formative feedback to program implementers, to ascertain the degree to which Fellows acquired targeted skills, and to determine the effect of the program on the instructional practice and leadership behaviors of Fellows. By program design, Fellows of varying technology skill levels were accepted to the MTA Leadership Program. Prior to the Summer Institute, few Fellows reported having advanced skills, with most rating themselves somewhere in the intermediate range. However, following the MTA experience, many Fellows considered themselves to have advanced skills. One middle school English teacher who attended the 2000 MTA said that the hands-on time was the best part of the program as participants "didn't leave knowing *how* to do it, they left having *done* it!"

The MTA Leadership Program was quite successful in changing Fellows' attitudes and beliefs about the potential of technology and themselves as technology users. In particular, Fellows showed statistically significant gains in their comfort using technology in instruction, their confidence in having the necessary skills to effectively integrate technology into instruction, and their belief that technology could help them address the diverse learning needs of their students.

Fellows also gained a wide variety of technical and curriculum integration skills. In the follow-up survey, nearly 60% of Fellows reported being a great deal more familiar with the instructional potential of technology. About half indicated that they were a great deal more able to design collaborative, inquiry-based learning activities using technology and to design learning experiences using technology that are linked to curriculum goals and state assessments.

During the Summer Institute, Fellows gained confidence in their ability to use technology in instruction and to assist other educators. They retained that confidence long after the Institute ended. About three-quarters of the Fellows believed they were definitely more able to use technology effectively in instruction as a result of their participation in the program. About two-thirds believed they were definitely better equipped to help others. They were slightly less convinced of their ability to effect change at the end of the Institute, and they became less convinced over time.

The most dramatic changes were in the frequency of technology use for instruction. In a follow-up survey, more than 80% of Fellows reported using technology very frequently with students. They used technology in a range of ways, but most common uses were to gather information, create and publish text, create graphics and other visuals, and report results from investigations. Fellows also used technology in various ways to help low-achieving students succeed.

## Reflections on the three projects

The key feature of each of the projects described here is the central role of one or more higher education partners. Higher education institutions bring multiple benefits to K–12 technology professional development. Chief among these are interests in educational improvement, curriculum development, assessment, and evaluation; subject-matter and interdisciplinary expertise; technical expertise; time for planning, reflection, and implementation; state-of-the-art facilities and conducive learning environments; ready labor by graduate and undergraduate students; broad interests in community development and the wider educational system; and the capacity to sustain long-term projects involving multiple partners and locations. These projects would not be possible without the higher education partners and the resources provided by them. Each of the major higher educational institutions represented by the three projects described in this chapter—University of Chicago, University of Illinois at Chicago, Johns Hopkins University, and Towson University—have missions that include the improvement of their local communities as well as the production and dissemination of knowledge and expertise to the world at large. Each of these institutions also allows for the long-term employment of people who do not fit easily into the traditional roles of faculty member or school administrator; such people are critically important to the success of projects such as those described here. Positions with titles such as research associate, clinical professor, or project manager allow people without clearly defined duties to work as entrepreneurs and ambassadors of educational improvement, garnering resources and offering quasi-independent advice and support to institutions such as K–12 public schools that are often constrained by legislated mandates and rigid job descriptions, resulting in projects that better meet the needs of K–12 teachers and their students.

## LITERATURE ESSENTIALS

### Professional development partnerships

Professional development partnerships are an important component of educational reform, particularly those related to technology integration. This is confirmed by the Preparing Tomorrow's Teachers to Use Technology (PT[3]) grant program as well as the International Society for Technology in Education's (ISTE) Essential Conditions. Key indicators for the PT[3] program include both interdisciplinary and K–16 partnerships. As such, all PT[3] grantees incorporated partnerships into their programs. ISTE defines partnerships as "engaged communities" and states that they are a necessary condition to leveraging the potential of technology for learning, designed to ensure that all participants have opportunities to observe, explore and implement technology integration (http://cnets.iste.org/teachers/t_esscond.html).

Partnerships strengthen the potential for reforms because they invite collaboration between people with diverse backgrounds and professional expertise who nonetheless share common goals. Yet, partnerships are challenging to organize and implement. The literature illuminates the complex nature of external partnerships and provides insight into how such partnerships can be structured for success.

At the outset, partners must recognize the different cultures in which they work. These cultures have unique structures of organization, discourse communities, and disciplinary expertise (Ilmer & Kirby, 2007; Richmond, 1996). It is challenging for partners to learn each others' routines, language, and institutional constraints. *Dialog* is necessary for establishing the personal relationships conducive to learning, uncovering differing perspectives and creating a culture of respect. Strategies for facilitating dialog include both face-to-face interactions and online discussion communities (Ilmer & Kirby, 2007; Borthwick, Pierson, Anderson, Morris, Lathem, & Parker, 2004).

*(Continued)*

## LITERATURE ESSENTIALS

*(Continued)*

Partners create a community of practice characterized by individuals engaging in *joint activity* which leads to shared experiences (Wenger, 1999). This includes defining who shall benefit from the partnership, the joint outcomes partners hope to achieve, and the actions that participants will undertake (Ilmer & Kirby, 2007; Aworuwa, Worrell, & Smaldino, 2006; Strudler, Archambault, Bendixen, Anderson, & Weiss, 2003). This shared social practice enables partners to alternatively teach and learn from one another (Wenger, 1999; Borthwick, 2001).

*Artifact and product development* is an effective strategy for creating shared experiences. This provides opportunities for participants to engage in hands-on exploration of the technology, collaborate with their peers, and reflect on their learning (Ringstaff & Kelly, 2002). Products are real and usable, and can seed future ideas to be implemented beyond those involved in the original partnership.

Although there is an organic and emergent nature to partnerships that cannot always be condensed to a few paragraphs, the literature discussed here can provide potential direction and ideas with which to begin.

It is important to stress that these higher education partners are not necessarily the schools of education that one might expect to be involved in such projects. Rather, the projects demonstrate that higher education institutions can be supportive of K–12 education even when such institutions have eliminated departments or schools of education or substantially altered their configurations. The K–12 partners of the projects described here were also critical to recruiting participants, ensuring ongoing follow-up support, and securing funding. Realizing that each participating institution has its own culture and body of knowledge, the K–12 partners recognized that persistence, perseverance, negotiation, mutual respect, and a dash of humor are essential to reaching common understanding and clarifying direction.

Each of the described projects evolved over multiple years, incorporating lessons learned along the way. We believe that multiyear professional development projects are preferable to one-time events, so that improvements can be made, and so that prior participants can be encouraged to return for more advanced study or to help provide instruction or leadership. Planning complex professional development activities such as these takes considerable time at the outset; ongoing attention to feedback and results is also needed. Multiyear projects, however, involve complex funding issues, and also require hosting institutions to maintain capacities over a longer period of time. This capacity must provide for ongoing follow-up support, including making server accounts available to participants long after the professional development institutes have ended.

Having participants design and create authentic products, including lesson plans, curriculum webs, and other materials for integrating technology that can actually be used in instructional programs provided a clear focus for the relevance of the professional development to the instructional priorities. This approach allowed participants to focus on improving the quality of their instruction and the effectiveness of using technology on student performance. Building and sustaining a learning community that can support professional development and ongoing implementation efforts allows participants to share ideas, resources, questions, and concerns with other educators, thereby strengthening their network of expertise and support. Finally, to meet the needs of adult learners, a continuum of differentiated levels of professional development for using technology should be offered. The diversity in background and skills in each of these projects required differentiated instruction to accommodate those participants who had only basic skills, as well as those with more advanced skills.

Evaluating the effectiveness of various models of professional development is crucial. Without evaluation, little can be learned and applied within multiple contexts. Yet evaluation is challenging. Using multiple evaluation strategies is important, as technology integration is embedded into other aspects of teaching. No one evaluation strategy will capture this complexity. Therefore, multiple evaluation strategies must be incorporated to reflect not only the outcomes of workshop activities on K–12 instruction, but also the processes involved in planning that instruction and adapting it once it has been implemented.

Finally, in a collaborative approach to professional development, evaluation strategies must cross university and school boundaries. In this way, outcomes can provide important information related to not only participants' satisfaction with professional development activities, but whether and how what was learned has impacted participants' actual classroom practice and, in turn, how that is tied to K–12 student achievement.

## GETTING STARTED RESOURCES

The Web sites of the three projects described in this chapter offer many materials and practices that can be adapted by other projects.

Cunningham, C. (2004). The Web Institute for Teachers. Retrieved October 15, 2007 from webinstituteforteachers.org

> The Web Institute for Teachers (WIT) is an intensive summer seminar designed to help preK–12 teachers integrate the World Wide Web into their curriculum.

eTech Ohio. (2005). *Evaluating professional development, Dr. Thomas Guskey (02/05)*. Retrieved October 16, 2007 from www.etech.ohio.gov/programs/interview/guskey.jsp

> This is an interview (available as a transcript and audio clips) by Dr. Thomas Guskey that addresses questions related to effective evaluation of technology professional development for teachers.

*The Maryland Technology Academy*. (2008). Retrieved January 15, 2008 from www.mdtechacademy.org

> The Maryland Technology Academy is an intensive professional development opportunity designed to provide a cadre of K–16 teachers throughout Maryland with professional development opportunities that focus on using technology to significantly increase student learning and promote school improvement.

McKenzie, J. (2001). How teachers learn technology best. *From Now On: The Education Technology Journal, 10*(6). Retrieved October 15, 2007 from http://fno.org/mar01/howlearn.html

> This article provides a number of guidelines for the development of strong professional development programs.

*Teachers Infusing Technology in Urban Schools*. (2004). Retrieved October 17, 2007 from the University of Illinois at Chicago Web site: www2.ed.uic.edu/pt3/

> Project TITUS (Teachers Infusing Technology in Urban Schools) reforms teacher certification programs across colleges by integrating technology-infused instruction into preservice teaching courses for elementary and secondary programs.

## chapter 11

# How Do We Support Teacher Learning Online and On-site?

Lessons learned from Washington's Networked Learning Community

*Joanne Carney*
*Western Washington University*

## abstract

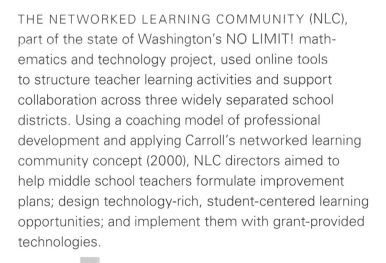

THE NETWORKED LEARNING COMMUNITY (NLC), part of the state of Washington's NO LIMIT! mathematics and technology project, used online tools to structure teacher learning activities and support collaboration across three widely separated school districts. Using a coaching model of professional development and applying Carroll's networked learning community concept (2000), NLC directors aimed to help middle school teachers formulate improvement plans; design technology-rich, student-centered learning opportunities; and implement them with grant-provided technologies.

With the emergence of a host of new online learning technologies and a scarcity of funds to pay for teacher professional development, many of those charged with meeting teachers' learning needs are looking for ways to combine school- and district-based resources with materials and support available via online tools. I studied one such project as an outside evaluator for a technology and mathematics initiative in Washington State. In this chapter I will share some of the lessons the project directors and I learned about how to provide professional development both online and on-site—through cyberspace and from down the hall.

# The Networked Learning Community (NLC)

In 2003, Washington State's Networked Learning Community (NLC) began a project designed to help middle school teachers use technology to enhance their teaching of mathematics—incorporating more active learning strategies and bringing their instructional approaches in line with National Council of Teachers of Mathematics (NCTM) standards. This NLC project was part of a larger grant—New Outcomes: Learning Improvement in Mathematics Integrating Technology (NO LIMIT!), a statewide initiative begun in 2001. The NLC project, led by directors David Tucker and Ken Bakken, aimed to implement Carroll's (2000) conception of a networked learning community:

> A Networked Learning Community is constructed as its members collaborate to achieve common goals, learning together as they develop solutions for problems they are addressing in common. As the learning community grows, the members of the community develop new knowledge and skills through their participation and contributions.

Because the three school districts participating in the NLC were widely separated geographically and distant from the directors' base of operations in Washington's northwest corner, the directors knew it was essential that a Web-based technology be used for communication among learning community members and for access to learning resources. In addition to the online component, though, the NLC actively built upon the existing mentoring networks within participating schools and districts. In fact, Tucker and Bakken conceived of their own role as that of coach, rather than director, emphasizing that view by using the title Project Coaches. Thus, the NLC offers an interesting hybrid model for those who seek to design effective professional development in educational technology: it combines both online and on-site coaching for integration of technology into enhanced instructional practices.

- How do various online technological tools support or fail to support teacher learning?

- What kinds of professional development activities or tasks are effective for teacher learning?

- How can geographically distant professional development providers coordinate their efforts with local, site-based teacher professional development efforts?

- What school and district practices or policies contribute to the effectiveness of a networked learning community?

It is hoped that information about the NLC will aid others in choosing effective tools for coaching and communication, structuring appropriate learning activities for teachers, and identifying factors in a local setting that may support or hinder their efforts.

The experiences of the participants in this learning community—both their successes and challenges—shed light on a number of important questions for professional developers:

## NO LIMIT! Organization and approach

Before telling the story of the NLC, the reader should know about the larger organization within which it has operated. NO LIMIT! is a Washington State initiative begun in 2001 with Technology Literacy Challenge Fund (TLCF) money, later becoming an Enhancing Education Through Technology (EETT) program. The overarching objective of NO LIMIT! was to enhance mathematics teaching and learning in the middle grades through integration of technology and the alignment of pedagogical practice with the NCTM 2000 standards. Mathematics at the middle grades was targeted due to the poor performance of Washington students on standardized tests at this level.

The NO LIMIT! project typically provided each teacher-participant with approximately $10,000 for equipment and software purchases over a two-year period as a way to encourage teachers to try technology-enhanced instructional approaches for teaching mathematics. The project also gave impetus to the creation of local professional learning communities and helped middle-level teachers develop a deeper understanding of mathematics.

## Project evaluation

A team of evaluators at Western Washington University acted as external evaluators of NO LIMIT! Much of the evaluation of the larger project was based upon bimonthly teacher logs completed by teacher participants. Several in-depth case studies of selected projects were completed annually. My role as evaluator was to do an annual case study on the NLC. Data sources for case study evaluation included:

- Classroom observation
- Observation during training sessions
- Semi-structured interviews of selected teacher participants and project directors
- Focus group interviews of district teams
- Bimonthly teacher logs
- Online communication

- Teacher lesson design projects
- Teacher conference presentations
- A limited number of student work samples
- Washington Assessment of Student Learning (WASL) scores

This chapter is based upon insights derived from these data.

## LITERATURE ESSENTIALS

### Online learning communities

Information about the theory, design, learning in, and methodology for evaluation of Web-based learning communities can be found in an edited text by Barab, Kling, and Gray (2004). Writers identify the challenges and complexities of process and practice in various types of online learning communities. The chapter by Schlager and Fusco draws upon the community of practice literature to examine the processes and structures of effective professional development for teachers and how local professional norms and practices support or inhibit those projects. Guideposts for technology design that supports system-wide improvement are also offered as a conceptual framework for analysis and research on online infrastructure to support education communities of practice. Those guideposts include: (1) learning processes; (2) history and culture; (3) membership identity and multiplicity; (4) community reproduction and evolution; (5) social networks; (6) leaders and contributors; (7) tools, artifacts, and places; and (8) the practice.

How are learning and cognitive change fostered by online communities? Renninger and Shumar (2002) help one consider the theory and practice of Internet community-building. Case studies on *The Math Forum* and *Tapped In* are of particular interest, because these are two initiatives to enhance teachers' knowledge and practice, and other chapters focus on online forums for different audiences and purposes.

Dede (2006) provides advice about choosing and designing effective professional development for teachers. Exemplary online programs are examined and compared, with conclusions aimed both at those who develop online programs and for teachers and administrators searching for good professional development. Dede offers suggestions for research that shed light on how online teacher professional development might play a transformative role in improving education.

*(Continued)*

**LITERATURE ESSENTIALS**

*(Continued)*

Carroll (2000) contends that a learning revolution, sparked by powerful new interactive communication technologies, is underway—and schooling as we know it must either change or become marginalized. In networked learning communities, everyone is a learner, and the distinctions between students and teachers fade away. Schools have traditionally focused on knowledge transmission; however, in a networked learning community, two other dimensions are achieved: knowledge adaptation and knowledge generation. Carroll outlines the roles, assessment, rules, relationships, boundaries, and tools of a networked learning community, and suggests that to implement his ideas for learning communities, we must prepare educators who themselves are expert learners able to implement the practices he has explained and envisioned.

The perspective of Hall and Hord (2001) on facilitating the change process in organizations is specifically applicable to an online professional development model. Understanding individuals' affective and behavioral characteristics during a change process can help even online professional developers avoid common potholes and attune their support to learners' needs.

## Networked learning community goals

The NLC sought to achieve the following goals:

- Help a school develop a comprehensive systemic change effort for their mathematics program.

- Help a school implement new, standards-aligned math curriculum, improved research-based teaching skills, and technology integration.

- Help a school implement a building-wide staff development program consistent with math curriculum and technology goals, assisting individual teachers to identify and implement specific professional improvement.

Four professional development strands were part of the NLC approach: (1) online coaching by project directors and associates, (2) periodic on-site coaching by project directors, (3) ongoing support from school- or district-based learning communities, and (4) summer institutes where teams from the various local sites could interact and see models of technology-rich math instruction.

# Engaging in meaningful learning activity

Teachers are busy people. Those who are planning teacher-learning activities must first deal with teachers' time constraints and, frequently, with their unwillingness to engage in tasks they do not find valuable. Teachers are also often reluctant to make changes in their practices when they are unable to see how an innovation might benefit them or their students. For this reason, NLC coach Bakken repeats the mantra, "They [teachers] have to see the value."

NLC coaches used a three-part strategy for showing teachers the value, and motivating them to engage in the development of "technology-rich" math projects:

1. Give teachers a vision for how they might engage their students in technology-supported inquiry in mathematics.

2. Situate the learning activity within teachers' own work.

3. Provide an impetus to action by defining an authentic audience for presentation of the teachers' work.

Each of these strategies will be explained in the sections that follow.

## Providing a vision

NLC Coaches aimed to give participating teachers a vision of how technology might enhance their mathematics instruction, as well as some practical methods for implementing that vision, during the project's annual Summer Workshop. During this two-day gathering, coaches modeled a technology-supported inquiry project—engaging teachers as learners and then guiding them in an analysis of the model lesson's methods. Guest speakers who could expand teachers' knowledge of mathematics, technology, or pedagogical methods were also invited.

For example, during the first year's Summer Workshop, Brian Harpel (2004) was invited to present his methods for teaching mathematics through writing. Harpel's approach proved to have wide impact among NLC teachers and students. One teacher reported:

> The three of us [teachers] are using a writing response to problem solving … We all learned that this summer and adapted it somewhat … More of my students are willing to read off of that how they got the solution, because now they have words other than just looking at their math and going, "I got this, but I don't know how." They have words now that tell how. Students I would not have expected to volunteer to read their solutions have done so. It helps them put the correct words to what they were doing mathematically.

Harpel's writing-based instructional strategies gave teachers a basic tool for engaging students in mathematical inquiry, and they could see the benefit of those methods for their students.

NLC teachers in one participating school district were so appreciative of Harpel's approach that they used district professional development funds to bring him back for two additional presentations to all district teachers. Other teachers spoke of sharing Harpel's methods informally with colleagues. In this manner, NLC best-practice strategies for teaching mathematics gradually percolated through participating schools and districts.

## Situating learning in teachers' work

To help teachers see the value of each year's learning activity, NLC coaches situated it within each teacher's own work. At the Summer Workshop, teachers chose one area of their curriculum they felt could be enhanced by the combination of technology and new instructional approaches, and they collaboratively worked to redesign that lesson. Because the task was self-chosen and focused on teachers' desire to be more effective in teaching their curriculum, these instructional design projects were likely to be much more engaging than tasks defined by administrators or inservice providers.

NLC coaches developed a Training Model to structure the annual learning activity. This model (Figure 11.1) includes the following steps:

1. Goal setting,

2. Collaborative planning,

3. Instructional design by an eCoach (a tool that will be described in a subsequent section),

4. Pilot testing in the teacher's classroom,

5. Evaluation by means of a feedback loop, and

6. Presentation to an authentic audience.

How were the teachers—time-constrained and sometimes stressed by the demands of learning new technologies and pedagogies—motivated to complete and implement their technology-enhanced lesson? NLC coaches provided monetary incentives at each stage of the process and an authentic audience for the presentation of their work. It turned out that defining an authentic audience proved to be the most powerful inducement for teachers to persevere.

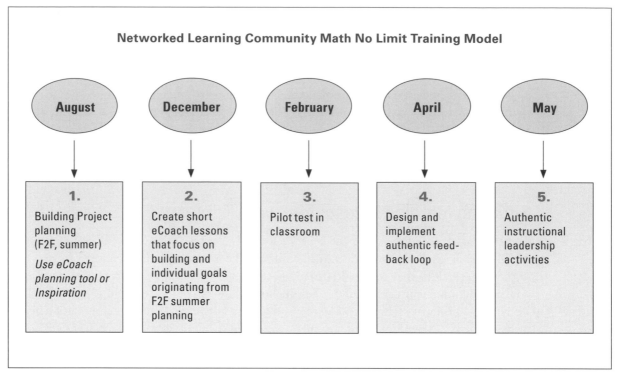

FIGURE 11.1. NLC training model

## Providing an impetus to change

Each year NLC coaches arranged for teacher-participants to have an authentic audience for reporting the results of their instructional innovation. During the project's first year, teachers were to identify some area in their math curriculum that could be taught more effectively with the use of technology, design a technology-rich math lesson for that content, implement the lesson, and then report on it in a group session at the Northwest Council for Computer Education (NCCE) conference. The task and conference presentation requirement provided situated contexts and authentic audiences of students, educators, and technologists—creating a need for genuine change and for corresponding teacher learning.

The task of designing and presenting a technology-rich math project caused NLC teachers great anxiety at the beginning of the year. Most were technology novices with limited math content knowledge and little experience presenting at professional conferences; yet later, they reported this was the most powerful and valuable learning experience of the year. A situated learning perspective (Putnam & Borko, 2000) provides a good explanation as to why this NCCE technology-rich math project was such an effective learning experience:

1. The task was meaningful because it was derived from teachers' own curriculum and involved a presentation to an authentic audience;

2. It challenged teachers' *frames* [of reference] (Schön, 1987) and modeled the kind of authentic, project-based activities they were asked to devise for their own students;

3. The task prompted teachers to seek mentoring from coaches and more knowledgeable peers in their local learning communities;

4. Teachers were given the opportunity for structured, collaborative sharing; and

5. Teachers presented their work at a large regional conference, which enhanced their professional self-image and resulted in additional learning.

During Year 2 (2004–2005), NLC coaches faced budgetary pressures and sought to provide an authentic audience online, rather than funding conference travel for all teachers. Although this seemed to be a reasonable adaptation, it proved to be far less successful—for reasons the project directors had not anticipated, as will be explained in the next section, which considers the online tools used by the NLC.

# Using an online tool for learning and communication

When the project began in 2003, NLC coaches had anticipated that popular course management software would provide a place where teachers could obtain resources and assignments from Coaches, exchange files, and communicate with other NLC teachers at the three district sites across Washington State. It was hoped that the software would facilitate collaborative sharing and peer mentoring. This did not occur. Instead, teachers were frustrated by the tool, finding it time-consuming to use and difficult to locate materials. NLC coaches soon recognized that using software designed for a higher-education coursework model was inappropriate for their learning community of K–12 teachers. For the second year of the project, NLC coaches adopted My eCoach—an online environment designed specifically for teacher professional development—and used the eCoach Custom Builder feature to have teachers design an inquiry lesson or unit to enhance some aspect of their math curriculum.

## My eCoach: An online environment for professional development

Analyzing features that teachers and coaches found useful in this particular online environment may help others choose and evaluate their own online professional development tools.

Built around a baseball metaphor, the eCoach online learning environment has many features for mentored, collaborative teacher learning: coaching and course management tools, online lesson and curriculum builders, standards alignment tools, a searchable eLibrary of resources, discussion boards, instant messaging, internal e-mail, an e-portfolio builder, and a blog. Teachers can add co-authors to a project, invite comments, and receive ongoing feedback from a Coach.

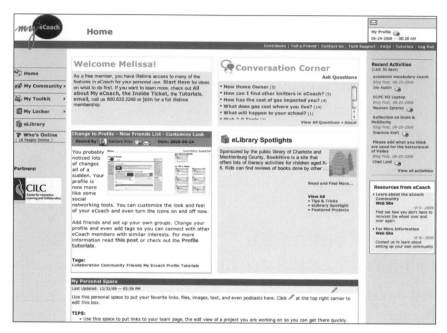

**FIGURE 11.2.** eCoach Home Field page

NLC teachers, having used the other software previously, responded positively to the eCoach interface, saying it was much easier to use because nearly everything could be found on the "Home Field" entry page (Figure 11.2).

Highly useful for achieving the goals of the NLC project was the standards alignment tool in eCoach—a pull-down menu that enabled teachers to easily align learning objectives with standards.

Teachers with limited technology skills appreciated the Web-publishing feature of eCoach. With it, they could fill in various templates to create Web resource pages or instructional units. Being able to upload resource files for those units to the eCoach server was helpful, because in some cases, the school district server did not allow teachers sufficient storage space. Technology novices also benefited from model projects and lesson plans in the eLibrary—a fairly extensive collection of juried projects and resources posted by other teachers. NLC coaches appreciated how they could structure teacher learning activities with eCoach and provide all the resources teachers would need to complete their project—while modeling the kind of standards-based instructional design they wanted teachers to emulate.

Teachers did experience some rather expected difficulties in using eCoach to design a technology-enhanced mathematics unit, however: those with limited technology skills had to spend more time learning the tool than working on lesson design; there was dissatisfaction with the internal message feature in place of school e-mail; and there was dissatisfaction with the constraints of certain software features, such as Builder templates. Yet the greatest difficulties the second year of the project were not due to tool features, but instead were a result of the online audience defined for publication of teachers' work and the complexity of the task coupled with an unfamiliar tool. Not only were teachers learning eCoach software, but they were often learning new technologies and writing a fully developed unit plan simultaneously. Rarely had many of them engaged in such complex unit planning.

## Tool-based dilemmas and challenges

NLC Coaches' identification of an authentic audience of teacher peers who would have access to the finished instructional units proved to be problematic. Recall that due to budgetary constraints, the Coaches had told teachers they would be presenting their technology-integrated math projects to other teachers online—sharing their lesson designs by publishing them on eCoach. This proved to be a source of great concern: telling teachers they were creating an online product not only to use with their students, but also to share with their peers was quite intimidating. Many teachers do not regularly write for such authentic audiences and find such a task time-consuming, frustrating, and ultimately unnecessary for teaching a good lesson. We found that some with aptitudes in math were not necessarily good writers. NLC Coaches found themselves having to spend a great deal of time offering suggestions about writing for an audience and doing extensive editing of teachers' written products rather than focusing on the math content or pedagogical aspects of the lesson.

Yet, on the other hand, telling teachers that the product they were creating so laboriously would not be shared with other teachers online prompted a different type of protest: "Why are we spending so much time on this if we're not sharing it with other teachers? I don't need to write all these steps out if it's just for me and my students!" Thus, the online nature of the tool, which allowed for publication (though it was not required), proved to be a problem. Coaches had not anticipated this authentic audience dilemma. In the end, for this second year, NLC coaches were forced to simplify the instructional design task; instead of a fully developed instructional unit, teachers used eCoach to create a much simpler Web resource.

During the project's third year, NLC coaches came back to the authentic audience that had proven so motivating during the first year—presentation at a regional technology conference. (Fortunately, supplemental funds were made available for this travel by the NO LIMIT! project director.) This time they used eCoach as a presentation tool, as well as a model of the kind of standards-based instructional unit eCoach could scaffold. The learning activities devised by teachers for their own classroom use, presentation screens, as well as other resource materials that might be helpful to audience members were provided online via eCoach.

## Lessons learned about using an online tool for learning and communication

Professional developers ought to be prepared for the probability that their tools will have unanticipated effects. Some of the challenges faced by the NLC—the authentic audience dilemma, teachers' limited writing experience, and the challenges of learning a new tool while engaging in complex or unfamiliar tasks—are issues to anticipate. Professional developers ought to keep in mind Helen Barrett's (2001) caution, "When learning new tools, use familiar tasks; and when learning new tasks, use familiar tools."

# Coordinating with local, site-based programs and policies

How does an online professional development initiative effectively coordinate efforts with local, site-based initiatives? When school or district programs and policies are in alignment with the outside professional development initiative, the result can be a powerful synergy. When local practices or policies are at odds with the initiative, the project's goals can be hindered. The NLC was able to coordinate their activities with local efforts in a number of ways: working with established school and district learning communities, building upon curriculum reform efforts, and leveraging existing technological resources.

## Working with established learning communities and peer experts

This synergy was most apparent at Ridgefield Elementary School in District 1, where a learning community had flourished (90% staff involvement) for at least four years prior to the NLC's inception. The building principal herself was an active participant, providing vision, support, and leadership. The NLC capitalized on this pre-existing learning community, paying two teachers at the school to be mentor-leaders and benefiting from already-established relationships and processes.

In schools where strong learning communities had not been established, NLC coaches encouraged teachers to assist each other. This was a primary reason why districts were required to identify school-based teams of teachers who would participate in the initiative. Teachers, especially those who were technology novices, reported the assistance of more knowledgeable peers (in both technology and math) as being crucial for the development and implementation of their technology-rich learning activities.

## Building on district curriculum reform efforts

Hargreaves, Earl, Moore, and Manning (2001) have noted that in schools where teachers make significant changes in their practices, something compelling occurs, giving teachers an urgent need for change. For example, district adoption of the Investigations math curriculum (TERC, 1997) propelled change among Ridgefield's NLC teachers during the first year of the project.

Investigations emphasized mathematical inquiry applied to real-life problems, mathematical reasoning, and the use of technological tools for investigation and communication—an approach quite different from the district's previous math curriculum, which had emphasized computation skills. Thus, district elementary teachers could no longer teach math using traditional methods. In order to help students practice mathematical problem-solving, teachers had to give up the certainty of answer keys and algorithms and become inquirers along with their students, not a comfortable process for some teachers. However this change did contribute to the achievement of NLC goals, as project coaches suggested ways to integrate technology into the new ways of teaching mathematics that investigations had prompted.

## Leveraging resources

Where changes in teachers' methods for teaching math were driven forward by a new curriculum in one district, in another small rural district, NLC efforts were leveraged by a grant that provided laptops to all seventh- and eighth-grade students. This sudden access to ubiquitous technology prompted NLC teachers to search for appropriate ways to use the laptops: "I've been looking for math sites that the students can be involved in and we have these laptops, so … it has been important … how can we get the laptop or computer use interjected into the math?" In response, NLC coaches suggested technologies the teachers may not have been familiar with, and helped them devise inquiry-based learning activities to integrate new hardware and software.

## Lessons learned about coordinating with local programs

A professional development effort can get more bang for its buck by coordinating local programs. Strategies include working with established learning communities and peer support structures, building on existing district instructional improvement efforts, and leveraging resources where they are available.

## Dealing with local barriers to change

Pre-existing learning communities, aligned curricular and professional development initiatives, support personnel, and technological resources can create a synergy between online and on-site professional development; however, it is far too common that local factors instead conspire to weaken the efforts of an outside project such as the NLC. Those factors for the NLC included changing district priorities and insufficient resources.

## Changing district priorities

Often changes in district personnel or the pursuit of other initiatives can alter a school's or district's priorities, weakening its commitment to an existing project. Teachers and professional development leaders must prioritize where to use their time and energy.

For example, in District 1, a promising first year in which district programs and policies were in alignment with NLC goals was followed by a change in focus: district administrators turned their staff professional development efforts away from mathematics after the district received a large literacy grant. Subsequently, many of the informal school supports (e.g., student teacher assignments, team meeting time, release time) that had been provided to NLC teachers during the project's first year were cut back and used to support the reading initiative.

In their attempt to solve this problem of changing district priorities, NLC coaches drew more heavily upon the project's on-site mentors, who could use their personal relationships with teacher-peers to prompt and support project efforts, but their effectiveness was significantly impaired.

## Insufficient resources

Another common barrier to professional development initiatives is a lack of necessary local resources. Resources important to the success of a project such as NLC include: incentives for participation (e.g., money, hardware or software, release time, etc.), adequate district technology infrastructure and technical support, and policies both to reward and hold teachers accountable for their professional development. Because the NO LIMIT! grant itself provided some incentives in the form of $10,000 worth of new hardware or software, time proved to be the resource most in demand. As project director Bakken noted, "It often doesn't matter what the incentives are—teachers just don't have time." *All* of the NLC teachers complained about a lack of time to accomplish their projects and to meet with team members.

Although both NLC Coaches pointed to the need for a drastic restructuring of the school day for integrated, long-term teacher professional development, Tucker suggested Web-based technologies might be a partial solution to the time challenge:

> If you ask any teacher in the business nowadays, one of the problems they have is that they don't have time to be professionally trained. I know of only one way to reduce that problem a little bit and that is Web-based collaboration. So I think the Web is going to be a mainstay.

The new, collaborative Web-based technologies Tucker had in mind collectively are termed *Web 2.0.*

# New technologies for collaboration and learning—Web 2.0

NLC Coaches continued using eCoach for the duration of the project; however, they also considered how emerging technologies might support a learning community. Tucker envisions using various Web 2.0 applications as needed, in a flexible, teacher-centered model of professional development:

> We ended up with eCoach, because eCoach did a whole bunch of things: it aligned to the standards; it allowed reflections and it allowed dialoging to occur. [Now there are] new Web services, free services, that you could build into your network learning community ... like Flickr, like Writely, like Bloglines. Tom Carroll's view of a networked learning community was very human-focused. The resources were living people that could do certain tasks. Well, it is not that way anymore. Now there is a computer server somewhere that can do this for you and do it well ... and save you time.

Evolving Web-based collaborative technologies may indeed transform professional learning. Yet one might ask: With the teacher at the center, constructing his or her own Networked Learning Community, how does one give the teacher a vision of what might be possible, instructionally, with technology? In many cases, teachers do not know these technologies exist, or they cannot imagine how they would fit into a lesson. They also are often at a loss as to how to integrate technology into constructivist, inquiry-based learning activities, and sometimes they are afraid to try. Teachers have concerns about classroom management, about adequately covering curriculum, and about standardized testing. How then, do they obtain the vision for how technology might enhance their instruction, as it was enhanced for NLC middle-school mathematics teachers, and how do they receive the support they need to put all the pieces together? This is the formidable challenge for teacher professional development seeking to incorporate technology into enhanced classroom practice.

A further challenge for evaluation of teacher professional development is documenting whether or not changes in teacher practice are occurring, and whether those changes have resulted in improvements in student learning.

# Evaluating impact on teacher practice and student learning

Both teachers' self-reported survey data and observation documented change in the practices of NLC teachers. Data also demonstrated a greater confidence in the use of technology for teaching mathematics. In some cases, teachers made dramatic changes in their practice—evolving from the nonuse of technology and traditional mathematics pedagogy based on algorithms and rote knowledge, to the use of technology for enhanced, inquiry-based mathematics. Far more common, however, was the teacher who during the course of the NLC initiative developed an exceptional lesson or unit, but continued with day-to-day teaching practices largely unchanged. Whether the learning prompted by the NLC will continue to percolate and result in incremental changes over a period of time cannot yet be determined, because evaluation concluded with the end of the three-year project. Furthermore, evaluators were unable to substantiate enhanced student learning through test scores, although teacher surveys and student interviews offered evidence of enhanced engagement.

# Conclusion

It is common for school districts to establish mentoring, coaching, and peer-support models of professional development for teachers. Yet few school districts have sufficient capacity to provide teachers with ready access to all the resources and support they will need to learn new technologies and integrate them into a more constructivist pedagogy. The Washington State Networked Learning Community provides professional developers with both insights and caveats in combining online coaching with local resources to support a professional learning community.

Factors vital for the establishment of such a learning community include: (1) the choice of an appropriate tool for communication, (2) structured learning activity, (3) access to sufficient resources, and (4) continuing support from more expert learners. Also important for success is the coordination of professional development efforts online and on-site. Coaching, mentoring, and involvement in a professional learning community on the school and district level support and extend professional development efforts from outside the local setting. Such external efforts are complemented by a consistency of focus and allocation of sufficient resources from within the school and district.

Despite their successes, NLC Coaches Tucker and Bakken would admit they have not yet achieved Carroll's vision of a networked learning community; yet, through their efforts, they have indeed opened up the world for some teachers and their students:

> I can tell you with this grant, there have been times when I've sat down to work with it and thought "What am I doing?! This is not in my comfort zone!" But I know that the kids are going to enjoy it. They are going to have a piece of technology in their hands and they are going to get something from that in middle school that, when they go to high school, those concepts are just going to be that much easier, because it is a springboard … in this age group, it is just like a springboard. The world opens up wide and their parameters, their boundaries of what they think they can do, you know—expand.

## GETTING STARTED RESOURCES

Bull, G. (2006, April). Collaboration in a Web 2.0 environment. *Learning & Leading with Technology. 33*(7) pp. 23–24.

> Bull explains how syndicated feeds and other Web 2.0 tools can be used to follow multiple student postings, facilitate collaborative writing, share images associated with group projects, and track news topics related to a subject area.

Carroll, T. G. (2000). If we didn't have the schools we have today, would we create the schools we have today? *Contemporary Issues in Technology and Teacher Education* [Online serial], *1*(1). Retrieved August 20, 2007 from www.citejournal.org/vol1/iss1/currentissues/general/article1.htm

> Carroll suggests that networked learning communities might transform education.

eCoach. (2008). *Making Learning Personal*. Retrieved October 17, 2007 from http://my-ecoach.com

> My eCoach is an online learning environment that offers collaboration, communication, curriculum, standards, resources, and various coaching tools.

Maxwell, M., Kimball, W. H., Moore, J., & Petty, P. (2007). Tips for providing online instruction and professional development. Workshop at the National Educational Computing Conference in Atlanta, June 24, 2007. Materials retrieved January 2008 from www.pampetty.com/boutique.htm

> This workshop sponsored by ISTE's Special Interest Group for Teacher Educators (SIGTE) provides teacher educators with specific methods of creating online learning communities, providing online professional development, and online courses. Materials from the workshop and other resources are available from the Petty and Maxwell Web site: A Boutique Approach to Online Instruction: Different Paths to Exemplary Online Instruction.

Salpeter, J. (2003, August). Professional development: 21st century models. *Technology & Learning. 24*(1). Retrieved August 28, 2007 from www.techlearning.com/story/showArticle.php?articleID=13000492

> This article profiles three forward-looking staff development programs to explore the question: What do successful professional development communities look like? And what role does technology play in supporting them? Useful Web links to online professional development resources are provided.

## chapter 12

# Ensuring Integration of Teacher Changes

What practices will make sure
that professional development
takes a hold?

*Dianna L. Newman*
*University at Albany/SUNY*

## abstract

THIS CHAPTER SUMMARIZES major strategies and
indicators needed to ensure successful transfer of
skills, abilities, and knowledge acquired during professional development into K–12 educational settings.
Based on a meta-analysis of over 50 case studies, the
author uses the Three I Model of Systems Change to
highlight basic and advanced strategies that promote
greater technology integration. Key areas emphasized
include: changes in policies and procedures; changes
in infrastructure; and changes in delivery of curriculum
and instruction. Within each area, the author discusses
successful practices of initiating, implementing, and
impacting change as schools attempt to integrate
technology into their educational culture.

Creating sustained and substantial change in any system, especially within education, is highly complex and requires a system-wide effort. Examples identifying levels of change effort may be found within related literature (e.g., Hawley, 1997; Schalock, Fredericks, Dalke, & Alberto, 1994; & Shrag, 1996) but little is known of how to support and document change as an ongoing process. Newman (2001) and colleagues have developed a model for documenting systems change that shows it as a continuous, cyclical process of integrating reform into an organization. In this model, change is viewed as an active process, not a completed outcome. The Three I Model of System Change assesses the process according to three developmental levels—initiation, implementation, and impact. Within each of these levels, activities, learning, uses, and outcomes occur that build and support system-wide change. Documentation of these indicators can be used to not only show successful systems change but also to provide exemplary practices that can be used by others when enhancing their own systems.

---

### LITERATURE ESSENTIALS

## Systems change

Systems change is increasingly being recognized as a central component of program implementation and evaluation. This is especially evident in externally sponsored projects where the focus of funding is to not only to implement a process, but also to integrate it into the grantees' organization. First, let us begin with a generic definition of systems change adapted from that used by the Addictions Technology Transfer Centers (2000): "Systems change is the moving of knowledge, skills, abilities, and proven practices into an organization by showing that these facets are accepted, incorporated, and maintained" (Newman & Lobosco, 2007).

Multiple theories and definitions abound of what constitutes systems change and how to achieve it. Bridges (1986) proposed a model that views the process as an evolving cycle of change. Based on two major assumptions (change is a necessary demand of life and people resist change), Bridges emphasized the need for a visioning stage that encompasses culture change, negotiation, planning, and validation. Hegguland et al. (1985) also proposed that systems change is a multiphase process, but emphasizes the need for a bottom-up, participatory approach if true change is to occur and persist. This approach begins with an entry phase where stakeholders identify what is wrong and what needs to be fixed, followed by a mobilization phase where stakeholders develop a vision of the correct approach or process and decide who will implement the vision and, equally important, who will be affected by the changes. This is followed by planning and implementation phases in which strategies for developing the vision are designed and the required resources and activities provided. At the end of these phases, stakeholders then review what happened and if all participants are happy with the results.

*(Continued)*

---

## LITERATURE ESSENTIALS

*(Continued)*

Similarly, the Chaos Model of Systems Change (Schalock et al., 1994) assumes that the whole of the system is greater than the sum of its parts, that change is a long-term process, and that this process incorporates considerable disequilibria. This unbalance creates short-term randomness and chaos that refocuses to become meaningful change in the long term. This model also assumes that the various aspects of a system are interrelated, including leadership, polices, resources, environment, structures, personnel, information, decisions, and clients, and that as a result, the system is dynamic and change will be heavily influenced by old and new relationships, power structures, and conflicts. Consequently, the process must include conscious definition of new roles and validation of concerns.

The works of Fullan (1993, 1999, 2000) note that every organization has a set of internal values and that lasting change must acknowledge and reflect these values or else change of the values must be part of the process. Shula, Lee, and Van Melle (2001) address the requirements for sustainable change indicating the need for:

- a clear rationale that links change to outcomes,

- the use of an integrated approach to implementation,

- the creation of ongoing institutional support,

- changes in budgeting and evaluation that reflect importance of the process and outcomes,

- a sense of partnership and collaboration on the part of participants.

This chapter presents a summary of major change indicators for successful instructional technology integration. It is based on the results of over 50 systems change case studies conducted as part of Title III, Title IID, and Goals 2000 grant-supported efforts. As part of these grants, school districts utilized multiple types of professional development such as those discussed in the previous chapters in this book. A typical project included grant-supported trainings, planning sessions, and embedded professional development. Teachers designed interdisciplinary curricula and created the means to implement those curricula using software, Internet technologies, and multimedia hardware and systems. In addition, a technical support structure involving follow-up training and embedded professional development was available. Expanded hardware and software resources also were made available at some sites.

A key objective established for each grant was to document sustainable systemic change at the school-wide level and to identify best practices in creating and sustaining systemic change. As a result, over 50 concurrent multiyear case studies were conducted of schools, their teachers, the professional development offered and its subsequent implementation, and students' outcomes. Data sources included: (1) pre-, post-, follow-up and end-of-project surveys and interviews with stakeholders to assess perceptions regarding technology usefulness, proficiency, and confidence with various technologies, preference for instructional methods, and outcomes of instruction; (2) repeated observations of classrooms and alternative learning settings to document utilization of technology in instructional settings; (3) reviews of curricular units to document areas of instructional content and the associated technology utilized; and (4) a review of district and building archival records to document changes in policies, procedures, and technology infrastructure. These data were used to develop a Three I Systems Change Matrix for each of the buildings. A meta-analysis of these matrices was then conducted to document strategies and indicators of successful systems change that supported sustainable efforts in technology integration. This chapter provides a summary of indicators that support change in policies and procedures, infrastructure, and the delivery of curriculum and instruction. Professional developers should look for these basic and advanced indicators and use them as guidelines as they work toward successful educational technology integration.

## The Three I Model of Systems Change

The Three I Model of Systems Change (Newman, 2001) identifies multiple phases of systems change and key indicators of change within each phase as a means of delineating intra- and interrelationships among variables that support strategic planning and sustainability. The three primary phases of change are Initiation, Implementation, and Impact. The Initiation Phase considers those activities required to envision, design, and plan the program. The Implementation Phase includes the processes associated with managing the program activities and outcomes. Finally, the Impact Phase addresses long-term, change-based outcomes, the summative evaluation of these outcomes, and the subsequent refinement of the program's vision and goals.

Each of these phases identifies a series of dependent variables that support change. These include: activities (the detailed descriptions of the project components, including purposes and goals and structure); learning (the increased knowledge base and skills that may have been derived as a result of the activities); use (the actual implementation of the learning and its duration); and formative outcomes or outputs (the impact of the activity, through learning and use that feed further activities and steps). There are five basic areas in which change must occur for sustainability to be evidenced: policies and procedures; the supporting infrastructure; delivery of services (in educational settings, generally, the development or revision of curricula and instructional practices); expectations of consumers (teachers, administrators, parents, students, and the community); and the organizational climate. Use of this process results in a series of 15 tables (Initiation, Implementation, and Impact for each of the five areas) for each project. In cross-site evaluations, these data can be used to form a composite table that represents the most common elements across projects. A visual summary of the model may be found in Figure 12.1, and a sample Three I Matrix that resulted from the meta-analysis conducted for this chapter is presented in Table 12.1.

**Table 12.1** | Example of a Three I Matrix: key indicators of change to curriculum development and instruction in the initiation phase*

| Activity | Learning | Use | Outcome |
|---|---|---|---|
| **VISION** | | | |
| **L** Identifying technology resources that can be used to enhance instruction | **L** Knowledge of the existence of limited technologies and professional development opportunities | **L** Decision to pursue additional information and opportunities to increase expertise in using computers within educational contexts | **L** Development of entry-level familiarity with technology and its potential roles |
| **L** Discussing best practices in technology integration with other teachers | **L** Recognition of ways in which technology can be used to enhance curriculum development and instruction | **H** Development of more extensive criteria for assessing value of technologies and training opportunities | **L** Perceived need to adapt to changes in technology and to use technology as means of varying instruction |
| **H** Distinguishing grade level and subject area appropriateness | **H** Basic understanding of age appropriateness and applicability of certain tools to the given curriculum | | **H** Capacity to set clear, detailed goals and objectives for improving technology integration efforts |
| **H** Prioritizing professional development and integration activities that can most effectively enhance student learning | | | |
| **OBJECTIVES** | | | |
| **L** Defining roles that technology should play in curriculum design, instruction, and student learning | **L** Knowledge of realistic potential roles of technology within the classroom and school contexts | **L** Setting practical and observable objectives for technology integration in lesson planning and execution | **L** Communication with technology staff and other educators for direction on type and amount of professional development and appropriate resources |
| **L** Identifying familiarity, confidence, and skill development as desired training outcomes | **L** Understanding of unique challenges posed by technology as an information source and means of productivity | **H** Teachers establishing benchmarks for themselves and their students within content and contextual frameworks | **H** Prioritization of student-centered learning in the process of learning to integrate technology |
| **H** Focusing on using technology applications in different contexts and teaching students to evaluate their effectiveness | **H** Analysis of student understanding and perceptions concerning technology | | **H** Professional technology-based goals and objectives match those delineated in school-wide technology planning |
| **H** Prioritizing seamless integration of key technologies over broad knowledge | **H** Identification of barriers to overcome in fostering seamless integration | | |
| **STRATEGIES** | | | |
| **L** Seeking training and regular technical support from both local and external experts | **L** Acquisition of skills | **L** Selection of tools for integration into curriculum development and instruction | **L** Planned inclusion of technology tools within overall curriculum |
| **L** Increasing exposure to available technologies | **L** Discrimination of most worthwhile tools and applications | **H** Individualized plans for inclusion and integration of technology that are reflective of the building-wide plan but that are adaptive to unique classroom needs | **L** Planned inclusion of technology in specified instructional practices |
| **H** Using technology applications regularly to maintain effective practices | **H** Increased skill in acquiring and sharing new knowledge and confidence in creating changes that meet individual needs | | **H** Teacher and classroom specific plans for implementation |

***L (Low)** represents characteristics of schools lacking evidence of systemic change or demonstrating only basic change.*
**H (High)** *represents additional characteristics seen only in schools demonstrating advanced and comprehensive evidence of systemic change.*

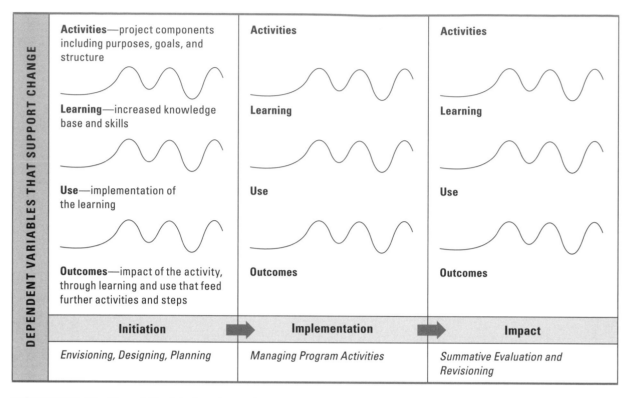

**FIGURE 12.1.** The Three I Model of systems change

## Indicators of systems change

The following sections summarize the key indicators for successful technology integration in educational systems that were identified as a result of the meta-analysis for policies and procedures, infrastructure, and the delivery of curriculum and instruction. These data represent 9 of the 15 meta-analysis tables developed for the overall study (including Initiation, Implementation, and Impact for each of the five components). As noted above, when developing these tables, we also made note of programmatic variations that resulted in low or basic change as well as those that resulted in major sustainable system-wide change. Low or basic indicators represent necessary change, while high or advanced indicators represent changes that led to deeper and more sustainable integration. Presentation of these changes also leads to the identification of best practices that will support and maintain professional development efforts when initiating educational technology reform, when implementing it, and finally when assessing the impact on the system. A brief summary of these results may be found in Figure 12.2.

| | | Policies and Procedures | Infrastructure | Curriculum and Instruction |
|---|---|---|---|---|
| **INDICATORS OF CHANGE** | **BASIC** | Technology support staff in charge of prioritizing resources, advocating technology growth, developing use policies, and evaluating current use<br><br>Dissemination of school-wide technology goals to staff<br><br>Technology curriculum has separate set of standards<br><br>Documented ineffective approaches are dropped from the list of possible uses | Reliance on in-house knowledge and support for technology infrastructure; a limited, if any, technology budget<br><br>Attending technology-based meetings and conferences is primary means of determining school needs<br><br>Development of stand-alone technology resources that are not embedded in content area needs | Identifying stand-alone tech instruction and curriculum as outcomes; review of technology standards not integrated with that of other standards<br><br>Professional development for specific technology skills<br><br>Identifying familiarity, confidence, and skill development as desired training outcomes |
| | **ADVANCED** | A school-wide committee develops a technology plan and conducts school-wide technology-based needs assessments and reviews data on a regular basis; resources for this review are part of the budget<br><br>Operational methods are in place to review and support specific grade level and subject area use<br><br>Administrators begin to use technology indicators as part of their review and hiring practices<br><br>Continued long-term review of uses and support for modifications and creative practices | Careful selection of equipment and establishment of criteria for evaluating impacts of infrastructure acquisition and utilization<br><br>Assessing infrastructure's capacity to meet emerging needs identified by stakeholders and through formal technology plan<br><br>Reorganization of space, budget, and personnel requirements to maximize best practice or to address new needs<br><br>Expanded and sustained infrastructure planning that will increase expectation of and satisfaction with student use<br><br>Technology needs are part of all professional development budgets, curriculum planning efforts, and staff review processes | Prioritizing professional development and integration activities by what is most effective in enhancing student learning<br><br>Implementing new technology-supported instructional methods based on student needs<br><br>Modeling, coaching, and self reflection become part of embedded professional development and instructional practices<br><br>Increase in technology uses to address standards, authentic assessment, and state testing; preparedness for regular modifications, initiation of new resource acquisition, and changes based on needs identified to support curriculum and instruction |

**FIGURE 12.2.** Basic and advanced indicators of change in the Three I Model. Low or basic indicators represent necessary change, while high or advanced indicators represent changes that led to deeper and more sustainable integration.

## Changes to policies and procedures

Changes in policies and procedures reflect the prominence of technology supported education within the legal and organizational supports of a system. This includes personnel selection, promotion criteria, budgets and long-term planning. Without changes to this leg of the system, short-term change may occur, but long-term sustained change will either not occur or not be consistent.

## Key indicators of change to policies and procedures in the initiation phase

In successful school districts, sustainable technology integration only occurred if it was accompanied by systemic change in polices and procedures backed by administrative support. This was facilitated by the use of needs assessments and formal or informal technology planning processes. In addition to administrative support, a key facilitator found in high change buildings within school-wide policies and procedures was the presence of an active technology coordinator who seamlessly: (1) connected educators with specific needs and curricula to appropriate technology applications, and (2) linked teachers to technology resources. The documentation of a detailed technology plan, including measurable technology-based objectives and observable performance indicators, also was prevalent among schools in which technology integration was successful. A basic process by which administrative changes were envisioned typically incorporated: (1) an increased understanding and acceptance of the possibilities inherent within new technology applications, and (2) a belief that technology changes must be planned and based on assessed needs and resources. The process of setting technology-based goals and objectives at the administrative level resulted in the identification of resources and possible applications of those resources, the dissemination of school-based initiatives to all staff members and upper-level administrators, and increased openness toward technology and congruency of perceptions concerning technology across the school. Administrative strategies for implementing technology-based policy or procedure changes often incorporated:

- the encouragement of teacher training,

- the investigation of infrastructure and support upgrades,

- the formation of collaborative partnerships among educators within and across schools, and

- the assessment and execution of formal, school-wide technology planning.

These strategies usually resulted in increased training and equipment acquisition, clearer technology expectations across the school, and increased educator cooperation in advancing technology-based goals.

## Key indicators of change to policies and procedures in the implementation phase

A variety of activities designed to influence the implementation of change in technology integration occurred at this stage. These included:

- prioritizing technology applications and infrastructure,

- engaging in both operational and strategic technology planning,

- integrating administrative and technology support staff knowledge of effective technology-based teaching into instructional supervision,

- using computer technologies for administrative tasks, and

- advocating for specific professional development opportunities based on grade-level and subject area needs.

Intermediate outcomes that were used to guide further implementation changes included: maintenance of effective polices and procures, increased interest in appropriate technology tools and applications across all grades and content, and identification of necessary reforms in technology uses and acquisition. In schools that evinced the greatest and most sustainable change, administrators indicated willingness and initiative in adapting technologies to the specific priorities of the school. In those sites with less sustainable change, however, technological resources were purchased and then building priorities were changed to match the technology. Buildings with more change also were more involved in continuous internal evaluation of their use of technology and its impact. In high change buildings, concrete planning processes included formative feedback, and both administrators and teachers were part of the data-gathering effort. Also in high change buildings, the process of shifting to sustainable in-house support and increased capacity for technology use in the classrooms was emphasized, as opposed to in computer labs; this resulted in greater self-determination for teachers and more support for policies and procedures that would benefit integrated classroom use with less emphasis on "who gets the lab when."

## Key indicators of change to policies and procedures in the impact phase

The long-term impacts of changes made to policies and procedures that led to technology integration were:

- permanent integration of technology in school-wide professional development schemes;

- the construction of a sustainable in-house support and professional development structure; and

- improvements in staff attitudes toward and expectations of technology utilization.

Although some degree of these changes were noted in most schools, their presence did not necessarily lead to sustained nor in-depth change as defined by integration in multiple content areas, grade levels, and specific individual needs. The process of technology planning alone, while basic to change, did not always lead to lasting change; instead, a revisioning process, by which administrators continued to analyze goals and objectives, was needed for sustainability. Those who provided evidence of revisioning indicated that they used both current information on educational technologies and previously implemented operational and strategic planning records to solicit new and appropriate support from outside sources, and to reestablish goals and objectives based on staff and infrastructure changes and student needs. This resulted in increased technology literacy, greater use, more diversification of technology resources and applications, and immediate consideration of student-centered learning when investigating innovative technologies.

As noted in Figure 12.2 column 1, changes in policies and procedures that supported sustainable, long-term systems change began with the development of a clear vision using databased decision-making that included all stakeholder groups. The resulting plan was supported by budget line items as well as internal review mechanisms that were included within administrative reviews. These changes became part of the permanent policies and procedures that supported not only technology but subsequent infrastructure and curriculum and instructional decision-making across the entire content domain.

## Changes to infrastructure

Lasting changes to K–12 infrastructure reflect the importance of technology and technology sustainability in the allocation and use of district resources. This includes the embedded, sustained acknowledgement that the switch to technology is never "done" but that it is a continuing evolution of professional development, equipment selection and replacement, and prioritization of staff and student needs. Without changes to this "leg" of the system, any other changes will rapidly fade or lose their own internal support.

### Key indicators of change to infrastructure in the initiation phase

Support for infrastructure growth within schools was typically initiated via assessments of needs and existing resources, comparisons of available technologies with those requested by trainees, and prioritization of several viable technology tools and support activities. In schools evidencing greater change, formal infrastructure planning often was conducted in coordination with district-wide technology planning, and resources were shifted, depending on availability, to meet the diverse needs of trained educators. This procedure led to the prioritization of infrastructure growth initiatives and the eventual identification of clear alternatives for resources and activities needed to build the infrastructure. In more advanced districts, infrastructure planning was initiated within school-wide technology planning, thus allowing for common visions for infrastructure development across administration, technical support, and teaching staffs. Goals and objectives for changes to the infrastructure were established based on what the school perceived a "trained" teacher would need. This led to a clearer understanding of the resources that existed within the schools and the capacities of the schools to support growth. Outcomes of the process of setting goals and objectives included the identification of areas in need of changes followed by the establishment of priorities for procurement. The prioritization was based on teachers', administrators', and technology staff members' formal and informal ratings of efficiency of specific resources (hardware and software) and their support for integrated instruction using these resources.

Strategies utilized to further infrastructure change initiatives included the following:

- clearly identifying the roles of technical support personnel or the school technology coordinator;

- defining essential, possible, and impractical support and equipment resources; and

- creating a formal plan for evaluating and upgrading the school's infrastructure.

This process helped to refine the selection of effective technologies and support activities and, in high change schools, adapt the infrastructure to the needs of stakeholders.

## Key indicators of change to infrastructure in the implementation phase

The implementation of systemic change to technology infrastructures typically included:

- the solicitation and integration of external grant-funded support,

- the maintenance and modification of equipment based on stakeholder skills and needs informs technology planning, and

- the expansion of the roles of technology coordinators or experts.

More complex change was sometimes manifested through broad reorganization of space and infrastructure schemes. In schools that featured infrastructure-based systemic change, technology planners often sought equipment, training, and technical support from external experts and acquired and implemented new tools to match the needs of stakeholders. The integration of upgrades and new equipment into schools' infrastructures promoted successful uses of technology across the buildings, especially when the capacities to meet technology demands were regularly assessed. Although all schools reported that support for participation continued and that technology personnel reacted appropriately to emerging resultant barriers, the most successful districts featured proactive approaches to meeting new demands. These included:

- shifting staff roles,

- standardizing equipment acquisition and use procedures, and

- integrating infrastructure assessment into formal technology planning.

As a result of these proactive changes, there was greater flexibility and accuracy in diagnosing new infrastructure-based problems and implementing solutions. The implementation of new means of managing technology infrastructures was formatively evaluated by collecting feedback from and observing equipment uses by teachers and students, conducting and assessing the strengths and benefits of equipment trials, and engaging technology committees or teacher decision-makers in collaborative planning. Through these processes, planners were able to identify gaps between the demands for and capacities of existing hardware and software and to formulate recommendations for broad and specific modifications to infrastructure. In general, key hardware and software revisions included the acquisition of resources that were deemed more suitable for schools following formative evaluation and the reorganization of space or equipment connections to maximize efficiency and to address needs or problems. This often resulted in more prompt and effective progress in infrastructure management and improvements in mastery of technology use across school buildings.

### Key indicators of change to infrastructure in the impact phase

In most schools, change was described in terms of shifts from uninformed acquisitions of resources to careful infrastructure-building based on projected needs and benefits. In those schools where change was the greatest and most lasting, the movement went further to feature a shift from rigid, long-term infrastructure planning to a system that allowed for regular modifications based on frequently changing conditions. The impact of these processes included:

- improved technology utility and monitoring of technology applications,

- increased stakeholder input into the infrastructure change process,

- administrative willingness to support flexible infrastructures, and

- potential for the infrastructures to grow to meet new demands of stakeholders.

Summative evaluation was used in a majority of schools to document these changes through periodic inspection of equipment and observations of uses. High change schools featured more formal evaluation efforts, such as planned discussions in technology committee meetings or in-depth surveys that solicited teachers' technology preferences, uses, skills, and perceived needs. In these buildings, technology coordinators used this information to inform their decision-making, particularly with regard to purchasing, updating, or phasing out resources and applications. It also was noted that only in those schools with the greatest change was summative evaluation used to predict or prevent future infrastructure failure and to assist in making changes in other local buildings. Those schools with the greatest change used this information as part of the process of creating or revising their vision and included discussions of the increased diversity of students and the relationship of diversity to technology needs and incoming technology competencies, as well as student, parent, and teacher knowledge of and satisfaction with ongoing efforts.

As noted in Figure 12.2 column 2, changes in infrastructure that supported long-term, sustainable systems change began with a clear vision of the resources needed to support an integrated approach to professional development and to subsequent use. The selection of resources was based on formal goals and objectives that reflected support for best practices of integrated use as well as flexibility that would meet growing and changing needs. These viewpoints became part of the regular review of the building's infrastructure and ongoing needs assessments related to professional development and curriculum and instruction.

## Changes to the processes of curriculum development and instruction (C & I)

Changes in the design and development of curriculum and instruction that reflect systemic support for technology integration are the easiest to envision but often take the longest to obtain and area the hardest to sustain. These changes encompass both major and minor alterations to the delivery of services to children, parents, and the community, and have the greatest impact on the key stakeholders. It is the vision of changes to this leg of the system that drives the other changes but that is also the most controversial and easiest to lose.

## Key indicators of change to curriculum development and instruction in the initiation phase

The process of systemic change that best led to altered curriculum development began with the identification of resources and best practices followed by a decision to increase personal and professional knowledge and skills. In those schools where the greatest change was noted, this identification was coupled with the distinguishing of grade/content/subject-area appropriateness and need, as well as the ability to develop individual goals that supported the building-wide technology plan. Specific indicators that were established as part of the envisioning process of changes in curriculum and instruction included the following:

- increased teacher confidence with using technology in instruction,

- increased general proficiency in the use of educational technologies,

- creation of technology-integrated curricula that reflect standards,

- identification of new interdisciplinary connections supported by technology,

- development of new means of using technology to teach problem solving and teaching technology as a tool for problem solving, and

- creation of technology-integrated authentic assessment activities.

The delineation of subsequent goals and objectives used these indicators to establish building-wide expectations. Moreover, in schools that had sustainable change, the indicators identified above were used to establish specific teacher and student goals. This included defining the role of technology within the broad curriculum and in specific curriculum units. Strategies ranged from acquisition of stand-alone skills and resources needed to support existing curricula to the creation of new knowledge and methods of integrating and sharing with others. The greatest growth was noted when the goals reflected not only teacher goals, but also student goals, including benchmarks and self-evaluation procedures established within the learning context. Curriculum plans that strove for both knowledge and changes in affect as well as cognitive outcomes also resulted in more detailed efforts that subsequently culminated in greater impact.

The initiation of such system-wide changes in instruction was a developmental process; it typically began through the identification of technology resources and the means by which they could be used to enhance teaching, as well as observations of best practices and exposure to professional development opportunities delivered by trained colleagues. Following the establishment of clear instructional and curricular goals, as well as intended outcomes of student technology use, educators then sought training and direct exposure to and experience with available tools with the assistance of school-wide technology experts and administrators. In buildings where the most progress in change was noted, educators transferred the knowledge into content- and age-appropriate learning from the beginning of training; they did not wait until they returned to the classroom. In most cases, this immediate transfer was planned as part of the professional development activity.

## Key indicators of change to curriculum development and instruction in the implementation phase

The implementation of systemic change in curriculum development and instruction yielded two divergent patterns of growth that reflected a continuum of change based on the following variables:

- perceptions of the process,
- changes to current practices,
- the value of technology and its role in instruction,
- the role and process of formative evaluation, and
- outcomes of evaluation.

Those systems that perceived the process as primarily a staff development initiative, whereby faculty would learn and implement new skills, had lower levels of intermediate outcomes and limited sustainable change. Those systems that viewed the process as encompassing changes to policies and infrastructure as well as the acquisition and implementation of new skills had more sustainable outcomes. Implementation activities resulting in long-term changes to curriculum and instructional practices reflected delivery of the strategies developed during training and later planning. At the lowest level of sustainability, this consisted of adding technology to previously developed lesson plans through the introduction of supporting materials and online resources. At the highest level, where more change and sustainability was noted, those who received training and support created new lesson plans and implemented new methods of teaching the content. In this context, technology became the tool whereby resources were used to design the curriculum, increase the knowledge shared, and empower the student to search for new knowledge. Intermediate outcomes documented by the teachers and by evaluation reflected the two divergent patterns.

The results of lower levels of integration were alternate modes of teaching content, more motivated students, and more plans for eventual expansion of technology use. Schools at the higher levels of sustainability, however, evidenced direct curriculum change outcomes plus an increased valuing of the process of change. In addition, schools at the higher levels of sustainable change used formative evaluation of the process of initiating curriculum and instructional changes to inform the process. This process took place at both the individual level and within teams; it consisted of examining the desired goals of specific changes and their expected outcomes and assessing their success. In those settings where lower-level change occurred, barriers to implementation were identified that reflected the need for more skills. In those settings where higher levels of change occurred, barriers and facilitators to improving skills, infrastructure, policy, and overall support were addressed. This resulted in two divergent outcomes of evaluation; in the low change settings, unsuccessful instructional integration approaches were immediately deemed not appropriate or not applicable and were dropped; in the more successful cases, resources were reallocated to allow for more support or modifications of the processes, thereby supporting continued testing and development of methods.

## Key indicators of change to curriculum development and instruction in the impact phase

Although the majority of schools were able to document some intermediate outcomes in the area of curriculum and instructional practices, not all showed evidence of long-term sustainable impact on variables identified in the above sections. Key strategies supporting sustainable change reflected the movement of technology away from stand-alone curriculum or the learning of skills only as a means of providing support for specific uses. In high change schools, technology was viewed as a resource that teachers should be using within and across multiple content and contextual settings. A philosophical change, noted in schools that exhibited sustainable integration, was that technology was a means of empowering both teachers and students in constructing their own knowledge. Those systems that addressed change as a direct, independent outcome resulting primarily from professional development for teachers tended to modify their vision to reflect the boundaries established by specific skills; this resulted in short-term change.

Those systems that addressed change as a holistic process encompassing professional development, infrastructure, and policies perceived it as an inclusive and dynamic method of changing curriculum and instruction. In these buildings, educators continually revisited and revised all areas based on the outcomes associated with changes in the other areas. The role of summative evaluation and revisioning also played an important role in those schools that experienced sustainable system-wide changes in curriculum and instruction. In these buildings, internal and external evaluation of the use of technology-integrated instructional practices became part of standard instructional reviews and personnel evaluations. These reviews were used to continually support clarifications of the role of technology within cross-classroom curriculum planning and in the development of grade and building wide expectations of use. These clarifications, in turn, fed the expectations of changes in policies and procedures and in the infrastructure needed to support curriculum and instruction.

As noted in Figure 12.2 column 3, curriculum and instruction that supported long-term systemic change moved from a vision of stand-alone technology and acquisition of technology skills to a unified, embedded approach. Both training and use reflected local student needs as well as curriculum requirements and learning standards. Support for embedded professional development was based on a philosophy of integrated and student-centered learning with technology as a tool for teaching and learning, reflected frequent reviews of infrastructure, and included development of flexible policies that would extend those uses.

# Summary

In-depth, cross-site analysis of the process of creating sustainable system-wide change related to technology integration in K–12 settings indicates that it is not merely a matter of offering professional development to teachers, administrators, and other instructional staff. Rather, the process must be viewed from a systems change perspective. Changes in the delivery of services—that is, curriculum and instruction—do not stand alone. Not only must educators be provided with and encouraged to use their new technology-based knowledge and skills, the school in which they work must also change. The development of a technology plan is not enough. *Policies and procedures* in support of that plan must be clearly identified and supported by all levels of staff and the community and these must be revisited in an ongoing manner. The *infrastructure* also must be developed in a manner that allows for flexible and creative use of technology resources and that allows for the redefinition of stakeholder roles. *Curriculum and instruction* must be viewed and supported at all levels as a dynamic process that is reflective of teacher, student, and community needs and that can be changed to meet those needs while maintaining integrity of delivery of instruction. If we are to ensure the transfer of professional development in technology into the classroom, we must foster changes in the supporting policies, procedures, infrastructure, and expectations that will in turn foster changes in instruction and learning.

## GETTING STARTED RESOURCES

Chinman, M., Imm, P., & Wandersman, A. (2004). *Getting to outcomes 2004: Promoting accountability through methods and tools for planning, implementation, and evaluation.* Santa Monica, CA: RAND Corporation

This document provides the user with an overview of program accountability, key steps in creating programmatic and systemic change, lessons learned from practice, and potential methodologies that can be used to support evaluation efforts.

Fullan, M. (1993). *Change forces: Probing the depths of educational reform.* New York: The Falmer Press.

In this and subsequent manuscripts, Fullan discusses the status of systems change in educational and social systems and why we must pay attention to key factors including the values and interrelationships of those involved in the change.

Newman, D. L. & Lobosco, A. F. (2007, November). *Participatory systems change evaluation: Involving all users in all stages of systems change assessment.* Paper presented at Evaluation 2007: The Annual Meeting of the American Evaluation Association, Baltimore, MD.

This paper and others available from the author describe the process of documenting systems change and the use of the Three I Model of Systems Change. Selected papers and reports on specific projects also are available that document the process of systems change as related to educational technology integrated instruction by contacting dnewman@uamail.albany.edu

Parsons, B. A. (1997). *Using a systems approach to building communities.* St. Louis, MO: Danforth Foundation. Retrieved October 29, 2007, from the Danforth Foundation Web site. www.muohio.edu/forumscp/policymakers

Funded by the Danforth Foundation, this document and the supporting material address stages of systems change, variables related to systems change, and areas that are in need of support if systems change is to occur.

United Way (1996). *Measuring program outcomes: A practical approach.* United Way of America.

This manual provides a step-by-step approach to evaluating and documenting program outcomes for health, human service, educational and other social service programs.

# Summary and Synthesis

## Lessons learned about successful professional development in educational technology

*Melissa Pierson*
*University of Houston*

*Arlene Borthwick*
*National-Louis University*

## Charting a path to success

Designing effective educational professional development is a lot like charting directions for a road trip, although it involves much more than simply lining up longitude and latitude and tracing your finger to the starred destination on a map. Sometimes what appears to be the most direct route is missing key information, such as unexpected construction or traffic patterns. Add to that uncertainty the human variable, and the inherent problem becomes ascertaining that, in the first place, everyone in the car wants to go to the same place in the same manner.

Mapping the journey to effective professional development for educational technology is often assumed to be straightforward, but Lawless and Pellegrino (2007) remind us that content, delivery, and duration of professional development are important only to the extent that PD activities impact program outcomes, teacher change, and student achievement. Although a district might have charted a "right" way to proceed based on available data, the true best route must take into consideration an entire range of variables. What happens if a backseat passenger wants to take the scenic route or an impromptu detour—by examining alternative software programs, for example. Linda Tafel (chapter 2) reminds us that designers of professional development cannot assume that a group of teachers begin the journey with an identical set of goals and motivations. A one-way street to professional development success doesn't exist!

In chapter 1, Bowe and Pierson reviewed early initiatives directed to understanding the elements of successful professional development in educational technology. Subsequent chapters in the book provided additional knowledge and theoretical frameworks that enabled us, as editors, to identify major lessons learned.

The table titled "Professional Development Models At a Glance" (found in the Preface of this book), includes a column on the right for "Selected Lessons Learned." That column provides a preview of specific lessons detailed below.

## MAJOR LESSON
# Systems change for sustained innovation

Professional development does not occur in a vacuum. Several chapter authors (Borthwick & Risberg; Warriner; Newman) refer to the complex, interconnected systems in which professional development activities occur. Senge's (2006) book, *The Fifth Discipline* (discussed in chapter 3) highlights the fifth and essential discipline as systems thinking. In our efforts to increase the use of technology by teachers and students, we must expect systemic changes (Newman; Warriner) in organizational policies and procedures, infrastructure, the delivery of curriculum and instruction, expectations of stakeholders, and organizational climate (Newman) to assure lasting impact.

Along the same lines, in constructing their model for school improvement, Mid-continent Research for Education and Learning (McREL) identified key components influencing student achievement—components that were found to influence one another, suggesting "that schools function as interconnected systems" (Cicchinelli, Dean, Galvin, Goodwin, & Parsley, 2006, p. 5). McREL's key components were based on multiple reviews of the literature (completed in 2000–2003) and research of schools with high-needs populations (completed in 2005) to determine what works in effective classroom instruction, schools, and leadership. As we plan for professional development focused on use of technology in classroom instruction, we must also consider a similar multitude of variables in play—distribution of leadership, resources, existing skill levels, social networks, and others—and how changing one variable affects the others. We must not only take into account local variables, but situate our school within the district, state, federal, and even global environment (Borthwick & Risberg, chapter 3).

## MAJOR LESSON
# Shift toward an emphasis on organizational learning

As Rob Bowe and Melissa Pierson remind us in chapter 1, the educational technology community has a history of understanding our work as a series of staged or leveled models of teacher development. These prior models had "fixed sequences of stages representing successively higher levels of knowledge and skills acquisition … based on a traditional notion of professional skill as a set of attributes, such as knowledge, skills, and attitudes" (Dall'Alba & Sandberg, 2006, p. 385). Inasmuch as early frameworks aimed to shift the focus from the technology tools to the teachers and their developmental needs, they addressed the uniqueness of learners who participate in any professional development session. The role of the school organization, then, was to respond to these individual needs.

However, the convergence of recommendations from authors in this book suggests that although assessing teachers' needs and understanding the types of assistance and concerns teachers might have based on developmental levels are indeed necessary first steps, the focus on a single teacher's needs cannot tell a complete learning story. In fact, the linear nature of these staged models may conceal "more fundamental aspects of professional skill development" (Dall'Alba & Sandberg, 2006, p. 383). Distilling professional development down to discrete technology skills removes learning from the important context of content and pedagogy, as well as from a supporting system frame of reflection, inquiry, collaboration, and sharing. As educators, we know too much about learning in context to assume that teacher-learning can be described otherwise.

A systems approach to change implies a shift from a mindset of individual learning to global thinking of how individuals fit into the larger organization and the learning that must take place on the organizational level. This resonates with Senge's (2006) notion of individual learning taking place within the learning organization, and boldly highlights Borthwick and Risberg's chapter 3 recommendations, such as those to balance organization change with individual change. Table S.1 diagrams this shift from the solitary focus on individual learning implied by stage models. Successful PD initiatives are characterized by an expanded, informed, and connected view of learning on the organizational level.

**Table S.1** | Staged individual learning models compared with systems approach

| Stage Models Emphasizing Individual Learning | Systems Approach |
| --- | --- |
| Individual learning | Culture of organizational learning |
| Focus on individual needs | Focus on sharing and collaboration; learning communities |
| Focus on teacher change | Focus on teacher as learner |
| Focus on teacher skills, attitudes, and use of technology | Focus on teaching-learning environment, supported by technology as appropriate |
| Focus on technology acquisition and use | Focus on school reform |
| Assessment in the form of identification of stages of teacher adoption or technology implementation | Assessment in the form of student achievement |

Clearly a learning organization perspective necessitates a reevaluation of how we have previously framed the nature of professional development. We do not suggest this shift toward a learning organization perspective as a shift away from a focus on individual learning or as a release from the need to assess individuals. Rather, we assert that the same solid understanding of individuals and subsequent attention to those needs are integral to a larger change effort. As Linda Tafel, author of chapter 2, summed it up, "We must adopt models for simultaneous learning—supporting the individual, the individual in relationship with others, and in relationship to the larger organization" (p. 29).

Such shifts in learning perspective can already be seen in initiatives that could influence PD efforts. For example, the refreshed National Educational Technology Standards for students (NETS•S) (International Society for Technology in Education, 2007), released in 2007, shift away from prescribing individual skills with technology and toward a global perspective of 21st-century skills for learning. This choice of emphasizing strands such as collaboration, research, and problem solving over sheer technology skills bodes well for the guidance we can expect from the corresponding standards for teachers, NETS•T.

## MAJOR LESSON
# TPACK framed by reflective inquiry and collaboration for job-embedded support

In search of an organizing framework to describe the meaningful use of technology in teaching and learning, the educational technology field has converged on the idea of *Technological Pedagogical Content Knowledge* (TPACK) (Mishra & Koehler, 2006; Pierson, 2001). Derived from Shulman's (1986) notion of teaching as the intersection of content knowledge and pedagogical knowledge, there is agreement in the field that technological knowledge must also be a component in the definition of 21st-century teaching. The National Technology Leadership Summit held its ninth annual meeting in fall 2007, bringing together leaders in education associations and educational technology journals, with corporate representatives and federal policy makers, for the express purpose of exploring "how teacher education programs can facilitate the development of TPACK in preservice and inservice teachers" (National Technology Leadership Coalition, 2007). During the summit, the group considered alternate phrasing for TPACK, landing on TPACK as the "total package" for 21st-century teaching. Teachers with this total package possess discipline-specific expertise, the ability to employ teaching strategies compatible with content, and the skill and ability to use a variety of technology tools and resources in meaningful ways to support and extend each content need through multiple teaching and learning roles.

However, even preparing teachers with a sound TPACK foundation and ample skills practice in context may not be enough to ensure that good teachers remain in the profession. In fact, beginning teachers are more likely to remain in their chosen occupation when they have access to more than just knowledge of what and how to teach, including resources like mentors and collaboration with other teachers (Smith & Ingersoll, 2004). The authors in this volume have demonstrated that professional development must situate teachers squarely within the interaction among content, pedagogy, and technology to engage them in an exploration of meaningful technology-supported teaching. Common features drawn from the models presented in this book further suggest that the TPACK conceptual model can be strengthened when supported by a surrounding "frame" of *Reflection, Inquiry, Collaboration, and Sharing* (see Figure S.1).

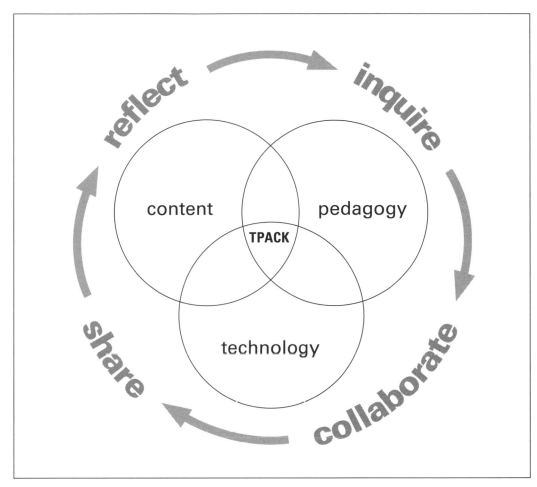

**FIGURE S.1.** The TPACK model framed by Reflection, Inquiry, Collaboration, and Sharing

We learn from Kara Dawson and her colleagues (chapter 7) that effective peer coaching initiatives must initially require time for *reflection* on "how technology can transform teaching and learning," thus establishing from the start a vision for teachers of the potential for the technology-supported strategies they are to learn through a PD session. Joanne Carney (chapter 11) and Dianna Newman (chapter 12) echo the need to establish a vision of how the use of technology can enhance instruction from the outset, further specifying that teachers are more likely to recognize the value of what they are learning if ties to their own work are made.

In chapter 9, Vince Ham, Derek Wenmoth, and Ronnie Davey describe three distinct projects with the common thread of *inquiry* woven throughout. These projects involved teachers identifying questions about their own practice with technology and action research activities undertaken to answer those questions. Dawson and his colleagues offer teacher inquiry as a tool to continually assess student learning as the outcome of PD initiatives, and Rae Niles (chapter 5) discusses the appreciative inquiry stance toward building on what is working.

The element of *collaboration* was present in most of the models in this book. From structuring time for collaboration (chapter 6), to collaboration with mentors (chapter 7), learning circles (chapter 8), learning communities (chapter 10), and even collaboration with students (chapter 5), these projects built success into their designs by simply having teachers work together. Not only did the collaboration encourage teachers to participate, it also ensured that teachers learned from one another in a job-embedded support model (chapter 7). Joanne Carney (chapter 11) describes how arranging for an authentic audience with which teacher participants can *share* their learning provides an "impetus to change" for teachers, giving them reason to engage. Sharing with one another the results of authentic tasks, such as the individual and group tales in chapter 8, also extends the learning exponentially. The use of teacher-authored real-life cases (Otto, chapter 4) enabled novice participants to grasp basic and potential applications of new technology.

This "framed" definition of technology-supported teaching positions TPACK as not only a conceptual model but also as a practical "total package" for ongoing support embedded in the work and culture of teaching. The definition acknowledges the role of such well-proven activities as reflection, inquiry, and collaboration as vital components to teacher development, especially related to educational technology.

**MAJOR LESSON**

## Ongoing assessment and action research to drive professional development choices

Bowe and Pierson (chapter 1) caution us that it is difficult to attribute changes in teaching and learning to professional development efforts. Unless we have a higher education partner (Cunningham et al., chapter 10), many of us may not have the resources or desire to design an experimental study (complete with control group) for a scientific study of what PD activities are the most effective in our context. Still, we want to know whether selected PD activities influence teacher behaviors and classroom instruction, and we need data to inform planning for our continuing PD work.

Each of the models presented in this book were accompanied by a description of how project leaders (or others) used a variety of tools to assess project outcomes and, thus, the effects of the professional development approaches that were used. Throughout the chapters in our book, we heard the almost mantra-like phrase guiding professional developers to "focus on student learning." This is not surprising in an age of accountability. The National Staff Development Council (NSDC) Standards are organized into three areas—the context, process, and content of staff development. All three subsets of standards are listed under identical introductory headings, focusing on "Staff development that improves the learning of all students" (p. 1). Further, one of the twelve NSDC standards states that "staff development that improves the learning of all students uses multiple sources of information to guide improvement and demonstrate its impact" (National Staff Development Council, 2001, p. 1).

As noted by Arlene Borthwick and Cathy Risberg (chapter 3), the professional developer should assess both classroom outcomes and organizational conditions. Guskey (2000) suggests that in addition to student learning outcomes, we should assess participants' reactions and learning, use of new knowledge and skills, and organization support and change. Dianna Newman (chapter 12) reminds us that outcomes identified within the various phases of professional development should be used to determine further steps and future activities. Similarly, McREL's overarching model for school improvement, *Success in Sight*, is a five-stage process that mirrors an action research approach: a cycle of taking stock, focusing on a solution based on existing research, taking collective action, monitoring and adjusting, and maintaining momentum (Cicchinelli et al., 2006).

Without inquiring into our own practice, we run the risk of driving up blind alleys. We agree with our New Zealand colleagues in chapter 9 who suggest that a self-study approach can not only be the PD method, but also lead to larger, common answers about student outcomes. The phases described in Tom Otto's Professional Development Framework (chapter 4), including Trial, Reflect, and Modify (phase 2) and Implement and Reflect (phase 3), also mirror the steps in a cycle of action research. Such a spiraled sequence uses the results of systematic inquiry to inform and lead into the next phase of questioning. These models imply that successful PD efforts must certainly have at their center the basic definitional components of TPACK elements (see above), but must also resemble the iterative action research cycle: encouraging teachers to begin any training by thinking about what they can learn from it and how what they are to learn is situated in the work that they already do; posing questions for how teaching and learning can improve; collaborating with peers and those more experienced to work to solve problems of practice; and evaluating and sharing findings with one another as part of an ongoing effort at collective improvement.

## Charting the route to PD success: Insider tips

Although the lessons described above are powerful ones, they are not the only lessons that may be gleaned from reading this text. Below are important yet perhaps less obvious recommendations to help you navigate the journey to PD success.

## TIP: Don't overplan

Tom Otto's model (chapter 4) for expanding teachers' use of ePortfolios teaches us two important lessons. First, the focus on an instructional and assessment strategy—ePortfolios—enabled teachers to learn (and want to learn) to use a variety of new technologies. Second, although a variety of PD activities were used as the project was disseminated across Queensland, Australia, the core design of the project included only four workshops each year. This long-term approach gave teachers time to grow over a period of years, without overwhelming them with PD activities.

## TIP: Choose your traveling companions wisely

No one wants to sit through mile after mile of a long car ride with someone whose company they don't enjoy. If you have any choice in the matter (and many a brother or sister wish they did) you should be able to choose your traveling companions. David Erickson and Sally Brewer (chapter 8) recommend traveling with the leadership of a change agent. This go-to person can serve multiple roles, including teacher, advocate—for both technology and professional development—and liaison with administration and the community. The advice for schools from Craig Cunningham and his colleagues (chapter 10) is to partner with someone who has the stamina to take the long driving shift. The authors help us to see the rich array of benefits that higher-education partners can bring to a school relationship, most notably the capacity for long-term commitment to projects, especially research-related activities vital to ongoing program evaluation and curriculum development. Finally, Judy DiLeo (chapter 7) suggests that the success of a mentor and mentee relationship is much more dependent on personal compatibility than on hailing from the same grade levels or content areas. Professional developers who devote time up front to matching mentors who actually want to be together will ensure a happier load of passengers, and ultimately, more commitment to the work at hand.

## TIP: Take turns driving (expand leadership and participation)

Working with Students Willing to Assist with Technology (SWAT) Team members, high school teachers in Sedgwick, Kansas, increased their skills, lesson integration, and comfort level with ICT. Thinking of students as a resource or asset readily accessible in our schools may require a paradigm shift, allocating a measure of leadership, voice, and power to our students. Yet, as described by Rae Niles (chapter 5), the outcomes achieved for students, teachers, and the community extended well beyond providing skill-based professional development for teachers. In effect, the SWAT program increased opportunities for student-centered and student-led instructional strategies.

Other authors (e.g., Borthwick & Risberg; Tafel; Warriner) remind us that it really is all right if we shake things up by switching what are considered the traditional leadership roles. Vince Ham (chapter 9) and one of his coauthors served as mentors in the projects on which they report. In this capacity, one of their approaches was to study their *own* practice as teacher educators at the same time that project teachers were action researching *their* individual teaching practices. Not only did this "self-study of self-study" serve as an ongoing formative evaluation, directly connecting project leaders with changing teacher needs, but it likely established a sense of authenticity in the action research model with which the teachers were being asked to engage. In yet another example, balancing online and on-site components, the project directors in Carney's chapter (chapter 11) actually conceived of themselves as coaches rather than as directors, emphasizing a "we're all in this together" mindset.

## TIP: Watch for road signs and gas stations along the way (nurture key elements that vary by project stage)

In their chapters, both George Warriner (chapter 6) and Dianna Newman (chapter 9) emphasize a systemic approach to sustaining technology innovation, Warriner through the lens of an activity system and Newman through use of the Three I Model. Based on an examination of schools across the country with high and low evidence of systemic change, Newman's Three I Model examined key indicators of change within three phases: initiation, implementation, and impact. Similarly, in his examination of the Instructional Technology Mentor Program (ITMP) in Sheboygan, Wisconsin, Warriner identified critical events and predictors of sustainability, and connected these to designing a framework for PD. The lesson for professional developers, then, is to be aware of how to structure for, support, and/or nurture key elements that may differ by phase or stage across the implementation of an innovation. Further, we should not be surprised to hit an implementation dip as we move ahead (Warriner, chapter 6). These road signs along the way should enable the developer to more accurately chart the path to success.

## Conclusion: Document your journey

As the reader of this book, you presumably are in a position to make choices about professional development strategies at some level. *This process must be collaborative; if the route is charted by one person, it may only include destinations that the one person desires to visit.* Harris (2007) recommends that making choices about the particular professional development methods and strategies is exactly what a school or district must do, selecting, combining and sequencing aspects to craft an overall approach based on its unique needs as a learning organization. The intention of our book is to assist this choice process by presenting multiple and varied cases of effective educational technology professional development strategies; however, in no way should it be interpreted as a complete list from which to select the single correct solution. Instead, the journey for a district toward effectively prepared technology-using teachers is one that must certainly consider individual needs and developmental levels of teachers, but within the larger context of where the district and community as a whole want to arrive in terms of using technology. And, along the way, Lawless and Pellegrino remind us that districts must make concerted efforts to systematically collect data, specifically regarding, "approaches, impact, and effectiveness across content areas and grade levels" (2007, p. 604). So, just as you might create a scrapbook of travel memorabilia to document vacation memories, a thorough evaluation that documents a professional development implementation will enable professional developers to review progress and effectiveness so that they can appropriately allocate resources for enhanced technology use by teachers and learners.

In a way, the professional development models presented in our book provide you with an atlas or travel guide, illustrating possible venues for you to consider in your PD journey. No matter which form(s) of travel you take—in-house leadership, peer coaching, learning circles, action research, partnering, networked learning communities—as you embark on your trip, remember to plan for passengers at the *individual and small group levels* (situated learning, job-embedded support, and reflective inquiry), and as participants in an *organizational system* of interactive processes that require ongoing assessment to establish professional development choices that sustain desired integration of technology uses in the teaching-learning environment.

# References

## A

Aamodt, A., & Plaza, E. (1994). Case-based reasoning: Foundational issues, methodological variations, and system approaches. *Artificial Intelligence Communications, 7*(1), 39–59.

Adamy, P., & Heinecke, W. (2005). The influence of organizational culture on technology integration in teacher education. *Journal of Technology and Teacher Education, 13*, 233–255.

Addiction Technology and Transfer Center. (2000). *The change book: A blueprint for technology transfer.* Kansas City, MO: Author.

Apple Inc. (2005). *Research: What it says about 1 to 1 learning.* Cupertino, CA: Author.

Argyris, C. (1999). *On organizational learning* (2nd ed.). Oxford, UK: Blackwell.

Argyris, C., & Schön, D. (1974) *Theory in practice: Increasing Professional Effectiveness.* San Francisco: Jossey-Bass.

Aworuwa, B., Worrell, P., & Smaldino, S. (2006). Working with partners: A reflection on partners and projects. *TechTrends 50*(3), 38–44.

Ayersman, D. J. (1996). Effects of computer instruction, learning style, gender, and experience on computer anxicty. *Computers in the Schools, 12*(4), 15–30.

## B

Bailey, G. D., & Lumley, D. (1997). *Staff development in technology: A sourcebook for teachers, technology leaders, and school administrators.* Bloomington, IN: National Educational Service.

Bain, J. D. (1999). Introduction to the special issue on evaluation of innovations. *Higher Education Research & Development, 18*(2), 165–172.

Bandura, A. (1986). *Social foundation of thought and action: A social cognitive theory.* Englewood Cliffs, NJ: Prentice-Hall.

Barab, S. A., Kling, R., & Gray, J. H. (Eds.). (2004). *Designing for virtual communities in the service of learning.* Cambridge, UK: Cambridge University Press.

Barrett, H. (2001). Electronic portfolio development: Combining multimedia development and portfolio development. Retrieved August 20, 2007 from www.thequest.state.la.us/resources/presentations/Barrett.pdf

Barrett, H. C. (2003, October 9). *The ePortfolio: A revolutionary tool for education and training?* Paper presented at the First International Conference on the ePortfolio, Poitiers, France.

Barth, R. (2006). Improving relationships within the schoolhouse. *Educational Leadership, 63*(6), 9–13.

Becker, H. J. (1994). How exemplary computer using teachers differ from other teachers: Implications for realizing the potential of computers in schools. *Journal of Research on Computing in Education, 26*(3), 291–321.

Bennett, W. J. (1999). *The educated child: A parent's guide.* New York: The Free Press.

Bober, M. J. (2001). Technology integration: The difficulties inherent in measuring pedagogical change. *TechTrends, 46*(1), 21–24.

Bond, L. (1998, May). *Doing what matters most: Investing in quality teaching.* Paper presented at the California Education Policy Seminar, Sacramento, California.

Bonifaz, A., & Zucker, A. (2004). *Lessons learned about providing laptops for all students.* Newton, MA: Northeast and the Islands Regional Technology in Education Consortium.

Borko, H. (2004). Professional development and teacher learning: Mapping the terrain. *Educational Researcher, 33*(8), 3–15.

Borthwick, A. (2001). Dancing in the dark? Learning more about what makes partnerships work. In R. Ravid & M. Handler (Eds.), *The many faces of school university collaboration* (pp. 23–41). Englewood, CO: Libraries Unlimited.

Borthwick, A., Pierson, M., Anderson, C., Morris, K., Lathem, S., & Parker, H. (2004). Building learning communities to increase faculty and preservice teacher use of technology. *Journal of Computing in Teacher Education, 21*(1): 23–32.

Borthwick, A. C., & Risberg, C. (2003, April). *New technologies and essential Conditions: Handheld computers in the classroom.* Paper presented at the Annual Meeting of the American Educational Research Association, Chicago.

Bradshaw, L. (2002). Technology for teaching and learning: Strategies for staff development and follow-up support. *Journal of Technology and Teacher Education, 10*(1), 131–150.

Bridges, W. (1986). Managing organizational transitions. *Organizational Dynamics, 15*(1), 24–33.

Brookfield, S. (1986). *Understanding and facilitating adult learning.* San Francisco: Jossey-Bass.

Brookfield, S. (1995). *Becoming a Critically Reflective Teacher.* San Francisco: Jossey-Bass.

Brooks, M., & Brooks, J. (1999). The courage to be constructivist. *Educational Leadership, 57*(3), 18–24.

Brown, S. (2003). Working models: Why mentoring programs may be the key to teacher retention. *Techniques: Connecting Education & Careers, 78*(5), 18.

Bull, G., Knezek, G., Roblyer, M. D., Schrum, L., & Thompson, A. (2005). A proactive approach to a research agenda for educational technology. *Journal of Research on Technology in Education, 37*(3).

Burney, D. (2004). Craft knowledge: The road to transforming schools. *Phi Delta Kappan, 85*(7), 526–531.

Byrom, E., & Bingham, M. (2001). *Factors influencing the effective use of technology for teaching and learning: Lessons learned from the SEIR\*TEC Intensive Site Schools* (2nd ed.). Durham, NC: SouthEast Initiatives Regional Technology in Education Consortium.

## C

Carr, W., & Kemmis, S. (1986) *Becoming Critical: Education, knowledge and action research.* Lewes, East Sussex, UK: Falmer.

Carroll, T. G. (2000). If we didn't have the schools we have today, would we create the schools we have today? [Electronic version]. *Contemporary Issues in Technology and Teacher Education, 1*(1), 117–140.

Christensen, R. (2002). Effects of technology integration education on attitudes of teachers and students. *Journal of Research on Technology in Education, 34*(4), 411–433.

Cicchinelli, L., Dean, C., Galvin, M., Goodwin, B., & Parsley, D. (2006). *Success in sight: A comprehensive approach to school improvement.* Denver, CO: Mid-continent Research for Education and Learning.

Cochran-Smith, M., & Lytle, S. L. (1993). *Inside/outside: Teacher research and knowledge*. New York: Teachers College Press.

Cole, K., Simkins, M., & Penuel, W. R. (2002). Learning to teach with technology: Strategies for inservice professional development. *Journal of Technology and Teacher Education, 10*(3), 431–455.

Collins, A. M., & Ferguson, W. (1993). Epistemic forms and epistemic games: Structures and strategies to guide inquiry. *Educational Psychologist, 28,* 25–42.

Cooperrider, D. L., & Srivastva, S. (1987). Appreciative inquiry in organizational life. *Research in Organizational Change and Development, 1,* 129–169.

Creighton, T. (2003). *The principal as technology leader.* Thousand Oaks, CA: Corwin Press.

Cuban, L. (1998). How schools change reforms: Redefining reform success and failure. *Teacher College Record, 99*(3), 453–477.

Cunningham, C. A. & Billingsley, M. (2006). *Curriculum Webs: Weaving the Web into teaching and learning,* (2nd ed.). Boston, MA: Allyn & Bacon.

Cunningham, C. A., Boxer, F., & Dairyko, E. (2000). The Web Institute for Teachers: Engaging teachers in developing Web-based curriculum. In C. Crawford et al. (Eds.), *Proceedings of Society for Information Technology and Teacher Education International Conference 2000* (pp. 2227–2232). Chesapeake, VA: Association for the Advancement of Computing in Education

Cunningham, C. A., & Joseph, D. (2004). Putting passion on-line: A protocol for building motivation into curriculum Webs. In C. Crawford et al. (Eds.), *Proceedings of Society for Information Technology in Teacher Education International Conference 2004* (pp. 1128–1132). Chesapeake, VA: Association for the Advancement of Computing in Education.

Cuttance, P. (2001). Executive summary. In P. Cuttance (Ed.), *School innovation: Pathway to the knowledge society* (pp. xiii–xxix). Canberra, ACT, Australia: DETYA.

## D

Daft, R. L. (1989). *Organizational theory and design* (3rd ed.). St. Paul, MN: West.

Dana, N. F., & Yendol-Silva, D. (2003). *The reflective educator's guide to classroom research: Learning to teach and teaching to learn through practitioner inquiry.* Thousand Oaks, CA: Corwin Press.

Dall'Alba, G., & Sandberg, J. (2006). Unveiling professional development: A critical review of stage models. *Review of Educational Research, 76,* 383–412.

Daloz, L. A. (1999). *Mentor: Guiding the journey of adult learners.* San Francisco: Jossey-Bass.

Darling-Hammond, L. (1998, February). Teacher learning that supports student learning. *Educational Leadership, 55,* 6–11.

Dawson, C., & Rakes, G. C. (2003). The influence of principals' technology training on the integration of technology into schools. *Journal of Research on Technology, 36*(1), 29–49.

Dede, C. (Ed.). (2006). *Online professional development for teachers: Emerging models and methods.* Cambridge, MA: Harvard Education Press.

Desimone, L. M., Porter, L. M., Garet, M. S., Yoon, K. S., & Birman, B. F. (2002). Effects of professional development on teachers' instruction: Results from a three-year longitudinal study. *Educational Evaluation and Policy Analysis, 24*(2), 81–112.

Dexter, S., Anderson, R. E., & Becker, H. J. (1999). Teachers' views of computers as catalysts for changes in their teaching practices. *Journal of Research on Computing in Education, 31*(3), 221–239.

Dobson, M., LeBlanc, D., & Burgoyne, D. (2004). Transforming tensions in learning technology design: Operationalising activity theory. *Canadian Journal of Learning and Technology, 30*(1).

Donaldson, G., Jr. (2006). *Cultivating leadership in schools: Connecting people, purpose and practice* (Rev. ed.). New York: Teachers College Press.

DuFour, R. (2004). What is a professional learning community? *Educational Leadership, 61*(8), 6–11.

DuFour, R., & Eaker, R. (1998). *Professional learning communities at work: Best practices for enhancing student achievement.* Alexandria, VA: National Education Service.

## E

Elliot, J. (1991). *Action Research for Educational Change.* Buckingham, UK: Open University Press.

eMINTS. (2004). *eMints fact sheet.* Retrieved (n.d.), from www.emints.org/faq/index.shtml

Engeström, Y. (1999). Activity theory and individual and social transformation. In Y. Engeström, R. Miettinen, & R.-L. Punamèaki-Gitai (Eds.), *Perspectives on activity theory* (pp. 19–38). Cambridge, UK: Cambridge University Press.

Ertmer, P. A. (1999). Addressing first- and second-order barriers to change: Strategies for technology integration. *Educational Technology Research and Development, 47*(4), 47–61.

Ertmer, P. A., Addison, P., Lane, M., Ross, E., & Woods, D. (1999). Examining teachers' beliefs about the role of technology in the elementary classroom. *Journal of Research on Computing in Education, 32*(1), 54–72.

## F

Fisher, S., & Dove, M. (1999, February-March). *Muffled voices: Teachers' concerns regarding technological change.* Paper presented at the Society for Information Technology and Teacher Education International Conference, San Antonio, TX.

Fishman, J. J., Marx, R. W., Best, S., & Tal, R. T. (2003). Linking teacher and student learning to improve professional development in systemic reform. *Teaching and Teacher Education, 19*, 643–658.

Florida Laptop for Learning Task Force. (2004). *Laptops for learning: Final report and recommendations of the Laptops for Learning Task Force.* Tallahassee: Florida State Department of Education.

Fouts, J. T. (2000). *Research on computers in education: Past, present and future.* Seattle, WA: Bill and Melinda Gates Foundation.

Friedman, T. (2006). *The world is flat.* New York: Farrar, Straus and Giroux.

Fullan, M. (1982). *The meaning of educational change.* New York: Teachers College Press.

Fullan, M. (1993). *Change forces probing the depths of educational reform.* New York: The Falmer Press.

Fullan, M. (1996) Professional culture and educational change. *School Psychology Review, 25*, 4, 496–501.

Fullan, M. (1999). *Change forces: The sequel.* New York: The Falmer Press.

Fullan, M. (2001). *Leading in a culture of change.* San Francisco: Jossey-Bass.

Fullan, M. (2004). *Leadership sustainability: System thinkers in action.* Thousand Oaks, CA: Sage.

Fullan, M., & Hargreaves, A. (Eds.). (1992). *Teacher Development and Educational Change.* London: Falmer.

Fullan, M., Hill, P., & Crévola, C. (2006). *Breakthrough.* Thousand Oaks, CA: Corwin.

# G

Garet, M. S., Porter, A., Desimone, L. M., Birman, B. F., & Yoon, K. S. (2001). What makes professional development effective? Analysis of a national sample of teachers. *American Educational Research Journal, 38*, 915–945.

Garmston, R. (1987). How administrators support peer coaching. *Educational Leadership, 44*(5), 18–26.

Glennon, T. K., & Melmed, A. (2000). Challenges of creating a nation of technology enabled schools. In Jossey-Bass (Ed.), *Jossey-Bass reader on technology and learning* (pp. 31). San Francisco: Jossey-Bass.

Greeno, J. G., & the Middle School Mathematics Through Applications Projects Group (1998). The situativity of knowing, learning, and research. *American Psychologist 53*(1), 5–26.

Grimmett, P. (1987). The role of district supervisors in the implementation of peer coaching. *Journal of Curriculum and Supervision, 3*, 3–28.

Grossman, P., Wineburg, S., & Woolworth, S. (2001). Toward a theory of teacher community. *Teachers College Record, 103*, 942–1012.

Guskey, T. R. (2000). *Evaluating professional development.* Thousand Oaks, CA: Corwin.

Guskey, T. R. (2002). Professional development and teacher change. *Teachers and Teaching, 8*(3), 381–391.

# H

Hall, G. E., & Hord, S. M. (2001). *Implementing change: Patterns, principles, and potholes.* Needham Heights, MA: Allyn & Bacon.

Ham, V., & Kane, R. (2004). Finding a way through the swamp: A case for self-study as research. In Loughran et al. (Eds.), *International handbook on self study in teaching and teacher education.* Amsterdam: Kluwer.

Ham, V., Mocau, P., Williamson-Leadley S., Toubat, H., & Winter, M. (2005). *ICTPD Through three lenses. An evaluation of the ICTPD School Clusters Programme 2001–2003. Supplement: Action researcher reports.* Wellington, New Zealand. Ministry of Education. Retrieved November 13, 2007 from www.educationcounts.edcentre.govt.nz/__data/assets/pdf_file/0006/7476/ICTPD3Lenses_Report.pdf

Hargreaves, A., Earl, L., Moore, S., & Manning, S. (2001). *Learning to change: Teaching beyond subjects and standards.* San Francisco: Jossey-Bass.

Hargreaves, A., & Fink, D. (2003). Sustaining leadership. *Phi Delta Kappan, 84*(9), 693–700.

Harpel, B. (2004, April). *How to really teach math through writing.* Workshop presented at the National Council of Teachers of Math Annual Conference, Philadelphia, PA.

Harper, D. (2006). *Vision to action: Adding student leadership to your technology plan.* GenYes.com. Retrieved July 1, 2007, from www.genyes.org/media/programs/how_to_include_students_in_tech_plan.pdf

Harper, D. (2007). *Generation YES Factsheet. Generation YES: Youth and educators succeeding.* Retrieved September 15, 2007, from www.genyes.org/media/freeresources/generation_yes_fact_sheet.pdf

Harris, J. (2007, June 25). *Educational technology professional development models: A taxonomy of combinable choices.* Paper presented at the National Educational Computing Conference, Atlanta, GA.

Hawley, C. (1997). Systemic Change in Education: A road map. *Educational Technology*, 57–64.

Hawley, W. D., & Valli, L. (1999). The essentials of effective professional development: A new consensus. In L. Darling-Hammond & G. Sykes (Eds.), *Teaching as the learning profession: Handbook of policy and practice* (pp. 127–150). San Francisco: Jossey-Bass.

Heggelund, M., Haring, N. G., Lynch, V., Pruess, J., Soltman, S., & Zodrow, N. (1985). Systems change: A case study. *Remedial and Special Education. 6*(3), 44–51.

Hirsh, S. (2001). We're growing and changing. *Journal of Staff Development, 22*(3), 10–17.

Hodas, S. (1993). Technology refusal and the organizational culture of schools. *Educational Policy Analysis Archives, 1*(10), 1–21.

Hughes, J. (2004). Technology learning principles for preservice and in-service teacher education. *Contemporary Issues in Technology and Teacher Education, 4*(3), 345–362.

Hughes, J. E., Kerr, S. P., & Ooms, A. (2005). Content-focused technology inquiry groups: Cases of teacher learning and technology integration. *Journal of Educational Computer Research, 32*(4), 367–379.

## I

Ilmer, S. & Kirby, P. (2007). *Urban K–12 school-university teacher preparation partnerships: An initiative of the Great Cities' Universities.* (ERIC Document Reproduction Service No. ED495718)

International Society for Technology in Education. (2000). *National educational technology standards for students: Connecting curriculum and technology.* Eugene, OR: International Society for Technology in Education.

International Society for Technology in Education. (2007). National Educational Technology Standards for Students. Retrieved November 13, 2007 from www.iste.org/NETS

Ishizuka, K. (2004, October). Teachers get a tech lesson. *School Library Journal.* Retrieved July 26, 2005, from http://schoollibraryjournal.com/index.asp?layout=articlePrint&articleid=CA456877

## J

Jakes, D. S., & Brennan, J. (2005). Digital storytelling, visual literacy and 21st century skills. Retrieved October 28, 2007 from www.techlearning.com/techlearning/pdf/events/techforum/ny05/Vault_article_jakesbrennan.pdf

Jenson, J., Lewis, B., & Savage, R. (2002). No one way: Working models for teachers' professional development. *Journal of Technology and Teacher Education, 10*(4), 481–496.

Jonassen, D. H. (1999). Designing constructivist learning environments. In C.M. Reigeluth (Ed.), *Instructional-design theories and models: A new paradigm of instructional theory* (vol. 2) (pp. 215–239). Mahwah, NJ: Lawrence Erlbaum.

Jonassen, D. H. (2000). *Computers as mindtools for schools: Engaging critical thinking* (2nd ed.). Upper Saddle River, NJ: Merrill.

Jonassen, D. H., & Hernandez-Serrano, J. (2002). Case-based reasoning and instructional design: Using stories to support problem solving. *Educational Technology Research and Development, 50*(2), 65–77.

Jonassen, D. H., & Rohrer-Murphy, L. (1999). Activity theory as a framework for designing constructivist learning environments. *Educational Technology Research and Development, 47*(1), 61–79.

Jonassen, D. H., Wang, F.-K., Strobel, J., & Cernusca, D. (2003). Applications of a case library of technology integration stories for teachers. *Journal of Technology and Teacher Education, 11*(4), 547–566.

Joyce, B. (2004). How are professional learning communities created? History has a few messages. *Phi Delta Kappan, 86*, 76–83.

Joyce, B. R., & Showers, B. (1980). Improving in-service training: The message of research. *Educational Leadership, 37*(5), 379–385.

Joyce, B. R., & Showers, B. (1988). *Student achievement through staff development.* New York: Longman.

Joyce, B. R., & Showers, B. (2002). *Student achievement through staff development* (3rd ed.). Alexandria, VA: Association for Supervision and Curriculum Development.

## K

Kajder, S., Bull, G., & Albaugh, S. (2005). Constructing digital stories. *Leading and Learning with Technology, 32*(5), 40–42.

Kegan, R. (1982). *The evolving self.* Cambridge, MA: Harvard University Press.

Kegan, R., & Lahey, L. (2001). *How the way we talk can change the way we work.* San Francisco: Jossey-Bass.

Kemmis, S., & McTaggart, R. (1988). *The Action Research Planner* (2nd ed.). Geelong, Victoria, Australia: Deakin University Press.

Kerr, S. T. (1991). Lever and fulcrum: Educational technology in teacher's thought and practice. *Teachers College Record, 93*(1), 114–123.

Killion, J. (2007). Web of support strengthens the effectiveness of school-based coaches. *Journal of Staff Development, 28*(1), 10–18.

Killion, J., & National Staff Development Council. (2002). *Assessing impact: Evaluating staff development.* Oxford, OH: National Staff Development Council.

King, K. P. (2003). Learning the new technologies: Strategies for success. *New Directions for Adult and Continuing Education, 98*, 49–57.

Knowles, M. S. (1973). *The adult learner: A neglected species.* Houston, TX: Gulf.

Knowles, M. S., Swanson, R. A., & Holton, E. F. (2005). *The adult learner: The definitive classic in adult education and human resource development* (6th ed.). Amsterdam: Elsevier Science and Technology Books.

Kuutti, K., & Arvonen, T. (1992). *Identifying potential CSCW applications by means of activity theory concepts: A case example.* Paper presented at the 1992 ACM conference on computer-supported cooperative work, Toronto, Ontario.

## L

Lachs, V. (2000). *Making multimedia in the classroom.* London: RoutledgeFalmer.

Laffey, J., & Musser, D. (1998). Attitudes of preservice teachers about using technology in teaching. *Journal of Technology and Teacher Education, 6*(4), 223–241.

Lawless, K. A., & Pellegrino, J. W. (2007). Professional development in integrating technology into teaching and learning: Knowns, unknowns, and ways to pursue better questions and answers. *Review of Educational Research, 77*, 575–614.

Lieberman, A. (1988). *Building a professional culture in schools.* New York: Teachers College Press.

Lim, C. P., & Khine, M. (2006). Managing teachers' barriers to ICT integration in Singapore schools. *Journal of Technology and Teacher Education, 14*(1), 97–125.

Lindstrom, P. H., & Speck, M. (2004). *The principal as professional development leader.* Thousand Oaks, CA: Corwin Press.

Little, J. W. (2002). Locating learning in teachers' communities of practice. *Teaching and Teacher Education, 18,* 917–946.

Loucks-Horsley, S. (1996). Professional development for science education: A critical and immediate challenge. In R.W. Bybee (Ed.), *National standards and the science curriculum: Challenges, opportunities, and recommendations* (pp. 83–95). Dubuque, IA: Kendall/Hunt Publishing Co.

Lovett, S., & Gilmore, A. (2003). Teachers' learning journeys: The quality learning circle as a model of professional development. *School Effectiveness and School Improvement, 14*(2), 189–211.

## M

Margerum-Leys, J., & Marx, R. W. (2004). The nature and sharing of teacher knowledge of technology in a student teacher/mentor teacher pair. *Journal of Teacher Education, 55*(5), 421–437.

Mattingly, C. (1991). Narrative reflections on practical actions: Two learning experiments in reflective storytelling. In D. A. Schön (Ed.), *The reflective turn: Case studies in and on educational practice* (pp. 235–257). New York: Teachers College, Columbia University.

Matzen, N. J., & Edmunds, J. A. (2007). Technology as a catalyst for change: The role of professional development. *Journal of Research on Technology in Education, 39,* 417–430.

McGrath, D., & Sands, N. (2004). Taking the plunge. *Leading and Learning with Technology, 31*(7), 34–36.

McNiff, J., Lomax, P., & Whitehead, J. (1996). *You and your action research project.* London: Routledge.

McPherson, S., Wizer, D., & Pierrel, E. (2006, February). Technology Academies: A professional development model for technology integration leaders. *Learning and Leading with Technology, 33,* 5.

Meltzer, J., & Sherman, T. M. (1997). 10 Commandments of tech staff development. *NASSP Bulletin, 81*(585), 23–32.

Merriam, S. B., Caffarella, R. S., & Baumgartner, L. M. (2006). *Learning in adulthood: A comprehensive guide* (3rd. ed.). San Francisco: Jossey-Bass.

Microsoft Corporation. (2004). *Peer Coaching Program.* Retrieved August 14, 2005, from http://pc.innovativeteachers.com/mpc_web/default.aspx

Microsoft Peer Coaching Evaluation (2005). *Evaluation overview* (pp. 135–157). Tampa, FL: Florida Center for Instructional Technology.

Miles, M., & Huberman, A. M. (1994). *Qualitative data analysis* (2nd ed.). Thousand Oaks, CA: Sage.

Mills, G. (2003). *Action research. A guide for the teacher researcher.* (2nd ed.). Upper Saddle River, NJ: Merrill Prentice Hall.

Mishra, P., & Koeher, M. J. (2006). Technological Pedagogical Content Knowledge: A new framework for teacher knowledge. *Teachers College Record, 108*(6), 1017–1054.

Mitchum, K., Wells, D. L., & Wells, J. G. (2003). Effective integration of instructional technologies (IT): Evaluating professional development and instructional change. *Journal of Technology and Teacher Education, 11*(3), 397–414.

Moersch, C. (1999). Assessing current technology use in the classroom: A key to efficient staff development and technology planning. *Learning and Leading with Technology, 26*(8), 40–45.

Mouza, C. (2003). Learning to teach with new technology: Implications for professional development. *Journal of Research on Technology in Education, 35*(2), 272–289.

Munby, H., & Russell, T. (1995). Towards rigour with relevance: How can teachers and teacher educators claim to know? In T. Russell & F. Korthagen (Eds), *Teachers who teach teachers: Reflections on teacher education.* London: Falmer.

## N

National Center for Education Statistics (2000). *Teachers' tools for the 21st century: A report on teachers' use of technology.* Washington, DC: U.S. Department of Education, Office of Research and Improvement.

National Council of Teachers of Mathematics (NCTM). (2000). *Principles and Standards for School Mathematics.* Reston, VA: Author.

National Staff Development Council. (1994). *National Staff Development Council standards for staff development.* Oxford, OH: National Staff Development Council (NSDC).

National Staff Development Council (2001). *NSDC's Standards for Staff Development.* Retrieved November 12, 2007, from www.nsdc.org/standards/index.cfm

National Staff Development Council. (2004). *National Staff Development Council's standards for staff development, revised: Advancing student learning through staff development.* Oxford, OH· National Staff Development Council (NSDC).

National Staff Development Council (2006). *Professional Development IQ Test.* Retrieved January 31, 2006, from www.nsdc.org/library/basics/pdiqan.cfm

National Technology Leadership Coalition. (2007). National Technology Leadership Summit IX. Retrieved November 19, 2007 from www.ntls.info

Nespor, J. (1987). The role of beliefs in the practice of teaching. *Journal of Curriculum Studies, 19*(4), 317–328.

Newman, D. L. (2001, November). *Evaluating systems change: A model of assessment.* Paper presented at Evaluation 2001: The Annual Meeting of the American Evaluation Association, St. Louis, MO.

Newman, D. L., & Lobosco, A. F. (2007, November). *Participatory systems change evaluation: Involving all users in all stages of systems change assessment.* Paper presented at Evaluation 2007: The Annual Meeting of the American Evaluation Association in Baltimore, MD.

New Zealand Ministry of Education (2006). *Towards a Framework for Professional Practice: INSTEP.* Unpublished Draft Report from the Inservice Teacher Education Project (INSTEP), Wellington, New Zealand.

Niesz, T. (2007). Why teacher networks (can) work. *Phi Delta Kappan, 88*(8), 605–610.

Niles, R. (2006). *A study of the application of emerging technology: Teacher and student perceptions of the impact of one-to-one laptop computer access.* Unpublished doctoral dissertation, University of Wichita (KS). Retrieved January 14, 2008, from Shocker Open Access Repository at Wichita State University Libraries.

North Central Regional Education Laboratory (2003). *enGauge 21st century skills: Literacy in the digital age.* Retrieved October 27, 2007, from www.ncrel.org/engauge/skills/skills.htm

## O

Orr, C. (2001). Building technology-based, learner-centered classrooms: The evolution of a professional development model. *Educational Technology Research and Development, 49*(1), 15–34.

Owen, A., Farsaii, S., Knezak, G., & Christensen, R. (2005, December/January). Teaching in the One-to-One Classroom: It's not about laptops, it's about empowerment. *Learning and Leading with Technology, 33,* 12–16.

Owston, R. (2003). School context, sustainability and transferability of innovation. In R. Kozma (Ed.), *Technology, innovation and educational change: A global perspective. A report of the second information technology in education study, Module 2* (pp. 125–161). Eugene, OR: International Society for Technology in Education.

## P

Pajares, M. F. (1992). Teachers' beliefs and educational research. *Review of Educational Research. 62,* 307–32.

Peery, A. B. (2004). *Deep Change: Professional development from the inside out.* Lanham, MD: ScareCrow Education.

Penuel, W. R., Sussex, W., & Korbak, C. (2005, October). *Mapping the distribution of expertise and resources in a school: Investigating the potential of using social network analysis in evaluation.* Paper presented at the Joint Conference of the Canadian Evaluation Society and the American Evaluation Association, Toronto, Ontario, Canada.

Peterson, K., (n.d.). *About the Puget Sound Center for Teaching, Learning and Technology.* Retrieved July 26, 2005, from www.psctlt.org/About_PSCTLT/overview.html

Pierson, M. E. (2001). Technology integration practice as a function of pedagogical expertise. *Journal of Research on Computing in Education, 33*(4), 413–429.

Pitler, H., Flynn, K., & Gaddy, B. (2004). *Is a laptop initiative in your future?* Retrieved January 14, 2008, from the Mid-Continent Research for Education and Learning Web site: www.mcrel.org/topics/products/182/

Polselli, R. (2002). Combining web-based training and mentorship to improve technology integration in the K–12 classroom. *Journal of Technology and Teacher Education, 10*(2), 247–272.

Poole, B. (2003). *Education for an information age: Teaching in the computerized classroom.* Retrieved November 10, 2007, from the University of Pittsburgh at Johnstown Web site: www.pitt.edu/~edindex/InfoAge6frame.html

Putnam, R. T., & Borko, H. (2000). What do new views of knowledge and thinking have to say about research on teacher learning? *Educational Researcher, 29*(1), 4–15.

## R

Radinsky, J., Smolin, L., & Lawless, K. (2005). Collaborative curriculum design as a vehicle for professional development. In C. Vrasidas & G. Glass (Eds.), *Preparing teachers to teach with technology: A volume in current perspectives on applied information technologies* (pp. 369–380). Greenwich, CT: Information Age Publishing.

Radinsky, J., Smolin, L., Lawless, K. A., & Newman, M. (2003). School-university collaborative design teams: Curriculum design as a vehicle for professional development in teaching with technology. *Proceedings for the annual meeting of the Society for Information Technology and Teacher Education, Albuquerque, NM, 1,* 3775–3778.

Ravitz, J. L., Becker, H. J., & Wong, Y. T. (2000). *Constructivist-compatible beliefs and practices among U.S. teachers*. Irvine, CA: Center for Research on Information Technology and Organizations, University of California.

Reeves, D. B. (2006). Of hubs, bridges, and networks. *Educational Leadership, 63*(8), 32–37.

Renninger, K. A., & Shumar, W. (Eds.). 2002. *Building virtual communities: Learning and change in cyberspace*. Cambridge, UK: Cambridge University Press.

Rhine, S., & Bailey, M. (2005). *Integrated technologies, innovative learning: Insights from the PT3 program* (1st ed.). Eugene, OR: International Society for Technology in Education.

Richardson, V. (1999). Teacher education and the construction of meaning. In G. Griffin (Ed.), *Teacher education for a new century: Emerging perspectives, promising practices, and future possibilities: Yearbook of the National Society for the Study of Education* (pp. 145–166). Chicago: University of Chicago Press.

Richardson, V. (2003). The dilemmas of professional development. *Phi Delta Kappan, 84*, 401–406.

Richmond, G. (1996). University/school partnerships: Bridging the culture gap. *Theory into Practice, 35*(3), 214–218.

Ringstaff, C., & Kelley, L. (2002). *The learning return on our educational investment*. San Francisco: WestEd RTEC.

Risberg, C. (2006). *Start with conversations and collaboration-strategies for building and connecting a School's Organizational Culture to Effective Technology Adoption and Staff Development*. Unpublished manuscript.

Robbins, N. (2000). Technology subcultures and indicators associated with high technology performance in schools. *Journal of Research on Computing in Education, 33*, 111–124.

Robinson, V. (1993). *Problem-Based Methodology: Research for the improvement of practice*. Oxford, UK: Pergamon.

Rogers, E. M. (2003). *Diffusion of innovations* (5th ed.). New York: Free Press.

Ropp, M. M. (1999, Summer). Exploring individual characteristics associated with learning to use computers in preservice teacher preparation. *Journal of Research on Computing in Education, 31*(4), 402–424.

## S

Sabelli, N., & Dede, C. (2001). *Reconceptualizing the goals and process of educational research and funding: Interconnecting scholarship and practice*. Retrieved January 23, 2005, from The Berkman Center for Internet and Society Web site: http://h2oproject.law.harvard.edu/educational_funding.pdf

Salomon, G. (1991). Transcending the quantitative/qualitative debate: The analytic and systemic approaches to educational research. *Educational Research, 20*, 10–18.

Salpeter, J. (2005). Telling tales with technology: Digital storytelling is a new twist on the ancient art of the oral narrative. *Technology & Learning, 25*(7), 18.

Sam, H. K., Othman, A., & Nordin, Z. S. (2005). Computer self-efficacy, computer anxiety, and attitudes toward the Internet: A study among undergraduates in Unimas. *Educational Technology and Society, 8*(4), 205–219.

Sandholtz, J. H., Ringstaff, C., & Dwyer, D. (1997). *Teaching with Technology: Creating student-centered classrooms*. New York: Teachers College.

Schacter, J. (1999). *The impact of educational technology on student achievement: What the most current research has to say.* Retrieved November 10, 2007 from the Milken Exchange on Educational Technology Web site: www.mff.org/pubs/ME161.pdf

Schalock, M. D., Fredericks, B., Dalke, B. A., & Alberto, P. A. (1994). The house that TRACES built: A conceptual model of service delivery and implications for change. *Journal of Special Education, 28,* 203–224.

Schmidt, M. R. (2000). You know more than you can say: In memory of Donald A. Schön (1930–1997). *Public Administration Review, 60*(3), 266–275.

Schmoker, M. J. (1999). *Results: The key to continuous school improvement* (2nd ed.). Alexandria, VA: Association for Supervision and Curriculum Development.

Schmoker, M. J. (2006). *Results now: how we can achieve unprecedented improvements in teaching and learning.* Alexandria, VA: Association for Supervision and Curriculum Development.

Schofield, J. W., & Davidson, A. L. (2002). *Bringing the Internet to school: Lessons from an urban district.* Somerset, NJ: Jossey-Bass.

Schön, D. (1983). *The Reflective Practitioner: How professionals think in action.* USA: Basic Books.

Schön, D. (1987). *Educating the reflective practitioner.* San Francisco: Jossey-Bass.

Schrader, P. G., & Lawless, K. (2004). The knowledge, attitudes, & behaviors approach: How to evaluate performance and learning in complex environments. *Performance Improvement, 43*(9) 8–15.

Senge, P. M. (2006). *The fifth discipline: The art & practice of the learning organization* (2nd ed.). New York: Doubleday.

Senge, P. M., Cambron-McCabe, N., Lucas, T., Smith, B., Dutton, J., & Kleiner, A. (2000). *Schools that learn: A fifth discipline fieldbook for educators, parents, and everyone who cares about education.* New York: Doubleday.

Senge, P. M., Scharmer, C. O., Jaworski, J., & Flowers, B. S. (2004). *Presence: Human purpose and the field of the future.* Cambridge, MA: The Society for Organizational Learning.

Shrag, J. A. (1996). Systems change leading to better integration of services for students with special needs. *School Psychology Review, 25,* 4, 489–496.

Shulha, L. M., Lee, M. W., & Van Melle, E. P. (2001, June). *The art of the possible.* An Unpublished report, Ontario Knowledge Network for Learning, Queens University, Ontario, Canada.

Shulman, L. S. (1986). Those who understand: Knowledge growth in teaching. *Educational Researcher, 15,* 4–14.

Shulman, L. S. (1987). Knowledge and teaching: Foundations of the new reform. *Harvard Educational Review, 57,* 1–22.

Smith, T. A., & Ingersoll, R. M. (2004). What are the effects of induction and mentoring on beginning teacher turnover? *Educational Evaluation and Policy Analysis, 26,* 681–714.

Smolin, L., Lawless, K., Newman, M., & Jullian, K. (2002). *Supporting technology experiences for preservice and inservice educators in urban programs: Report of a PT3 pilot project.* Paper presented at the annual American Educational Research Association conference, New Orleans, LA.

Smolin, L., Lawless, K., Radinsky, J. (2006, April). *A design-based approach to technology integration professional development for inservice teachers.* Paper presented at the annual meeting of the American Educational Research Association, San Francisco, CA.

Snow-Renner, R., & Lauer, P. (2005). *McREL Insights-Professional Development Analysis.* Aurora, CO: Author.

Somekh, B. (2005). *Action Research A Methodology for Change & Development*. Maidenhead, UK: Open University Press.

Sparks, D. (1998). Using Technology to improve teaching and staff development: An interview with Kathleen Fulton. *Journal of Staff Development, 19*(1), 9.

Sparks, D. (2003). Change agent: Interview, Michael Fullan. *Journal of Staff Development, 24*(1), 55–58.

Sparks, D. (2006). *Plugging educators into technology*. Retrieved January 31, 2006, from the National Staff Development Council Web site: www.nsdc.org/library/publications/results/res2-99tech.cfm

Sparks, D., & Hirsh, S. (1997). *A new vision for staff development*. Alexandria, VA: Association for Supervision and Curriculum Development and National Staff Development Council.

Spillane, J. P. (1999). External reform initiatives and teacher's efforts to reconstruct practice: The mediating role of teacher's zones of enactment. *Journal of Curriculum Studies, 31*, 143–175.

Spillane, J. P. (2006). *Distributed leadership*. San Francisco: Jossey-Bass.

Spitzer, B., & Stansberry, S. (2004, October). *Public school teacher use of instructional technology from an organizational culture perspective: An explanatory case study of two middle schools*. Paper presented at the Association for Educational Communications and Technology Conference, Chicago. (ERIC Document Reproduction Service No. ED485068)

Stein, M. K., & Wang, M. C. (1988). Teacher development and school improvement: The process of teacher change. *Teaching and Teacher Education, 4*, 171–187.

Stenhouse, L. (1981). What counts as research? *British Journal of Educational Studies, 29*, 103–113.

Strudler, N., Archambault, L., Bendixen, L., Anderson, L., & Weiss, R. (2003). Project THREAD: Technology helping restructure educational access and delivery. *Educational Technology Research and Development, 51*, 41–56.

## T

Tafel, L., & Bertani, A. (1992). Reconceptualizing staff development for systemic change. *Journal of Staff Development, 13*(4), 42–45.

Tatnall, A., & Davey, B. (2003). ICT and training: A proposal for an ecological model of innovation. *Educational Technology & Society, 6*(1), 14–17.

TERC. (1997). *Investigations in Number, Data, and Space*. Upper Saddle River, NJ: Pearson.

Thibeault, N. (2004, June). Multimedia madness-Improving professional development for instructional technology. *Proceedings of the 2004 Association of Small Computer Users in Education Conference*, Myrtle Beach, SC, 262–270.

## V

Valencia, S. W., & Killion, J. P. (1988). Overcoming obstacles to teacher change: Direction from school-based efforts. *Journal of Staff Development, 9*(2), 2–8.

Vanatta, R. A., Banister, S., Fischer, J., Messenheimer, T., & Ross, C. (2005). Pathways for change. In S. Rhine & M. Bailey (Eds.), *Integrated Technologies, Innovative Learning: Insights from the PT3 Program* (pp. 21–33). Eugene, OR: International Society for Technology in Education.

Vygotsky, L. S. (1978). *Mind in society: The development of higher psychological processes*. Cambridge, MA: Harvard University Press.

## W

Wagner, T., Kegan, R., Lahey, L., Lemons, R. W., Garnier, J., Helsing, D., et al. (2006). *Change leadership: A practical guide to transforming our schools.* San Francisco: Jossey-Bass.

Warlick, D. (2002). *Raw materials for the mind: teaching & learning in information & technology rich schools.* Raleigh, NC: The Landmark Project.

Warriner, G. D. (2005). A case study of an instructional technology mentoring program in a public school district: Characteristics of a sustained innovation. (Doctoral dissertation, Pepperdine University, 2005). *Dissertation Abstracts International, 67–04 A.*

Waxman, H. C., Connell, M. L., & Gray, J. (2002). *A quantitative synthesis of recent research on the effects of teaching and learning with technology on student outcomes.* Retrieved November 10, 2007 from the North Central Regional Education Laboratory Web site: www.coe.ufl.edu/Courses/eme5054/Foundations/Articles/waxman.pdf

Wells, J. G. (2007). Key design factors in durable instructional technology professional development. *Journal of Technology and Teacher Education, 15*(1), 101–122.

Wenger, E. (1999). *Communities of practice: learning, meaning, and identity.* Cambridge, UK: Cambridge University Press.

Wiggins, G. P., & McTighe, J. (2001). *Understanding by design.* Upper Saddle River, NJ: Merrill/Prentice Hall.

Willis, J. (1993). What conditions encourage technology use? It depends on the context. *Computers in schools, 9*(4), 13–32.

Wizer, D. R., & McPherson, S. J. (2005). The administrator's role: Strategies for fostering staff development. *Learning and Leading with Technology, 32*(5), 14–17.

## Z

Zeichner, K. M., & Liston, D. P. (1996). *Reflective teaching: An introduction.* Mahwah, NJ: Lawrence Erlbaum Associates, Publishers.

Zorfass, J., & Rivero, H. K. (2005). Collaboration is key: How a community of practice promotes technology integration. *Journal of Special Education Technology, 20*(3), 51–67.

Zuber-Skerritt, O. (1996). Introduction: New directions in action research. In Zuber-Skerritt, O. (Ed), *New Directions in Action Research* (pp. 3–6). London: Falmer Press.

# Index

*Page references followed by t or f indicate tables or figures, respectively.*